Truth, Love, and Nirvana

Gentleness, serenity, compassion, through liberation from selfish craving—these are the fundamental teachings of the great Oriental religion of Buddhism, fathered twenty-five centuries ago by Siddhartha Gautama, son of a wealthy ruler in India, and now practiced by millions all over the world—especially in Ceylon, Thailand, Burma, Indo-China, and Japan.

According to Buddhism, suffering in man's earthly life is caused by self-centered desire. The ultimate aim of the good—or religious—man should be the elimination of such desire—which can be attained through grasping the truth about reality and following the eight-fold path which leads to Nirvana (a state transcending the limitations of earthly existence). The steps in this path include right belief, resolve, speech, conduct, daily occupation, effort, alertness, and finally, the ecstasy of selfless meditation.

Here, Edwin A. Burtt, the Sage Professor of Philosophy at Cornell University, and author of many scholarly volumes, including *The Metaphysical Foundations of Modern Physical Science* and *Types of Religious Philosophy*, has collected the best translations of the basic texts in this great religion devoted to universal love and the way to its realization.

Of this book, Arnold J. Toynbee, world-famous historian, has said: "Believing as I do that religion is the most important thing in life, I feel that a mutual understanding on the religious level is the key to spiritual union. I am particularly glad to see the announcement of Professor E. A. Burtt's volume of *The Teachings of The Compassionate Buddha*."

Other Mentor Religious Classics

The Holy Bible in Brief *edited and arranged*
by James Reeves

The basic story of the Old and New Testaments told
as one clear, continuous narrative in the words of the
authorized King James text. (#Ms116—50¢)

The Meaning of the Glorious Koran
An Explanatory Translation
by Mohammed Marmaduke Pickthall

The complete sacred book of Mohammedanism, translated with reverence and scholarship by a British
Moslem. Full historical introduction and commentary.
Provides invaluable insight into one of the world's
great religions. (#Ms94—50¢)

The Song of God: Bhagavad-Gita, *with introduction*
by Aldous Huxley

The timeless epic of Hindu faith vividly translated for
Western readers by Swami Prabhavananda and Chris-
topher Isherwood—a unique literary experience as
well as a contemporary message which touches today's
urgent problems. (#M103—35¢)

The Way of Life: Tao Tê Ching, *by Lao Tzu*

A new translation by R. B. Blakney of a masterpiece
of ancient Chinese wisdom, presenting the philosophy
of Taoism, second only to Confucianism in its influence on Eastern thought and life. (#M129—35¢)

To Our Readers

We welcome your comments about Signet, Signet Key
or Mentor books as well as your suggestions for new
reprints. If your dealer does not have the books you want,
you may order them by mail, enclosing the list price plus
5¢ a copy to cover mailing costs. Send for a copy of our
complete catalog. The New American Library of World
Literature, Inc., 501 Madison Ave., New York 22, N. Y.

THE TEACHINGS OF

The Compassionate Buddha

Edited, with Introduction
and Notes by
E. A. BURTT

A MENTOR RELIGIOUS CLASSIC

Published by The New American Library

Published as a MENTOR BOOK

FIRST PRINTING, MAY, 1955

Library of Congress Catalog Card No. 55-5474

MENTOR BOOKS are published by
The New American Library of World Literature, Inc.
501 Madison Avenue, New York 22, New York

PRINTED IN THE UNITED STATES OF AMERICA

Contents

Preface

I wish here to express grateful acknowledgment to those whose co-operation has made this volume possible and who have helped to give it whatever virtues it possesses.

Several scholars who are more familiar with Buddhist literature than I have given me kindly counsel regarding the choice of selections and have kept me from making several mistakes that I might easily have fallen into without their help. Doubtless there are other mistakes which I have not avoided; these friends are not responsible for them. I wish especially to thank in this connection Professor Wing Tsit Chan of Dartmouth College, Professor Kenneth Chen of Harvard University, Professor Kenneth W. Morgan of Colgate University, Professor Clarence H. Hamilton of Oberlin College, Dr. Cecil W. Hobbs of the Reference Department of the Library of Congress, the Bhikkhu Sangarakstra of the Maha Bodhi Society in Calcutta, and Professors Walter Liebenthal and K. Venkataramanan of the Visva-Bharati University at Santiniketan, India.

Professor Hamilton and Professor Liebenthal have also given kind permission to use translations of their own which it would not have been possible otherwise to include in this volume (Part V, Selection 2; and Part VI, Selections 6 and 8).

The following publishers have given much appreciated permission to use material under their copyright:

The Philosophical Library, New York for selections from *Buddhist Texts Through the Ages*, edited by E. Conze and contributed to also by I. Horner and A. Waley. (Part III: Selection 6, pp. 95-100; Selection 7, pp. 106, 113-14; Selection 8, pp. 88-90; Selection 9, p. 34; Selection 10, pp. 37-8. Part IV: Selection I, pp. 190-94; Selection 2, pp. 119, 128-32. Part VI: Selection 1, pp. 202-06; Selection 7, pp. 295-98; Epilogue, pp. 285-86.) I have also used a few sentences from p. 70 of *An Introduction to Zen Buddhism*, by D. T. Suzuki. (Selection 9 of Part VI.)

The Pali Text Society, London, for selections from the *Psalms of the Early Buddhists,* edited by C. A. F. Rhys Davids, *passim* (Selection 2 of Part II), and from volumes II, III, and IV of *Sacred Books of the Buddhists,* edited by T. W. Rhys Davids and C. A. F. Rhys Davids. (Part I: Selection 7, pp. 106-09, 128 of Vol. III. Part III: Selection 4, pp. 67-95 of Vol. II; Selection 5, pp. 173-84 of Vol. IV.)

Routledge and Kegan Paul, London, for selections from:

E. J. Thomas, *Early Buddhists Scriptures,* pp. 29-33, 158-60. (Selection 1 of Part I, and Selection 3 of Part III.)

F. Max Müller, *Buddhaghosa's Parables,* pp. lv-clxx. This is his translation of the *Dhammapada,* later published in *Sacred Books of the East,* Vol. X. (Selection 1 of Part II.)

Paul Bigandet, *The Life or Legend of Gaudama,* Vol. II, pp. 167-76. (Selection 1 of Part III.)

S. Beal, *A Catena of Buddhist Scriptures from the Chinese,* pp. 286-353. (Selection 3 of Part V.)

Harvard University Press, Cambridge, for selections from Volumes 3 and 37 of the Harvard Oriental Series edited by C. R. Lanman:

H. C. Warren, *Buddhism in Translations,* pp. 117-22, 351-53 of Vol. 3. (Selection 2 of Part I and Selection 2 of Part III.)

Lord Chalmers, *Buddha's Teachings,* pp. 211-19, 37-39 of Vol. 37. (Selections 3 and 6 of Part I.)

Yale University Press, New Haven, for a selection from E. W. Burlingame, *Buddhist Parables,* pp. 92-94. (Selection 5 of Part I.)

Oxford University (The Clarendon Press), for selections from:

Sacred Books of the East, Vol. XVII, edited by T. W. Rhys Davids and H. Oldenberg, pp. 293-306. (Selection 4 of Part I.)

W. E. Soothill, *The Lotus of the Wonderful Law.* (Part IV: Selection 4, pp. 71, 85-94, 106-13, 125-28; Selection 5, pp. 200-06.)

John Murray, London, for selections from L. D. Barnett, *The Path of Light,* pp. 37-94 *passim.* (Selection 3 of Part IV.)

The Liberal Arts Press, Inc., New York, for a selection from C. H. Hamilton, *Buddhism, A Religion of Infinite Compassion* (Library of Religion, No. 1), pp. 126-32. (Selection 2 of Part V.)

The American Oriental Society, New Haven, for a selection from C. H. Hamilton, *Wei Shih Er Shih Lun; The Treatise in Twenty Stanzas on Representation-only by Vasubandhu* (American Oriental Series, Volume 13). (Selection 2 of Part V.)

The Buddhist Society, London, for selections from Chu Chan, *The Huang Po Doctrine of Universal Mind*, pp. 16-50. (Selection 4 of Part V.)

The Chionin Temple, Kyoto, for selections from Coates and Ishizuka, *Honen the Buddhist Saint*, pp. 402-06, 542-45. (Selection 3 of Part VI.)

The Shinshu Otaniha Shumusho, Kyoto, and D. T. Suzuki, for a selection from *A Miscellany on the Shin Teaching of Buddhism* by D. T. Suzuki, pp. 122-28. (Selection 4 of Part VI.)

D. T. Suzuki, for selections from *The Lankavatara Sutra*, pp. 157-60, 182-86, with excerpts from pp. 59, 86, 205. (Selection 6 of Part IV.)

Taylor's Foreign Press, London, and Dr. D. B. Schindler, editor, for a selection from *Asia Major*, New Series, Vol. III, Part 2 (1952), pp. 139-54. (Selection 8 of Part VI.)

My thanks go also to the editors of the New American Library of World Literature. Their unfailing enthusiasm and careful collaboration have been a steady source of support and encouragement.

E. A. BURTT

Ithaca, New York
January, 1955

General Introduction

I

Primitive religions are unlike the great religions of the civilized peoples of the world except in the one feature that is common to all religion—the emotional concern present when men find themselves dependent on powers that are mysterious and unpredictable. The hidden powers by which primitive peoples feel themselves to be surrounded and with which they deal, by magic rite or prayerful appeal, are for the most part local agencies residing in sun, earth, rain, sea, or some species of animal or plant. Such powers are the strange potencies in these natural objects in virtue of which they sometimes act in ways that satisfy man's needs and further his well-being, and sometimes in ways that bring him frustration or even disaster. There is obviously, to primitive man's experience, such a potency in the sun; at times his fructifying warmth pours genially upon the crops through a long growing season so that they yield a rich harvest, at times he burns them up with his fierce heat or hides so often behind the chilly clouds that they grow slowly and poorly. The aim of primitive rites and petitions is to induce these uncertain powers to behave in ways that support man's struggle for life and prosperity instead of in ways that are unco-operative or hostile. Typical of primitive addresses are such expressions as these:

"Sun! I do this so that you may be burning hot, and eat up all the clouds in the sky."

"O millet, thou hast grown well for us; we thank thee, we eat thee."

"Help us, Mother Earth! We depend on your goodness. Let there be rain to water the prairies, that the grass may grow long and the berries be abundant."

There is only the most meager sense in primitive man's mind of any divine powers in the universe that are greater than these potencies, or more awesome from a moral or spiritual point of view.

Why is this so? The answer is fairly simple when one puts himself in the position of a primitive society. Such a group lacks established scientific knowledge of the laws according to which natural processes go on; its members are desperately seeking to maintain existence, health, and security in the absence of such knowledge; their dominant emotions are determined by the threatening or kindly forces on which this struggle depends for its success and which primitive man can only locate in or behind these natural processes. Such potencies constitute the divinities of primitive cultures; there is no awareness of any others, except in the dimmest and vaguest fashion.

At an early period of their history civilized societies lived under the conditions and with the dominant concerns of primitive groups. Most of what is known about their religion at that early stage indicates that it revealed the main characteristics of primitive religion, although there are a few differences that anticipate in some measure the form of civilized religion that later emerged. But why do civilized cultures have any religion at all? The rise of civilization in any part of the world means that, among other things, the society achieving that status has gained at least a rudimentary scientific understanding about the laws governing the processes of nature. It knows how, through a confidently applied technology, to provide a regular food supply and the other resources on which continued existence and health depend. So far as this happens, the mysterious divinities of primitive thought and feeling disappear; they are replaced by the orderly sequences which the scientific mind sees operating everywhere in nature. The capricious rain god gives way to the laws of formation and interaction of high and low pressure areas as they move across the earth's surface; the diabolical monster swallowing the sun or moon disappears in man's awareness of the astronomical motions and relationships which permits an accurate prediction of eclipses. One might think that with the coming of civilization religion would lose its pertinence and fade away—at least as soon as the emotional transformation brought about by the rise of scientific knowledge became complete.

But it did not happen that way. And the historical reason is that the victories gained by man in the emergence of civilization, through providing a solution of the dominant problem faced by primitive man, created another problem—equally challenging but different in kind. The societies that mastered the arts of civilization three thousand or more years ago— in China, India, Persia, Mesopotamia, Egypt, and a little later in southern Europe—became by that fact capable of rapid expansion not possible before. They absorbed less advanced peoples on the periphery of their territory, who were usually enslaved or at least reduced to the status of an inferior caste.

In course of time they came in conflict with other civilized societies who were reaching out in the same way; and the evils of war in its civilized form began to haunt man—first, war for supremacy over a continental region, e.g., Western Asia, then over the Mediterranean world, then over an entire continent or hemisphere, and now in our own day for worldwide supremacy. Within each civilized culture there gradually appeared a vast diversification of economic functions and vocational groups; men were thrown into complex forms of dependence on each other and interaction with each other. In this situation the dominant problem they had to face was very different from that which absorbed the attention and mastered the emotions of primitive man. Primitive groups were struggling to win a greater measure of security against the threatening forces of subhuman nature; on that struggle their physical survival and well-being depended. Civilized societies, by becoming civilized, have solved that problem, sufficiently at least so that the emotions of their leaders are no longer preoccupied and controlled by it. The challenging concern that more and more dominates their minds is how man can find a way to live in peace and harmony with his fellows; it becomes increasingly clear that the capacity of civilized life to survive (let alone rise to new heights of enduring achievement) depends on the successful meeting of this challenge.

Now, just as the essential characteristics of primitive religion reflect the limited understanding and the emotional tension present when men are dominated by that first problem, with the area of mystery which it involved, so the essential characteristics of the great civilized religions reflect the distinctive nature of the second major concern, and the somewhat different area of mystery which a serious and persistent effort to meet it proved to involve. Let us make this difference more explicit; there are four obvious and striking ways in which the orientation toward life and the universe of the civilized faiths diverges sharply from that of a typical primitive religion.

The first and foremost concerns the basic moral attitude of men. Primitives, with the rarest of exceptions, feel no sense of moral obligation toward anyone outside of their small cultural group, and this feeling is freely expressed in their religion. Just as a primitive religionist prays to a divine power: "Let this family prosper, let us be kept in health, let our food grow"; so he can also pray, without any sense of inconsistency: "Great Quahootze! Let me live, find the enemy, not

be afraid of him, find him asleep, and kill many of him."
Civilized religions, on the contrary, accept the principle of
universal moral responsibility, to be expressed toward all men
simply because they are men. This alteration of attitude is
most clearly revealed in their acceptance, without any qualification, of the Golden Rule as the norm of right conduct
in one's relations with his human fellows.

The second concerns man's basic conviction about the universe. Primitive thought takes for granted a cosmological
pluralism. There are many and diverse powers, familiar or more
elusive, that control the way things happen in the processes of
nature; there is no unity of force or law pervading them all.
Civilized theology, philosophy, and science assume, however,
an ultimate monism in the structure of things. There is a single
source and determiner of all reality, or a single principle of
order which gives systematic coherence to the modes of action
of everything that exists. In the theistic religions this unitary
source is conceived as a personal God, who is the creator of
the world and who embodies in perfect form the moral virtues of justice and love implied in sincere commitment to the
Golden Rule. In other religions it may take the form of a
cosmic extension of the moral law, or a superpersonal One
transcending the experienced world and all that it contains.

The third concerns the conception of the human soul. Primitive ideas assume that the soul is a physical or quasi-physical
entity, identified with the breath that animates a living body
or the shadow that it casts as it moves along the ground. The
leaders of civilized religion abandon this notion, finding it
hopelessly unsuited to their experience and their need. In
accepting as valid a universal moral law, and in responding
to the divine as interpreted in monistic terms, they have discovered in themselves, and they ascribe to all men, a spiritual
capacity of which primitive man knows almost nothing. It
is this capacity that constitutes the human soul for them—
the power to respond in feeling and conduct to a supreme
moral ideal and to realize harmony with a Divine Being em-
bodying that ideal. This potency in man gives meaning to
the civilized concept of "self" or "spirit"; it is something invisible and nonmaterial but none the less—as making up the
core of one's personality—it is that in him which is most real
and of greatest value.

The fourth concerns the belief that is held with respect to
the nature of human happiness—the kind of experience in
which man's true well-being and essential integrity lie. The

typical primitive belief on this matter is quite simple. Happiness consists in satisfying our natural desires, as fully and successfully as we can. There is no awareness that the part of our personality which readily identifies itself with these instinctive drives may not be our true self but only an immature, and in the long run unacceptable, substitute for it. But the pioneers of civilized religion have discovered that these spontaneous cravings are quite undependable guides to happiness; they are the causes of much misery and suffering, in ourselves and in others. True happiness consists in identifying ourselves with something that transcends these instinctive urges. In liberating oneness with that transcendent reality, they are sure, we become capable of a joy quite incomparable with the unstable gratifications of those primitive drives that apart from such pioneering discoveries constitute the only happiness man knows. In the language of one of the civilized religions, Christianity, our "old man"—the part of our nature which aggressively seeks these childish gratifications—must be crucified with Christ, so that the new man, which is Christ living in us, may come to birth and show its presence by the fruits of the spirit, such as truthfulness, peace, fearlessness, and love, which then are the spontaneous expression of our transformed nature.

Happily for the full realization of the varied spiritual potentialities of mankind, each of the great civilized religions of the world exemplifies these common characteristics in a somewhat distinctive way. And now that the violent hostility of adherents of one religion toward others is passing away, and is being replaced by an increasing eagerness to appreciate what is significant and valuable in each of them, a magnificent opportunity is open for all men to participate in that realization and to add to their own limited experience and understanding something of the insight achieved by spiritual explorers in other areas of the world.

II

The form in which these characteristics appear in Buddhism as one of the great civilized religions of the East is naturally influenced by its background in the earlier religious thought of India and by the historical situation which Buddha found himself challenged to meet. It was also, of course, largely determined by the unique genius of his own personality.

The earliest religion in India about which we have any definite information is that displayed in the ancient scriptures known as the Vedas, and especially the *Rig Veda*. This is, generally speaking, a form of primitive religion; the divinities addressed and celebrated are the personified forces of nature displayed in the sun, the earth, the rain, the sacrificial fire, the intoxicating libation, the sky, the wind. But beginning about 800 B.C. a novel kind of document appears, the *Upanishads*. The sages presented in these writings are struggling to work out a mystical philosophy of the universe and of human nature, with profound implications touching the way that man must follow to find salvation.

What is meant by a "mystical philosophy," when this term is used not to express vague condemnation but to describe a definite type of orientation in religion and metaphysics? Such an orientation constitutes a minor historical strand in several great religions, e.g., Christianity, Islam, and Confucianism. In Taoism and the Indian religions it is the primary and basic strand, determining the role and meaning of everything in the experience of their adherents and in their theological interpretations. Well, for the mystical way of thinking, one's salvation consists in leaving behind the separate, fearful, self-centered individual that in his finitude he now finds himself to be, and becoming one with the universal and absolute reality—leaving behind the realm of the unstable, transitory, and illusory, and becoming identified with the ultimate and eternal ground of all that exists. The passion of the Indian saint is the passion of the fragment for the whole—the longing to throw off the hampering limitations of finite existence and to achieve union with the infinite.

One of the most popular prayers of the *Upanishads* reads:

> From the unreal lead me to the real;
> From darkness lead me to light;
> From death lead me to deathlessness.

Here speaks the spirit of Indian religion. The problem of life, for this way of thinking, is rooted in the here and now of our daily existence, but the envisioned solution reveals an unquenchable audacity. There is a sense of the limitless possibilities of man, in comparison with which everything that he has already experienced before he becomes poignantly aware of them must be pronounced illusory rather than real, darkness rather than light, death rather than life. The task of man is to leave behind the cramping world of his present acquaintance, leave behind his limited self and all that belongs with it, and become one with transcendent reality—with the divine source of all that is great and good and true. Religion reveals the way of this arduous ascent; anything that does less than this will not, for the Indian mind, deserve to be called religion. Its task is to discover, and make available to men, a new dimension of human potentiality which apart from the insight of religious pioneers would never have been glimpsed.

Plato's famous allegory of the cave[1] presents in poetic and philosophic form the Indian concept of the way to salvation—as a tortuous passage from the darkness of unreality to the brilliant light of the truly real. But a reader of Plato might be left with the impression that this process of emancipation is a purely intellectual one, and that it can be accomplished only by those endowed with high philosophic gifts. To the Indian theologians an intellectual insight is indeed necessary, but the realization as a whole is by no means merely intellectual. It is a remolding of the whole personality—a genuinely new birth, except that it cannot be achieved suddenly but only as a result of long and patient discipline. Its essence is liberation from attachment to the demands and longings that now hold us captive, and to the shrinking self that erects a protective wall of separation between itself and all other forms of life; for it is these that pose the formidable obstructions that stand in the way of our realizing the Infinite and Eternal Being that we truly are. What the world thinks of as life is really death; our task is to escape from it to that which is truly life—the kind of life of which man is intrinsically capable and for which he is divinely destined.

Now the distinctive genius of Buddhism as a civilized religion can best be approached by a brief explanation of the fundamental concepts in which this mystical philosophy which first gains expression in the *Upanishads* is formulated. A mastery of their meaning is essential to a comprehension of Buddha's teaching and of the course of its development in the thought of his followers.

First and quite central is the concept of Brahman, the metaphysical absolute. Out of Brahman come all things; to Brahman all things return. In himself, Brahman is unknown and unknowable, but as taking form and meaning for us men he is *Sat-chit-ananda*—the source and embodiment of reality, knowledge, and bliss. Second, there is the concept of *atman*, the soul or self. And the very meaning of this concept is determined by the central Hindu conviction that the true self

[1] In his *Republic*, Book VII.

of each human being is identical with Brahman, and that
when that identity is realized the quest for salvation is fulfilled.
When the individual soul that has not realized its oneness
with Brahman is discussed, it is referred to as *"jivatman"*
or by the entirely different term *"purusha."* The crucial
stage in the process of gaining this realization is *moksha,*
which means "release" or "liberation." The key idea here
is that what makes possible the realization of identity with
Brahman is the freeing of the self from control by longings which bind it to the needs of the body and to other transitory concerns. Now only in rare cases will an individual be
sufficiently purged of these cravings in his present existence
so that he can hope for *moksha* before the death of the body
which his soul now tenants. But his soul will survive this
event and continue to exist, taking new forms one after another until the purgation is complete; in fact, it has existed
in innumerable forms in the past. This continued transmigration in the "ocean of births and deaths," which inevitably
goes on as long as any taint of self-demandingness is left, is
samsara. And what determines the form that will be taken
in each new existence is the law of *karma.* By this concept
Indian thought expresses the idea that the principle of causality operates in man's moral and spiritual experience, and
does so in a particular way. The state of one's achievement
at the end of his previous existence is the cause whose effect
is the form taken by his present existence; similarly, the state
achieved at the end of the present existence will decide the
form to be taken in the next. Or, stated more generally (so that
it will apply within the sequence of events experienced by
each form of existence as well as between one form and its
successor), *the law of* karma *is the principle that good choices,
earnest efforts, good deeds, build good character, while bad
choices, inertia, and evil deeds build bad character.* In the
latter case one is lengthening and making less hopeful the
round of successive existences, for there is no magical way
by which an evil character can be suddenly transformed into
a good one, whereas in the former case one is shortening it
and making it more hopeful. He is systematically doing what
each person can do to eliminate the moral obstructions that
bind him to the wheel of birth, suffering, and death, and thus
to make the law of *karma* work toward his ultimate release
and his blissful union with Brahman.

To these five concepts should be added a sixth, namely,
dharma. This word has a wide range of meanings in Indian

thought; perhaps the most general meaning, which underlies all of the more specific ones, is "the way that man should follow in order to fulfill his true nature and carry out his moral and social responsibilities." As taken over by Buddhism, this concept undergoes a most extraordinary development, the main features of which will be indicated in the sequel.

Buddha accepted, as essentially sound, the ideas expressed in the concepts of *moksha, samsara,* and *karma,* although some reinterpretation of them proved to be demanded by the principles involved in other aspects of his teaching. The concept of Brahman, as referring to a transcendent source of all reality, he rejected because of the metaphysical position which seemed to him required by a loving commitment to the practical well-being of all men. As marking the goal of the religious quest, Brahman is transformed rather than rejected; that goal is entrance into Nirvana instead of union with Brahman. The term *atman,* being interpreted by the theologians of his day as meaning a changeless and substantial self, he also rejected in favor of a more dynamic conception of human personality. We shall have to clarify later the famous *anatta* ("no soul") doctrine of Buddhism and the problems involved in the concept of Nirvana. What is basic in this area of his thought is that all forms of phenomenal existence, including living creatures, are in constant change and must in time perish. The fact that Buddha accepted so much but not more of the religious, philosophical and psychological framework of thought that was being developed in the *Upanishads* at the time he lived indicates both the degree to which his thinking was embedded in the Indian heritage and the degree to which he was ready to criticize that heritage and strike out along radically novel lines.

What were the main features of the broader human situation that he confronted? In general, that situation was one of radical social readjustment and deepening religious need. Wars were frequent between the petty princes and rival clans in northern India, and the organization of society was moving more and more in the direction of a rigid caste system. The struggle to rise above one's present social status and win a larger sphere of opportunity in life was becoming increasingly difficult. Religious insight was being obstructed by the dead hand of the past; the Vedas were frequently taught as a collection of authoritative texts rather than as living truths to be tested and reinterpreted (if need be) in the present. Heavy and probably increasing emphasis was placed on the correct performance of rite and ceremony. Religious thinkers, in the attempt to satisfy their metaphysical curiosity, were championing varied cosmological systems, each visionary claiming truth for his pet theory and heaping argumentative scorn on the theories of his opponents. Worst of all, perhaps, from Buddha's standpoint, religion was straying through these and other vices away from the insistent, poignant, practical needs of men and women. It was not leading them toward true fulfillment and more dependable happiness; it was becoming mired in obstructive tradition, repetitious rite, and dead or cantankerous dogma. He conceived it as his task to break through or sweep away these obstructive tangles, to find an enduring solution to the real problems of men, and to bring to India and the world a saving message of light and love.

Buddha was born a prince of the Sakya clan, which at that time (the first half of the sixth century B.C.) inhabited a part of the territory now embraced by Nepal and the adjoining area of North India; its capital city was Kapilavastu. His family name was Gautama (or Gotama), and his given name Siddartha. Few people, however, now know about these names, or make any use of them. Just as Jesus of Nazareth became to his devoted followers and to later generations in the Western world the Christ—the "Anointed One" of God, destined to be the Saviour of the world—so this great religious and philosophical pioneer of India became to later centuries the Buddha—the "Illumined One," destined to bring truth and joy and peace to a large fraction of civilized humanity since. And we shall need to be familiar with two other titles that are likewise derived from his religious significance in history. One is easily understood; he is Sakyamuni, the prophetic sage of the Sakyas. The other is haunted by much mystery; he is Tathagata. What this title means is more fully determined than any of the others by devout Buddhist feeling, as it lovingly centers upon him and becomes enriched through time. We may render it, "He who has fully come through," or, more simply and briefly, "the Perfect One"—the one who has attained spiritual perfection.

How glad the student of religion would be if it were possible to penetrate the mixture of legend and history that partially discloses, partially shrouds, the life of this great man! In Buddhist tradition an idealizing and moving story confronts us, filled with all the detail suggested by grateful projection and pious imagination. If the reader wishes to follow such a story, let him turn to the pages of Sir Edwin Arnold's *Light of Asia,* based on the life of Buddha as recounted by Buddhist biographers who lived five to six hundred years after the time of Buddha himself.

What do we know that can be set down with confidence as sober fact? Very little; but that little is deeply significant. Siddartha grew to young manhood amid scenes of luxury and surrounded by all the paraphernalia of sensuous enjoyment; he was protected by his father from learning about the sorrows and frustrations and perplexities to which ordinary flesh is heir. Somehow, when in his early twenties, be became acquainted with the sad facts of old age, of disease, and of death; for the first time he knew the major miseries to which human nature is inevitably subject in a world of decay and dissolution. This experience moved him to anxious and puzzled reflection, and then—having also met a monk full of wisdom, insight, and serenity—to determined, undiscouraged action. He must learn the meaning of life in such a strange world. He left his father's palace with its constant stimulations to self-centered indulgence, left his beautiful wife and newborn son, and wandered into the forest—the accepted haunt in India for those who have found the ways of ordinary life spiritually cramping. His purpose was to discover the truth— the essential and saving truth—about life and death, about sorrow and happiness. For seven years he sought and struggled, in relentless, torturing self-experiment. He inquired of renowned hermit sages. As would be the case in India, with its traditional insistence on renunciation, he tried ascetic denial of the body's demands in extreme form, finally succumbing to the dull blankness of a starving swoon. When he returned to consciousness again he was convinced that this was not the right way—such radical punishment of the body brings, he saw, not spiritual illumination and peace, but exhaustion, torpor, and impotence of mind. Gradually he found more successful clues to the understanding and liberation he sought. After being persistently tempted by the clever demon Mara, his quest reached its culmination in a long period of meditation under a spreading tree, which became for that reason to Buddhists the sacred Bodhi tree, not far from the present city of Gaya in northeastern India.

According to the historical tradition of Southern Buddhism this, the greatest event in all human history, occurred at the full moon of May, 544 B.C., which means that this volume of selections is appearing a year before the 2500th anniversary of that momentous occasion if we accept the Southern chronology.[2] In the joy of assured enlightenment he rose, and, after a brief delay, wandered slowly toward the sacred city of Benares, two hundred-odd miles to the west. How could he make his discovery intelligible and persuasive to others, so that it might guide them also toward true happiness and peace? Apparently there was a strong temptation to keep his illumination to himself, but it became clear that he must make the attempt. It meant formulating the basic truth about life in the halting, inadequate medium of human speech; and then it meant speaking that truth in love, so that others capable of responding to it would sense the answer to their living need too, and would not rest until they had mastered its promise and its power. At Sarnath, a few miles from the river near Benares, he preached his first sermon and won his first converts. Then for forty-odd years he continued to proclaim his message, expanding it in its bearing on the problems that sincere inquirers raised, and adapting it to the special needs of all who found hope and cheer in his presence. At the age of eighty he passed away in the arms of Ananda, his beloved disciple, with the words: "Decay is inherent in all compound things. Work out your own salvation with diligence."

What sort of person did the man whose biography has thus been briefly sketched impress others as being? Gautama the Buddha seems to have combined in high degree two qualities that are rarely found together and each of which is rarely exemplified in high degree. On the one hand he was a man of rich and responsive human sympathy, of unfailing patience, strength, gentleness, and good will. His friendliness, to all who came to him in sincere search, was genuine and un-reserved. He therefore aroused in his followers a wondering, eager, affectionate devotion such as only the greatest leaders of men have awakened. On the other hand, he was a thinker, of unexcelled philosophic power. His was one of the giant intellects of human history, exhibiting a keenness of analytic understanding that has rarely been equaled. He probed through the virtues and the deceptions of the thought of his day, adopting it where it seemed to him clearly sound and abandoning or radically revising it when he saw that it was missing the true and the good. It is in virtue of this characteristic of the Master that Buddhism is the only one of the great religions of the world that is consciously and frankly based on a systematic rational analysis of the problem of life, and of the way

---

[2] The actual date was more likely about fifteen years later, according to the consensus of competent historians.

to its solution. Buddha was a pioneering lover of men, and a philosophic genius, rolled into a single vigorous and radiant personality.

In the brief introductions to the parts into which this book is divided, and to specific selections, I shall add what further comments are needed to enable the reader to understand and appreciate the scriptures here included. In bringing this general introduction to a close I shall summarize briefly the history of Buddhism after the death of its founder.

Given its initial push by Gautama's dynamic personality, Buddhism spread rapidly. In a little more than two centuries after Buddha's death, Asoka, the first Buddhist emperor of India, came to power. Through his influence the new religion not only swept large areas of India but spread to Ceylon and other neighboring regions, especially to the east and the northwest. For a millennium it was a powerful force in molding the religious, moral, artistic, educational, and social life of India. But by the end of that thousand-year period its decline in the subcontinent had begun, and in another five hundred years it had practically disappeared from the land of its birth. But Buddhism lived and continued to grow because of its missionary fervor. The eagerness of its followers to carry the saving way to others had by this time spread it far and wide through northern and eastern Asia. In the west and northwest it was in time met and checked by the surging tide of Islam, but it remained the dominant religion of Ceylon, Burma, Thailand, and some other areas in southeast Asia; it became one of the living religions of China and Korea; it won Tibet and contended successfully with Shinto for the soul of Japan.

In this process of missionary expansion it was itself profoundly transformed, and the most significant steps in this transformation we shall later need to follow. During the early centuries of that period—from about 200 B.C. to A.D. 200—a cleavage into the two great schools of subsequent Buddhist history, Mahayana and Hinayana Buddhism, was taking place. Since these two terms themselves reflect the Mahayana viewpoint (Mahayana meaning "the greater vehicle" of salvation, and Hinayana "the lesser vehicle") I shall refer to the Hinayana school by a different term that is nonprejudicial and is acceptable in the Hinayana countries, namely "Theravada" Buddhism ("the way of the elders"). In general, the farther Buddhism spread, in space and in time, from the locus and date of its origin, the deeper the remolding it underwent. By keeping this fact in mind we shall be prepared for the novel ideas and emphases which will be revealed, especially in the selections expressing the devotional spirit of Chinese and Japanese Buddhism.

At the present time Buddhism is adjusting itself to the challenging impact of Western culture upon the East, and to all the varied forces that have broken loose in the modern world. So far as concerns the general situation in the Buddhist countries, two encouraging signs for the future are at hand. One is the formation of a World Buddhist Fellowship, drawing upon Buddhists in all countries, Theravada and Mahayana, for its membership; it has already held two conferences at which a united Buddhist orientation toward the world has been expressed. The other is the convening of the Sixth Buddhist Council at Rangoon, in a series of meetings extending for two years from May 1954 and focusing upon the commemoration of the 2500th anniversary of Buddha's illumination, during which it is expected that the first complete edition of the canonical Buddhist scriptures (the *Tripitaka* or "Three Baskets") will be published.

III

A few words, now, with regard to problems confronted by the editor in selecting and arranging material for the present volume.

For Theravadins, in a significant sense, the *Tripitaka* constitutes the scriptural canon of their religion. But for Buddhism as a whole there is no canon comparable to the Bible for Christianity or the Koran for Islam. Accordingly, I have interpreted the title of this volume in a very broad fashion; a more descriptive title would be "Teachings Expressing Varied Historical Trends in the Development of Buddhism." If Mahayana Buddhism is to be included at all, such a broad interpretation can hardly be avoided; and all of these trends spring from the inspiration of Gautama the Buddha. The reader will find, therefore, selections whose dates vary from the time when the earliest discourses were committed to writing to the thirteenth century A.D., when the latest sects influential in Japanese Buddhism were founded.

Thus interpreted, the field from which selection can be made is vast. Much of it has not yet been rendered available for detailed and comparative study, and by no means all of what is accessible has as yet been translated into English. Moreover, even of the translations now at hand only a very few combine all of the three virtues that are essential to a good translation of religious writings: scholarly accuracy, deep spiritual perceptiveness, and thorough familiarity with the conceptual framework presupposed by thinkers who use the language of the translation. This unhappily limiting situation is now being remedied, and with increasing rapidity; one may expect that within a very few years much more relevant material will be available in English, and that translations superior to those now at hand will be published in increasing number.

Under the restrictions of the present situation I have made the most judicious choices that I was able to make, with the specific purpose of this volume constantly in mind. Since so few available translations exemplify all of the desired virtues, I have been guided by my own sense of the wise balance between them. I have not hesitated at times to pick a more readable translation instead of one that is presumably more accurate from a scholarly standpoint; I have even used one or two rather free renderings which express the substance and the religious spirit of the thought at some cost in terms of other virtues. In both these situations, however, I have endeavored, with the kindly aid of scholar friends, to correct any serious errors that might have crept into these translations. Where the chief defect of a document that I wished to use was lack of familiarity on the translator's part with the linguistic framework now taken for granted by philosophers and theologians who write in English, I have made what changes seemed to be essential for ready intelligibility.

Since this book aims to reach the general reading public rather than scholars, I have dispensed with the diacritical marks to which those acquainted with Sanskrit and Pali are accustomed, for distinguishing between vowels and consonants represented by the same English letter. Readers who proceed —and I hope many will—to a more systematic study of Buddhist literature will need to become familiar with these marks, but then rather than now will be the appropriate time.

I have not found it necessary, for the purpose of this volume, to pass any judgment on the interesting question: Of the various scriptures which were, presumably, committed to writing quite early, which come closest to communicating the actual words of Gautama himself, and which reveal changes that had slowly taken place during the several generations or centuries that elapsed before this material was written down? However, I could not avoid judging as to which of the teachings contained in these scriptures most likely constitute his basic doctrines. This judgment is reflected in the material contained in Part I. Most of the writings drawn upon in the first three parts are of approximately equal age and canonical authority.

With this comment, the division of the selections that follow into the two books with their six parts will be self-explanatory. A further consideration guiding this division was the desire to limit each part to such a length that it can be read at a single relatively brief sitting. Any reader may, however, dip here and there into various parts as the mood of the moment leads him.

I wish to give specific mention to two of the sources from which the materials selected are drawn. Readers who undertake a more extensive study in this field will find great help in Edward Conze's *Buddhist Texts Through the Ages,* published, 1954, by Philosophical Library. Another valuable group of selections will be found in C. H. Hamilton's *Buddhism,* published in 1952 by the Liberal Arts Press.

A brief bibliography and a glossary of Sanskrit and Pali terms used in these selections are given at the end of the volume.

In closing, I wish to dedicate this book to the living memory of the towering personality whose beneficent influence through subsequent centuries it attempts in its modest way to reveal. His climactic experience happened twenty-five hundred years ago, but its spiritual radiance has not faded nor its illuminating power weakened. May this humble work contribute toward a wider knowledge of the great religion which he founded, and a deeper appreciation of the insight into saving truth that the world owes to him.

Book One

THE EARLY SCRIPTURES OF BUDDHISM

PART I: Some Basic Doctrines of the Buddha

Introduction

This section consists of especially basic and revealing teachings of Gautama given after his enlightenment. Although much, if not all, of this material was first committed to writing several generations after his death, I believe that it expresses the substance of his major doctrines and authentically discloses his keen and winsome personality.

Being a philosopher as well as a great spiritual pioneer, Buddha discarded all claims to special revelation and all appeals to authority or tradition. He found his standard of truth, and his way of discriminating it from error, in the common reason and experience of men as they can be brought to bear on the universal problem of life. And what is that problem? Well, its nature is set, he was sure, by the harassing ills that life in a world of unceasing generation and destruction inevitably brings, and by the fact that in trying to deal with these ills men and women mistake the way to true happiness for themselves and for others. But Buddha was confident that by the clarifying application of reason to the lessons of experience we can discriminate the conditions of genuine health of personality from their meretricious counterparts, and can likewise discriminate the qualities of mind that dependably further those conditions from qualities that fail to do so or are hostile to them. Especially was he confident that a rational analysis of the basic lessons taught by experience can locate the root of evil as it lies in the inner nature of each human being—that root whose uprooting is necessary and sufficient if any person is to find true well-being for himself and become a source of true well-being for others. This analysis yields the specifically Buddhist understanding of the universal problem of man, and the way of this uprooting is the way to salvation as Buddha conceived that goal.

The gist of the basic analysis is given in the famous sermon at Benares with which Buddha's sharing of his insight with others opened. Perhaps the reader will comprehend better the significance of that discourse if I, in anticipation, translate what I take to be the essence of his meaning into more familiar Western terms. It consists of the "Four Noble (Aryan) Truths," which I shall state as follows:

I. Existence is unhappiness.
II. Unhappiness is caused by selfish craving.
III. Selfish craving can be destroyed.
IV. It can be destroyed by following the eightfold path, whose steps are:
    1. Right understanding
    2. Right purpose (aspiration)
    3. Right speech
    4. Right conduct
    5. Right vocation
    6. Right effort
    7. Right alertness
    8. Right concentration

What is it that Buddha is telling the world here? First, that by the mere fact of being born under the conditions of finite existence every living creature is subject to the evils of sickness, old age, and death, and to the sadness that comes when his loved ones are stricken by these ills. These inevitable occasions of unhappiness (*dukha*) constitute the problem of life. But they would not make us unhappy were it not for the blind demandingness (*tanha*) in our nature which leads us to ask of the universe, for ourselves and those specially dear to us, more than it is ready or even able to give. Moreover, it is this same unrealistic and selfish craving which, frustrated as it inevitably becomes, moves us to act in ways that increase the unhappiness of others. Hence this is the factor in us which each person is responsible for bringing under control, in order that he may be a source of true and dependable well-being to himself and to others. Now, nothing short of complete destruction of this factor will do, for as long as any taint of it is left it cannot help affecting our action and poisoning our mental state. And under the Bodhi tree Buddha had discovered that such complete destruction is possible; others, too, who have followed him have made the same discovery, and their achievement gives further proof.

The way to such destruction lies in treading resolutely the eight steps of the right path. The first two of these are preliminary conditions that are essential; without a right understanding of the problem of life and a settled purpose to achieve the solution no further progress can be expected. The third, fourth, and fifth steps constitute a pledge of one's readiness to order his daily life in a manner consistent with his announced goal, and constitute the moral foundation on which progress toward the goal can be built. Even while one is still a spiritual novice he can use words as a medium of thorough honesty, he can follow the basic rules of moral conduct, he can earn his living in a way that is ethically reputable; and if he is not able to take these steps what ground for hope can there be of his capacity to undergo the deeper forms of renunciation that will be required? The last three steps are fundamental conditions of systematic progress toward the goal. They culminate in the achieved power of absolute concentration, by which the mind shows itself completely free from the sudden promptings and unpredictable flittings due to selfish craving. The person who has reached this stage is no longer subject to rebirth; he enters Nirvana, which is to be conceived not as sheer extinction but as the state naturally produced by the destruction of *tanha*—a state marked on the positive side by a sense of liberation, inward peace and strength, insight into truth, the joy of complete oneness with reality, and love toward all creatures in the universe.

1. The Sermon at Benares

Thus have I heard: at one time the Lord dwelt at Benares at Isipatana in the Deer Park. There the Lord addressed the five monks:—

"These two extremes, monks, are not to be practised by one who has gone forth from the world. What are the two? That conjoined with the passions and luxury, low, vulgar, common, ignoble, and useless; and that conjoined with self-torture, painful, ignoble, and useless. Avoiding these two extremes the Tathagata[1] has gained the enlightenment of the Middle Path, which produces insight and knowledge, and tends to calm, to higher knowledge, enlightenment, Nirvana.

[1] The Perfect One, i.e., the Buddha. See above, p. 20.

"And what, monks, is the Middle Path, of which the Tathagata has gained enlightenment, which produces insight and knowledge, and tends to calm, to higher knowledge, enlightenment, Nirvana? This is the noble Eightfold Way: namely, right view, right intention, right speech, right action, right livelihood, right effort, right mindfulness, right concentration. This, monks, is the Middle Path, of which the Tathagata has gained enlightenment, which produces insight and knowledge, and tends to calm, to higher knowledge, enlightenment, Nirvana.

"(1) Now this, monks, is the noble truth of pain: birth is painful, old age is painful, sickness is painful, death is painful, sorrow, lamentation, dejection, and despair are painful. Contact with unpleasant things is painful, not getting what one wishes is painful. In short the five groups of grasping[2] are painful.

"(2) Now this, monks, is the noble truth of the cause of pain: the craving, which tends to rebirth, combined with pleasure and lust, finding pleasure here and there; namely, the craving for passion, the craving for existence, the craving for non-existence.

"(3) Now this, monks, is the noble truth of the cessation of pain, the cessation without a remainder of craving, the abandonment, forsaking, release, non-attachment.

"(4) Now this, monks, is the noble truth of the way that leads to the cessation of pain: this is the noble Eightfold Way; namely, right views, right intention, right speech, right action, right livelihood, right effort, right mindfulness, right concentration.

" 'This is the noble truth of pain': Thus, monks, among doctrines unheard before, in me sight and knowledge arose, wisdom arose, knowledge arose, light arose.

" 'This noble truth of pain must be comprehended.' Thus, monks, among doctrines unheard before, in me sight and knowledge arose, wisdom arose, knowledge arose, light arose.

" 'It has been comprehended.' Thus, monks, among doctrines unheard before, in me sight and knowledge arose, wisdom arose, knowledge arose, light arose. [Repeated for the second truth, with the statement that the cause of pain

[2] The five *skandhas,* factors which make up an individual. See below, p. 86.

must be abandoned and has been abandoned, for the third truth that the cessation of pain must be realized and has been realized, and for the fourth that the Way must be practised and has been practised.]

"As long as in these four noble truths my due knowledge and insight with the three sections[3] and twelve divisions was not well purified, even so long, monks, in the world with its gods, Mara,[4] Brahma,[5] its beings with ascetics, brahmins, gods, and men, I had not attained the highest complete enlightenment. This I recognized.

"And when, monks, in these four noble truths my due knowledge and insight with its three sections and twelve divisions was well purified, then monks . . . I had attained the highest complete enlightenment. This I recognized. Knowledge arose in me, insight arose that the release of my mind is unshakable: this is my last existence; now there is no rebirth."

Thus spoke the Lord, and the five monks expressed delight and approval at the Lord's utterance. And while this exposition was being uttered there arose in the elder Kondanna the pure and spotless eye of the doctrine that whatever was liable to origination was all liable to cessation.

Thus when the Wheel of the Doctrine was set turning by the Lord, the earth-dwelling gods raised a shout: "This supreme Wheel of the Doctrine has been set going by the Lord at Benares at Isipatana in the Deer Park, a Wheel which has not been set going by any ascetic, brahmin, god, Mara, Brahma, or by anyone in the world." The gods of the heaven of the four Great Kings, hearing the shout of the earth-dwelling gods, raised a shout . . . The gods of the heaven of the Thirty-three, hearing the shout of the gods of the four Great Kings . . . the Yama gods . . . the Tusita gods . . . the Nimmanarati gods . . . the Paranimmitavasavattin gods . . . the gods of the Brahma-world raised a shout:[6] "This supreme Wheel of the Doctrine has been set going by the Lord at Benares at Isipatana

___

[3] These appear to refer to the three ways in which each of the four truths is treated: (1) there is pain, (2) it must be comprehended, (3) I have comprehended it.
[4] The great tempter, in Indian thought. See above, p. 21.
[5] See above, pp. 17 ff.
[6] The terms in capital letters refer to supernatural regions recognized in Indian mythology.

in the Deer Park, a Wheel which has not been set going by any ascetic, brahmin, god, Mara, Brahma, or by anyone in the world."

Thus at that very time, at that moment, at that second, a shout went up as far as the Brahma-world,[7] and this ten-thousandfold world system shook, shuddered, and trembled, and a boundless great light appeared in the world surpassing the divine majesty of the gods. . . .

2. Questions Not Tending to Edification

What was Buddha's position on metaphysical questions? West-
ern students have generally believed that it was a form of
agnosticism, since it has some similarities with that viewpoint
which is familiar to them. But it should more properly be
described as an avoidance of commitment to any of the alter-
native doctrines on these matters. And his radically practical
reason for such avoidance is brought out in many passages,
especially in the following selection from Sutta 63 of the
Majjhima-Nikaya.[8]

Thus have I heard.

On a certain occasion the Blessed One was dwelling at Savatthi in Jetavana monastery in Anathapindika's Park. Now it happened to the venerable Malunkyaputta, being in seclusion and plunged in meditation, that a consideration presented itself to his mind, as follows:

"These theories which the Blessed One has left un-explained, has set aside and rejected—that the world is eternal, that the world is not eternal, that the world is finite, that the world is infinite, that the soul and the body are identical, that the soul is one thing and the body an-other, that the saint[9] exists after death, that the saint does not exist after death, that the saint both exists and does not exist after death, that the saint neither exists nor does not exist after death—these the Blessed One does not ex-

[7] The highest of these regions.
[8] As translated by H. C. Warren. I have substituted the word "explain" where he uses the vaguer and more puzzling word "elucidate."
[9] The *arahat*, person who has gained liberation.

plain to me. And the fact that the Blessed One does not explain them to me does not please me nor suit me. Therefore I will draw near to the Blessed One and inquire of him concerning this matter. If the Blessed One will explain to me, either that the world is eternal, or that the world is not eternal, or that the world is finite, or that the world is infinite, or that the soul and the body are identical, or that the soul is one thing and the body another, or that the saint exists after death, or that the saint does not exist after death, or that the saint both exists and does not exist after death, or that the saint neither exists nor does not exist after death, in that case will I lead the religious life under the Blessed One. If the Blessed One will not explain to me, either that the world is eternal, or that the world is not eternal . . . or that the saint neither exists nor does not exist after death, in that case I will abandon religious training and return to the lower life of a layman."

Then the venerable Malunkyaputta arose at eventide from his seclusion, and drew near to where the Blessed One was; and having drawn near and greeted the Blessed One, he sat down respectfully at one side. And seated respectfully at one side, the venerable Malunkyaputta spoke to the Blessed One as follows:

"Reverend Sir, it happened to me, as I was just now in seclusion and plunged in meditation, that a consideration presented itself to my mind, as follows: 'These theories which the Blessed One has left unexplained, has set aside and rejected—that the world is eternal, that the world is not eternal . . . that the saint neither exists nor does not exist after death—these the Blessed One does not explain to me. And the fact that the Blessed One does not explain them to me does not please me nor suit me. I will draw near to the Blessed One and inquire of him concerning this matter. If the Blessed One will explain to me, either that the world is eternal, or that the world is not eternal . . . or that the saint neither exists nor does not exist after death, in that case will I lead the religious life under the Blessed One. If the Blessed One will not explain to me, either that the world is eternal, or that the world is not eternal . . . or that the saint neither exists nor does not exist after death, in that case will I abandon religious training and return to the lower life of a layman.'

"If the Blessed One knows that the world is eternal, let the Blessed One explain to me that the world is eternal; if the Blessed One knows that the world is not eternal, let the Blessed One explain to me that the world is not eternal. If the Blessed One does not know either that the world is eternal or that the world is not eternal, the only upright thing for one who does not know, or who has not that insight, is to say, 'I do not know; I have not that insight.' " . . .

"Pray, Malunkyaputta, did I ever say to you, 'Come, Malunkyaputta, lead the religious life under me, and I will explain to you either that the world is eternal, or that the world is not eternal . . . or that the saint neither exists nor does not exist after death'?"

"Nay, verily, Reverend Sir."

"Or did you ever say to me, 'Reverend Sir, I will lead the religious life under the Blessed One, on condition that the Blessed One explain to me either that the world is eternal, or that the world is not eternal . . . or that the saint neither exists nor does not exist after death'?"

"Nay, verily, Reverend Sir."

"So you acknowledge, Malunkyaputta, that I have not said to you, 'Come, Malunkyaputta, lead the religious life under me and I will explain to you either that the world is eternal, or that the world is not eternal . . . or that the saint neither exists nor does not exist after death'; and again that you have not said to me, 'Reverend Sir, I will lead the religious life under the Blessed One, on condition that the Blessed One explain to me either that the world is eternal, or that the world is not eternal . . . or that the saint neither exists nor does not exist after death.' That being the case, vain man, whom are you so angrily denouncing?

"Malunkyaputta, any one who should say, 'I will not lead the religious life under the Blessed One until the Blessed One shall explain to me either that the world is eternal, or that the world is not eternal . . . or that the saint neither exists nor does not exist after death';—that person would die, Malunkyaputta, before the Tathagata had ever explained this to him.

"It is as if, Malunkyaputta, a man had been wounded by an arrow thickly smeared with poison, and his friends and companions, his relatives and kinsfolk, were to procure for him a physician or surgeon; and the sick man were to say, 'I will not have this arrow taken out until I have learnt whether the man who wounded me belonged to the warrior caste, or to the Brahmin caste, or to the agricultural caste, or to the menial caste.'

"Or again he were to say, 'I will not have this arrow taken out until I have learnt the name of the man who wounded me, and to what clan he belongs.'

"Or again he were to say, 'I will not have this arrow taken out until I have learnt whether the man who wounded me was tall, or short, or of the middle height.'

"Or again he were to say, 'I will not have this arrow taken out until I have learnt whether the man who wounded me was black, or dusky, or of a yellow skin.'

"Or again he were to say, 'I will not have this arrow taken out until I have learnt whether the man who wounded me was from this or that village, or town, or city.' . . .

[Many other possibilities are mentioned.]

"That man would die, Malunkyaputta, without ever having learnt this.

"In exactly the same way, Malunkyaputta, any one who should say, 'I will not lead the religious life under the Blessed One until the Blessed One shall explain to me either that the world is eternal, or that the world is not eternal . . . or that the saint neither exists nor does not exist after death';—that person would die, Malunkyaputta, before the Tathagata had ever explained this to him.

"The religious life, Malunkyaputta, does not depend on the dogma that the world is eternal; nor does the religious life, Malunkyaputta, depend on the dogma that the world is not eternal. Whether the dogma obtain, Malunkyaputta, that the world is eternal, or that the world is not eternal, there still remain birth, old age, death, sorrow, lamentation, misery, grief, and despair, for the extinction of which in the present life I am prescribing. . . .

"Accordingly, Malunkyaputta, bear always in mind what it is that I have not explained, and what it is that I have explained. And what, Malunkyaputta, have I not explained? I have not explained, Malunkyaputta, that the world is eternal; I have not explained that the world is not eternal; I have not explained that the world is finite; I have not explained that the world is infinite; I have not explained that the soul and the body are identical; I have not explained that the soul is one thing and the body another; I have not explained that the saint exists after death; I have not explained that the saint does not exist after death; I have not explained that the saint both exists and does not exist after death; I have not explained that the saint neither exists nor does not exist after death. And why, Malunkyaputta, have I not explained this? Because, Malunkyaputta, this profits not, nor has to do with the fundamentals of religion, nor tends to aversion, absence of passion, cessation, quiescence, the supernatural faculties, supreme wisdom, and Nirvana; therefore have I not explained it?

"And what, Malunkyaputta, have I explained? Misery, Malunkyaputta, have I explained; the origin of misery have I explained; the cessation of misery have I explained; and the path leading to the cessation of misery have I explained. And why, Malunkyaputta, have I explained this? Because, Malunkyaputta, this does profit, has to do with the fundamentals of religion, and tends to aversion, absence of passion, cessation, quiescence, knowledge, supreme wisdom, and Nirvana; therefore have I explained it. Accordingly, Malunkyaputta, bear always in mind what it is that I have not explained, and what it is that I have explained." . . .

3. Truth Is Above Sectarian Dogmatism

Why was Buddha so confident that concern with metaphysical theories is unprofitable and does not tend toward spiritual edification? The basic reasons are vividly disclosed in the following selection from the Sutta-Nipata.

In the first place, no particular theory on such matters can be clearly established, as against alternative views. All alike are spun from sense data whose perception, in the case of each metaphysician, inevitably reflects his variable passions and egoistic demands. Thus, in the second place, the assertion of any such theory naturally provokes the assertion of counter-theories by others; this process generates heated and contentious argument, with its accompanying unresolved hostilities and mutual recriminations. It does not promote the humble self-searching and unity of understanding that are essential if the true spiritual goal is to be reached.

Any supposed truth that cannot be spoken in love and inward peace is not truth.

The Enquirer: Fixed in their pet beliefs,
    these divers wranglers bawl—
  "Hold this, and truth is yours";
  "Reject it, and you're lost."

  Thus they contend, and dub
  opponents "dolts" and "fools."
  Which of the lot is right,
  when all as experts pose?

The Lord: Well, if dissent denotes
  a "fool" and stupid "dolt,"
  then all are fools and dolts,
  —since each has his own view.

  Or, if each rival creed
  proves lore and brains and wit,
  no "dolts" exist,—since all
  alike are on a par.

  I count not that as true
  which those affirm, who call
  each other "fools."—They call
  each other so, because
  each deems his own view "Truth."

The Enquirer: What some style "truth," the rest
  call empty lies;—strife reigns.
  Pray, why do anchorites
  not speak in unison?

The Lord: There's one sole "Truth" (not two),
  to know which bars men's strife.
  But such a motley crowd
  of "truths" have they evolved,
  that anchorites, perforce,
  speak not in full accord.

The Enquirer: What makes these "experts" preach
"truths" so diverse? Is each
inherited? or just
a view they've framed themselves?

The Lord: Apart from consciousness,
no diverse truths exist.
—Mere sophistry declares
this "true," and that view "false."

The senses' evidence,
and works, inspire such scorn
for others, and such smug
conviction *he* is right,
that all his rivals rank
as "sorry, brainless fools." . . .

Delight in their dear views
makes sectaries assert
that all who disagree
"miss Purity and err."

These divers sectaries
—these sturdy advocates
of private paths to bliss—
claim Purity as theirs
alone, not found elsewhere.
Whom should the sturdiest
venture to call a "fool,"
when this invites the like
retort upon himself?

Stubborn in theories
which they themselves devised,
these wrangle on through life.
—Leave then dogmatic views
and their attendant strife! . . .

No dogmatist can win,
by self-concocted views,
the way to Purity.
Mere prepossessions point
his road to "Light"; he "sees"
his old-time "Purity." [1]

[1] I.e., the mistaken idea of purification determined by his dogmatic
prejudices.

No "Brahmin true" attains
the goal by mere research;
no partisan is he,
nor brother-sectary;
all vulgar theories
—which others toil to learn—
he knows, but heeds them not.

From earthly trammels freed,
aloof from party broils,
at peace where peace has fled,
the'unheeding sage ignores
what others toil to learn.

From whilom cankers purged,
with no fresh growths afoot,
from lusts and dogmas free,
quit too of theories,
he goes his stainless way,
devoid of self-reproach.

4. How Buddha Met a Schism Among His Disciples

Disputes broke out among Buddha's disciples from time to time, even while he was still among them. The following selection from the Maha-Vagga *reveals how he dealt with one such unhappy situation.*

At first, apparently, he left them in the midst of their wrangling, after general warnings about the causes and dangers of division, hoping that they would find the resources to end the discord themselves. This hope proved too optimistic, and the quarrel led to hostile words and even blows. The culmination of the incident is the story of Prince Dirghayu. Buddha's aim, in this story, was not merely to clarify the futility and grief-producing character of hatred, and by contrast the hopeful promise of renouncing hatred, but also to elicit in them a willingness to prefer the ends of loving understanding to those which would result if each group uncompromisingly maintained its partisan position.

And the Blessed One addressed the bhikshus[2] and told them the story of Prince Dirghayu. He said:[3]

"In former times, there lived at Benares a powerful king whose name was Brahmadatta of Kashi; and he went to war against Dirgheti, the king of Kosala, for he thought, 'The kingdom of Kosala is small and Dirgheti will not be able to resist my armies.'

"And Dirgheti, seeing that resistance was impossible against the great host of the king of Kashi, fled, leaving his little kingdom in the hands of Brahmadatta, and having wandered from place to place, he came at last to Benares, and lived there with his consort in a potter's dwelling outside the town.

"And the queen bore him a son and they called him Dirghayu.

"When Dirghayu had grown up, the king thought to himself: 'King Brahmadatta has done us great harm, and he is fearing our revenge; he will seek to kill us. Should he find us he will slay us all three.' And he sent his son away, and Dirghayu having received a good education from his father, applied himself diligently to learn all arts, becoming very skilful and wise.

"At that time the barber of king Dirgheti dwelt at Benares, and he saw the king, his former master, and being of an avaricious nature betrayed him to king Brahmadatta.

"When Brahmadatta, the king of Kashi, heard that the fugitive king of Kosala lived with his wife, unknown and in disguise, a quiet life in a potter's dwelling, he ordered him and his queen to be bound and executed; and the sheriff to whom the order was given seized king Dirgheti and led him to the place of execution.

"While the captive king was led through the streets of Benares he saw his son who had returned to visit his parents, and, careful not to betray the presence of his son, yet anxious to communicate to him his last advice, he cried: 'O Dirghayu, my son! Do not look long, do not look short, for not by hatred is hatred appeased; hatred is appeased by not-hatred[4] only.'

[2] Mendicant monks.
[3] This is a condensed rendering of the original, omitting repetitions and minor incidents.
[4] A better rendering for "not-hatred" would be "the renouncing of hatred," here and on the following pages.

"The king of Kosala was cruelly executed together with his wife, but Dirghayu their son bought strong wine and made the guards drunk. When the night arrived he laid the bodies of his parents upon a funeral pyre and burned them with all honors and religious rites.

"When king Brahmadatta learned of it, he became afraid, for he thought, 'Dirghayu, the son of king Dirgheti, will take revenge for the death of his parents, and if he espies a favorable occasion, he will assassinate me.'

"Young Dirghayu went to the forest and wept to his heart's content. Then he wiped his tears and returned to Benares. Hearing that assistants were wanted in the royal elephant stable, he offered his services and was engaged by the master of the elephants.

"And it happened that the king heard a sweet voice ringing through the night and singing to the lute a beautiful song that gladdened his heart. And having inquired among his attendants who the singer might be, he was told that the master of the elephants had in his service a young man of great accomplishments, and beloved by all his comrades. They said, 'He was wont to sing to the lute, and he must have been the singer that gladdened the heart of the king.'

"And the king ordered the young man before him and, being much pleased with Dirghayu, gave him employment in the royal castle. Observing how wisely the youth acted, how modest he was and yet punctilious in the performance of his work, the king very soon gave him a position of trust.

"Now it came to pass that the king went ahunting and became separated from his retinue, young Dirghayu alone remaining with him as his driver. And the king, worn out from the hunt, laid his head into the lap of young Dirghayu and slept.

"And Dirghayu thought: 'This king Brahmadatta had done us great injury; he robbed us of our kingdom and slew my father and my mother. He is now in my power.' Thinking thus he unsheathed his sword.

"Then Dirghayu thought of the last words of his father: 'Do not look long, do not look short. For not by hatred is hatred appeased. Hatred is appeased by not-hatred alone.' Thinking thus, he put his sword back into the sheath.

"The king became restless in his sleep and he awoke, and when the youth asked 'Why do you look frightened,

O king?' he replied: 'My sleep is always restless because I often dream that young Dirghayu comes upon me with his sword. While I lay here with my head in your lap I dreamed the dreadful dream again; and I awoke full of terror and alarm.'

"Then the youth laying his left hand upon the defenceless king's head and with his right hand drawing his sword said: 'I am Dirghayu, the son of king Dirgheti, whom you have robbed of his kingdom and slain together with his wife, my mother. The time of revenge has come.'

"The king seeing himself at the mercy of young Dirghayu raised his hands and said: 'Grant me my life, my dear Dirghayu, grant me my life, my dear Dirghayu!'

"And Dirghayu said without bitterness or ill-will: 'How can I grant you your life, O king, since my life is endangered by you. It is you, O king, who must grant me my life.'

"And the king said: 'Well, my dear Dirghayu, then grant me my life, and I will grant you your life.'

"Thus, king Brahmadatta of Kashi and young Dirghayu granted each other life and took each other's hands and swore an oath not to do any harm to each other. And on their return from the hunt the king was true to his word.

"And king Brahmadatta of Kashi said to young Dirghayu: 'Why did your father say to you in the hour of his death: "Do not look long, do not look short, for hatred is not appeased by hatred. Hatred is appeased by not-hatred alone,"—what did your father mean by that?'

"The youth replied: 'When my father, O king, in the hour of his death said: "Not long," he meant, let not your hatred last long. And when my father said, "Not short," he meant, Do not be hasty to fall out with your friends. And when he said, "For not by hatred is hatred appeased; hatred is appeased by not-hatred," he meant this: You have killed my father and mother, O king. If I should deprive you of your life, then your partisans would deprive me of life; my partisans again would deprive those of life. Thus by hatred, hatred would not be appeased. But now, O king, you have granted me my life, and I have granted you your life; thus by not-hatred hatred has been appeased.'

"Then king Brahmadatta of Kashi thought: 'How wise is young Dirghayu that he understands in its full extent the meaning of what his father spoke so concisely.' And the king gave him back his father's kingdom and gave him his daughter in marriage."

Having finished the story, the Blessed One said:

"Now, O bhikkhus, if such can be the forbearance and mildness of kings who wield the sceptre and bear the sword, so much more, O bhikkhus, must you so let your light shine before the world that you, having embraced the religious life according to so well-taught a doctrine and a discipline, are seen to be forbearing and mild. . . .

"Enough, O bhikkhus, no altercations, no contentions, no disunion, no quarrels!"

5. The Parable of the Mustard Seed*

The reader must not allow the brevity of this little story of Kisa Gotami to obscure its profound revelatory and spiritual significance. Two of Buddha's most important doctrines are taught in it. The source[1] from which it comes is not as ancient, presumably, as the scriptures drawn upon in the rest of this section, but there seems every reason to believe that these main lessons authentically reflect his teaching.

The first can be stated very briefly. Everything in the realm of phenomenal existence is in change and is transitory. Whatever becomes, passes away; whatever is born must die. Every living creature, like other things, is a compound of elements; sooner or later they must dissolve. Hence a realistic acceptance of death is an essential part of true adjustment to reality.

But, and here we come to the second lesson, this story reveals the essential connection, in Buddha's experience and teaching, between a realistic acceptance of death and the realization of an outgoing compassion toward all living beings who, like ourselves, are subject to such ills.

As long as one is completely absorbed in his own grief, arising from the death of a dear one, there is no way of gaining victory over pain or release from the numbing bitterness of loss. He may gradually forget, as most people do, but that is to accept the numbness rather than fully to adjust to

* E. W. Burlingame *Buddhist Parables*, Copyright, 1922, Yale University Press, pp. 92-94.
[1] The Anguttara Commentary. The story, in varied forms, appears in other sources.

*reality. If, instead, one can identify in feeling with the experi-
ence of others who similarly suffer, he will be freed from his
own grief by and in a compassionate oneness with all living
beings. This oneness intrinsically brings an enduring peace and
joy that are superior to grief—superior because they spring not
from hopelessly trying to evade its causes or stoically steeling
the mind to its impact, but through overcoming the evil to
oneself by the good of a deep and fully satisfying love for
others.*

*Buddha, sensing the spiritual capacity in Kisa Gotami, used
the occasion of her overwhelming sorrow to guide her into
an experience that would realize her power of tender, and
therefore liberating, identification with others who sorrow too.*

Gotami was her family name, but because she tired easily,
she was called Kisa Gotami, or Frail Gotami. She was
reborn at Savatthi in a poverty-stricken house. When she
grew up, she married, going to the house of her husband's
family to live. There, because she was the daughter of a
poverty-stricken house, they treated her with contempt.
After a time she gave birth to a son. Then they accorded her
respect.

But when that boy of hers was old enough to play and
run hither and about, he died. Sorrow sprang up within her.
Thought she: Since the birth of my son, I, who was once
denied honor and respect in this very house, have received
respect. These folk may even seek to cast my son away.
Taking her son on her hip, she went about from one house
door to another, saying: "Give me medicine for my son!"

Wherever people encountered her, they said, Where did
you ever meet with medicine for the dead? So saying, they
clapped their hands and laughed in derision. She had not
the slightest idea what they meant.

Now a certain wise man saw her and thought: This
woman must have been driven out of her mind by sorrow
for her son. But medicine for her, no one else is likely to
know—the Possessor of the Ten Forces alone is likely to
know. Said he: "Woman, as for medicine for your son—
there is no one else who knows—the Possessor of the Ten
Forces, the foremost individual in the world of men and
the worlds of the gods, resides at a neighboring monastery.
Go to him and ask."

The man speaks the truth, thought she. Taking her son on her hip, when the Tathagata sat down in the Seat of the Buddhas, she took her stand in the outer circle of the congregation and said: "O Exalted One, give me medicine for my son!"

The Teacher, seeing that she was ripe for conversion, said: "You did well, Gotami, in coming hither for medicine. Go enter the city, make the rounds of the entire city, beginning at the beginning, and in whatever house no one has ever died, from that house fetch tiny grains of mustard seed."

"Very well, reverend sir," said she. Delighted in heart, she entered within the city, and at the very first house said: "The Possessor of the Ten Forces bids me fetch tiny grains of mustard seed for medicine for my son. Give me tiny grains of mustard seed."

"Alas! Gotami," said they, and brought and gave to her.

"This particular seed I cannot take. In this house some one has died!"

"What say you, Gotami! Here it is impossible to count the dead!"

"Well then, enough! I'll not take it. The Possessor of the Ten Forces did not tell me to take mustard seed from a house where any one has ever died."

In this same way she went to the second house, and to the third. Thought she: In the entire city this must be the way! This the Buddha, full of compassion for the welfare of mankind, must have seen! Overcome with emotion, she went outside of the city, carried her son to the burning-ground, and holding him in her arms, said: "Dear little son, I thought that you alone had been overtaken by this thing which men call death. But you are not the only one death has overtaken. This is a law common to all mankind." So saying, she cast her son away in the burning-ground. Then she uttered the following stanza:

No village law, no law of market town,
No law of a single house is this—
Of all the world and all the worlds of gods
This only is the Law, that all things are impermanent.

Now when she had so said, she went to the Teacher. Said

the Teacher to her: "Gotami, did you get the tiny grains of mustard seed?"

"Done, reverend sir, is the business of the mustard seed! Only give me a refuge!" Then the Teacher recited to her the following stanzas:

That man who delights in children and cattle,
That man whose heart adheres thereto,
Death takes that man and goes his way,
As sweeps away a mighty flood a sleeping village.[2] . . .

Though one should live a hundred years,
Not seeing the Region of the Deathless,
Better were it for one to live a single day,
The Region of the Deathless seeing. . . .

6. Universal Love and Good Will

The essence of spiritual realization, in relation to the blindly craving and frustrated unhappiness that precedes it, is liberation. As the preceding selection indicates, its culminating— that is, its dependably peace- and bliss-producing—quality, is love. And by love, here, Buddha meant no dependent attachment to a person or object through whom one hopes to find his longings satisfied, but an unlimited self-giving compassion flowing freely toward all creatures that live. Moreover, it is a condition of growth toward such an experience that one express, at each stage, as much of this ideal compassion as his spiritual progress permits.

The following selection from the Sutta-Nipata *is a hymn to love, expressed in the form of a universal benediction. It is the Buddhist "Thirteenth Chapter of First Corinthians."*

May creatures all abound

in weal and peace; may all
be blessed with peace always;
all creatures weak or strong,
all creatures great and small;

[2] See below, the *Dhammapada*, Chap. xx, p. 66.

creatures unseen or seen,
dwelling afar or near,
born or awaiting birth,
—may all be blessed with peace!

Let none cajole or flout
his fellow anywhere;
let none wish others harm
in dudgeon or in hate.

Just as with her own life
a mother shields from hurt
her own, her only, child, —
let all-embracing thoughts
for all that lives be thine,

—an all-embracing love
for all the universe
in all its heights and depths
and breadth, unstinted love,
unmarred by hate within,
not rousing enmity.

So, as you stand or walk,
or sit, or lie, reflect
with all your might on this;
—'tis deemed 'a state divine.'

7. Buddha's Farewell Address

*By the time oral tradition became committed to writing, much
material had accumulated about Buddha's acts and sayings
during the weeks preceding his death. Some of these reported
sayings seem out of harmony with each other, and it is difficult
for the student of Buddhism to decide which among them most
truly represent his farewell teaching. It is my judgment, however, that the following selection from the* Mahaparinibbana
Suttanta *brings out one major and authentic note.*[1]

[1] It is a part of the "Second Portion for Recitation," with a few con-
densations. The bit of verse at the end is from the Third Portion.

When the Blessed One had remained as long as he wished at Ambapali's grove, he went to Beluva, near Vaishali. There the Blessed One addressed the brethren, and said: "O mendicants, do you take up your abode for the rainy season roundabout Vaishali, each one according to the place where his friends and near companions may live. I shall enter upon the rainy season here at Beluva."

When the Blessed One had thus entered upon the rainy season there fell upon him a dire sickness, and sharp pains came upon him even unto death. But the Blessed One, mindful and self-possessed, bore them without complaint.

Then this thought occurred to the Blessed One,

"It would not be right for me to pass away from life without addressing the disciples, without taking leave of the order.[2] Let me now, by a strong effort of the will, bend this sickness down again, and keep my hold on life till the allotted time have come."

And the Blessed One, by a strong effort of the will, bent the sickness down, and kept his hold on life till the time he fixed upon should come. And the sickness abated.

Thus the Blessed One began to recover; and when he had quite got rid of the sickness, he went out from the monastery, and sat down on a seat spread out in the open air. And the venerable Ananda, accompanied by many other disciples, approached where the Blessed One was, saluted him, and taking a seat respectfully on one side, said: "I have beheld, Lord, how the Blessed One was in health, and I have beheld how the Blessed One had to suffer. And though at the sight of the sickness of the Blessed One my body became weak as a creeper, and the horizon became dim to me, and my faculties were no longer clear, yet notwithstanding I took some little comfort from the thought that the Blessed One would not pass away from existence until at least he had left instructions as touching the order."

And the Blessed One addressed Ananda for the sake of the order and said:

"What, then, Ananda, does the order expect of me? I have preached the truth without making any distinction between exoteric and esoteric doctrine;[3] for in respect of

[2] The community of monks who were his disciples.
[3] "Exoteric," shared with all; "esoteric," taught only to a few.

the truth, Ananda, the Tathagata has no such thing as the closed fist of a teacher, who keeps some things back.

"Surely, Ananda, should there be any one who harbors the thought, 'It is I who will lead the brotherhood,' or, 'The order is dependent upon me,' he should lay down instructions in any matter concerning the order. Now the Tathagata, Ananda, thinks not that it is he who should lead the brotherhood, or that the order is dependent upon him.

"Why, then, should the Tathagata leave instructions in any matter concerning the order?

"I am now grown old, O Ananda, and full of years; my journey is drawing to its close, I have reached the sum of my days, I am turning eighty years of age.

"Just as a worn-out cart can only with much difficulty be made to move along, so the body of the Tathagata can only be kept going with much additional care.

"It is only, Ananda, when the Tathagata, ceasing to attend to any outward thing, becomes plunged in that devout meditation of heart which is concerned with no bodily object, it is only then that the body of the Tathagata is at ease.

"Therefore, O Ananda, be ye lamps unto yourselves. Rely on yourselves, and do not rely on external help.

"Hold fast to the truth as a lamp. Seek salvation alone in the truth. Look not for assistance to any one besides yourselves.

"And how, Ananda, can a brother be a lamp unto himself, rely on himself only and not on any external help, holding fast to the truth as his lamp and seeking salvation in the truth alone, looking not for assistance to any one besides himself?

"Herein, O Ananda, let a brother, as he dwells in the body, so regard the body that he, being strenuous, thoughtful, and mindful,[4] may, whilst in the world, overcome the grief which arises from the body's cravings.

"While subject to sensations let him continue so to regard the sensations that he, being strenuous, thoughtful, and mindful, may, whilst in the world, overcome the grief which arises from the sensations.

"And so, also, when he thinks, or reasons, or feels, let him so regard his thought that being strenuous, thoughtful,

[4] These three terms refer to steps 6, 7, and 8 in the table on p. 28: right effort, right alertness, right concentration.

and mindful he may, whilst in the world, overcome the grief
which arises from the craving due to ideas, or to reasoning, or to feeling.

"Those who, either now or after I am dead, shall be a
lamp unto themselves, relying upon themselves only and
not relying upon any external help, but holding fast to the
truth as their lamp, and seeking their salvation in the truth
alone, shall not look for assistance to any one besides themselves, it is they, Ananda, among my bhikshus, who shall
reach the very topmost height! But they must be anxious to
learn. . . .

"My age is now full ripe, my life draws to its close:
I leave you, I depart, relying on myself alone!
Be earnest then, O brethren, holy, full of thought!
Be steadfast in resolve! Keep watch o'er your own hearts!
Who wearies not, but holds fast to his truth and law,
Shall cross this sea of life, shall make an end of grief."

PART II: Treading the Path to Nirvana

Introduction

One may master the teachings contained in the preceding discourses and still not quite catch the spirit communicated by
Gautama to his early disciples—the spirit which animated
Buddhism as it spread more and more widely and began to be
a significant force in the religious life of India. But no great
religion can be fully understood unless that spirit is apprehended. Only then does one realize what the essential emphases
are and how the basic ideas are related together; he sees only
then, in the case of Buddhism, what they meant in the living
experience of those who followed Buddha into the homeless
life to seek the spiritual goal, leaving behind the distractions
of the world in order to achieve the freedom and peace of
Nirvana.

For this purpose, one looks for a collection of hymns expressing the eager enthusiasm of Gautama's early disciples,
and for a document summarizing his teachings—not in terms

of the setting in which they were uttered, but as they were selected and arranged by someone who wanted them in the form of a manual capable of giving inspiration, support, and practical guidance in the daily lives of his devoted followers.

Happily, this need is ideally met in the ancient Buddhist scriptures. We find there the *Psalms of the Early Buddhists,* which express in very revealing fashion the grateful devotion and aspiring commitment of the monks and nuns who for the sake of Nirvana renounced the entanglements of ordinary life, as Buddha did, and gave themselves single-mindedly to their spiritual task. And we also find the *Dhammapada* (the "Way of Truth," or the "Way of the Doctrine"). No other compendium of Buddha's teaching gives such a clear disclosure of the dynamic zeal as well as the religious perspective which was absorbed from his energetic and winsome personality by his followers. The reader can hardly fail to catch the vigor of this spirit—especially the note of hopeful pursuit of the path of self-conquest, of aggressive alertness in face of the temptation to sloth and inertia, and of eager determination to allow nothing to block the way to the final achievement.

Let us take the *Dhammapada* first.

1. The Way of Truth

No one knows just when this magnificent document was composed. It forms a part of the Sutta Pitaka; *and it consists of selected utterances presumed to have been spoken by the Buddha, organized under topical heads and arranged in a sequence believed by the composer best to clarify the gospel of early Buddhism. It was apparently in existence by the time of the Emperor Asoka, 250 B.C., and it quickly became popular with all schools of Buddhist thought and practice. It is unmatched for its powerful use of the technique of partial repetition, and for the sustained note of moral earnestness which pervades it. Lin Yutang calls it "a great spiritual testimony, one of the very few religious masterpieces in the world, combining genuineness of spiritual passion with a happy gift of literary expression."[1] The selections that follow comprise approximately half of this religious classic. The Max Müller translation is used, with a few slight changes in the interest*

[1] *The Wisdom of China and India* (Random House, 1942), p. 326.

of greater readability and clarity.[2]

Shall we first orient ourselves by a brief summary of its message in terms such as a Westerner who had absorbed its dynamic challenge might use?

"I bring you great and good news. There is a way from the crushing miseries of this transitory life to real happiness, and it is open to all. But the way is hard, and there is no magical method of making it easy. It means strenuous and constant self-examination; it means renouncing all that you foolishly prize now—your present self, in fact, with all the ignorant cravings and blind urges that make it what it is. No one can tread this path for you, neither god nor man; you must tread it for yourself. So begin now. Be alert, and steadfastly alert. Make the most sustained effort of which you are capable. Let nothing entice you to dally by the wayside—neither self-indulgence, nor the mistaken urge to self-punishment, nor vain metaphysical curiosity, nor the desire for companionship with those not yet ready to enter upon the path. Face uncompromisingly toward the goal. And victory over self—the greatest of all victories, and the key to peace and joy in this life and beyond—will be won."

Chapter I.   THE TWIN VERSES

All that we are is the result of what we have thought: it is founded on our thoughts, it is made up of our thoughts. If a man speaks or acts with an evil thought, pain follows him, as the wheel follows the foot of the ox that draws the carriage.

All that we are is the result of what we have thought: it is founded on our thoughts, it is made up of our thoughts. If a man speaks or acts with a pure thought, happiness follows him, like a shadow that never leaves him.

"He abused me, he beat me, he defeated me, he robbed me"—in those who harbor such thoughts hatred will never cease.

"He abused me, he beat me, he defeated me, he robbed me"—in those who do not harbor such thoughts hatred will cease.

For hatred does not cease by hatred at any time; hatred ceases by love—this is an eternal law.

[2] These changes have been checked against recent scholarly translations.

The world does not know that we must all come to an end here; but those who know it, their quarrels cease at once.

He who lives looking for pleasures only, his senses uncontrolled, immoderate in his food, idle, and weak, Mara[1] will certainly overthrow him, as the wind throws down a weak tree.

He who lives without looking for pleasures, his senses well-controlled, moderate in his food, faithful, and strong, him Mara will certainly not overthrow, any more than the wind throws down a rocky mountain.

He who wishes to put on the yellow robe[2] without having cleansed himself from sin, who disregards also temperance and truth, is unworthy of the yellow robe.

But he who has cleansed himself from sin, is well-grounded in all virtues, and endowed also with temperance and truth: he is indeed worthy of the yellow robe.

They who imagine truth in untruth, and see untruth in truth, never arrive at truth, but follow vain desires.

They who know truth in truth, and untruth in untruth, arrive at truth and follow true desires.

As rain breaks through an ill-thatched house, passion will break through an unreflecting mind.

As rain does not break through a well-thatched house, passion will not break through a well-reflecting mind.

The evildoer mourns in this world, and he mourns in the next; he mourns in both. He mourns and suffers when he sees the evil result of his own acts.

The virtuous man delights in this world, and he delights in the next; he delights in both. He delights and rejoices, when he sees the purity of his own work.

The evildoer suffers in this world, and he suffers in the next; he suffers in both. He suffers when he thinks of the evil he has done; he suffers even more when going on the evil path.

The virtuous man is happy in this world, and he is happy in the next; he is happy in both. He is happy when he thinks of the good he has done; he is still more happy when advancing on the good path.

The thoughtless man, even if he can recite a large portion

[1] The great tempter.
[2] The garb of the Buddhist monk.

of the law,[3] but is not a doer of it, has no share in the religious life, but is like a cowherd counting the cows of others.

The follower of the law, even if he can recite only a small portion of it but, having forsaken passion and hatred and foolishness, possesses true knowledge and serenity of mind; he, attached to nothing in this world or that to come, has indeed a share in the religious life.

Chapter II ON EARNESTNESS

Earnestness is the path of Nirvana; thoughtlessness the path of death. Those who are in earnest do not die; those who are thoughtless are as if dead already.

Having understood this clearly, those who have progressed in earnestness delight in earnestness, and rejoice in the knowledge of the elect.

These wise people, meditative, steady, always exerting strong powers, attain to Nirvana, the highest happiness.

If an earnest person has roused himself, if he is not forgetful, if his deeds are pure, if he acts with consideration, if he restrains himself, and lives according to law—then his glory will increase.

By rousing himself, by earnestness, by restraint and control, the wise man may make for himself an island which no flood can overwhelm.

Fools follow after vanity. The wise man keeps his earnestness as his best jewel.

Follow not after vanity, nor after the enjoyment of sense pleasures and lust! He who is earnest and meditative obtains ample joy.

When the man of understanding drives away vanity by earnestness, he, the wise, climbing the terraced heights of wisdom, looks down upon the fools; free from sorrow he looks upon the sorrowing crowd, as one that stands on a mountain looks down upon them that stand upon the plain.

Earnest among the thoughtless, awake among the sleepers, the wise man advances like a racer, leaving behind the hack.

By earnestness did Maghavan [Indra] rise to the lordship

[3] The *dhamma,* or doctrine.

of the gods. People praise earnestness; thoughtlessness is always blamed.

A bhikshu who delights in earnestness, who looks with fear on thoughtlessness, moves about like fire, burning all his fetters, small or large.

A bhikshu who delights in earnestness, who looks with fear on thoughtlessness, cannot fall away from his perfect state—he is close to Nirvana.

Chapter III   THOUGHT

As a fletcher makes straight his arrow, a wise man makes straight his trembling and unsteady thought, which is difficult to guard, difficult to hold back.

As a fish taken from his watery home and thrown on the dry ground, our thought trembles all over in order to escape the dominion of Mara, the tempter.

It is good to tame the mind, which is difficult to hold in and flighty, rushing wherever it lists; a tamed mind brings happiness.

Let the wise man guard his thoughts, for they are difficult to perceive, very subtle, and they rush wherever they list; thoughts well-guarded bring happiness.

Those who bridle their mind, which travels far, moves about alone, is incorporeal, and hides in the chamber of the heart, will be free from the bonds of Mara, the tempter.

If a man's faith is unsteady, if he does not know the true law, if his peace of mind is troubled, his knowledge will never be perfect.

If a man's thoughts are not scattered, if his mind is not perplexed, if he has ceased to think of good or evil, then there is no fear for him while he is watchful.

Knowing that his body is fragile like a jar, and making his thought firm like a fortress, one should attack Mara, the tempter, with the weapon of knowledge; one should watch him when conquered, and should never rest.

Before long, alas! this body will lie on the earth, despised, without awareness, like a useless log.

Whatever a hater may do to a hater, or an enemy to an enemy, a wrongly-directed mind will do us greater mischief.

Not a mother, not a father, will do so much, nor any other relatives; a well-directed mind will do us greater service. . . .

Chapter v   THE FOOL

Long is the night to him who is awake; long is a mile[4] to him who is tired; long is life to the foolish who do not know the true law.

If a traveler does not meet with one who is his better, or his equal, let him firmly keep to his solitary journey; there is no companionship with a fool.

"These sons belong to me, and this wealth belongs to me"—with such thoughts a fool is tormented. He himself does not belong to himself; how much less sons and wealth?

The fool who knows his foolishness is wise at least so far. But a fool who thinks himself wise, he is called a fool indeed.

If a fool be associated with a wise man even all his life, he will perceive the truth as little as a spoon perceives the taste of soup.

If an intelligent man be associated for one minute only with a wise man, he will soon perceive the truth, as the tongue perceives the taste of soup.

Fools of poor understanding have themselves for their greatest enemies, for they do evil deeds which bear bitter fruits.

That deed is not well-done of which a man must repent, and the result of which he receives crying and with a tearful face.

No, that deed is well-done of which a man does not repent, and the reward of which he receives gladly and happily.

As long as the evil deed done does not bear fruit, the fool thinks it is like honey; but when it ripens, then the fool suffers grief.

[4] The word means really a distance of nine or twelve miles.

Chapter VI   THE WISE MAN

If you see a man who shows you what is to be avoided, who administers reproofs, and is intelligent, follow that wise man as you would one who reveals hidden treasures; it will be better, not worse, for him who follows him.

Let him admonish, let him teach, let him forbid what is improper!—he will be beloved of the good; by the bad he will be hated.

Do not have evildoers for friends, do not have blame-worthy people for friends: have virtuous people for friends, have for friends the best of men.

He who drinks in the law lives happily with a serene mind; the wise man rejoices always in the law, as preached by the elect.

Well-makers lead the water wherever they like; fletchers bend the arrow; carpenters bend a log of wood; wise people fashion themselves.

As a solid rock is not shaken by the wind, wise people waver not amidst blame and praise.

Wise people, after they have listened to the laws, become serene, like a deep, smooth, and still lake.

Good men walk warily under all circumstances; good men speak not out of a desire for sensual gratification; whether touched by happiness or sorrow, wise people never appear elated or depressed.

If, whether for his own sake, or for the sake of others, a man wishes neither for a son, nor for wealth, nor for lord-ship, and if he does not wish for his own success by unfair means, then he is good, wise, and virtuous.

Few are there among men who arrive at the other shore;[1] the other people here run up and down this shore.

But those who, when the law has been well preached to them, follow the law, will pass over the dominion of death, however difficult to cross.

A wise man should leave the dark state of ordinary life, and follow the bright state of the bhikshu. After going from his home to a homeless state, he should in his retirement look for enjoyment where enjoyment seemed difficult. Leaving all pleasures behind, and calling nothing his own,

[1] I.e., reach Nirvana. See below, p. 111 ff., 161 ff.

the wise man should purge himself of all the vices of the mind.

Those whose mind is well-grounded in the seven elements of knowledge, who without clinging to anything rejoice in freedom from attachment, whose appetites have been conquered, and who are full of light, they win Nirvana even in this world. . . .

Chapter VIII THE THOUSANDS

Even though a speech be a thousand [words], but made up of senseless words, one word of sense is better, which if a man hears, he becomes quiet.

Even though a poem be a thousand [words], but made up of senseless words, one word of a poem is better, which if a man hears, he becomes quiet.

Though a man recite a hundred poems made up of senseless words, one word is better, which if a man hears, he becomes quiet.

If one man conquer in battle a thousand times a thousand men, and if another conquer himself, he is the greatest of conquerors.

One's own self conquered is better than all other people conquered; not even a god could change into defeat the victory of a man who has vanquished himself. . . .

Chapter IX EVIL

A man should hasten toward the good, and should keep his thoughts from evil; if a man does what is good slothfully, his mind delights in evil.

If a man commits a sin, let him not do it again; let him not delight in sin—the accumulation of evil is painful.

If a man does what is good, let him do it again; let him delight in it—the accumulation of good is delightful.

Even an evildoer sees happiness so long as his evil deed does not ripen; but when his evil deed ripens, then does the evildoer see evil.

Even a good man sees evil days so long as his good deed does not ripen; but when his good deed ripens, then does the good man see good days.

Let no man think lightly of evil, saying in his heart, "It

will not come nigh unto me." Even by the falling of water drops a water pot is filled; the fool becomes full of evil, even if he gather it little by little.

Let no man think lightly of good, saying in his heart, "It will not come nigh unto me." Even by the falling of water drops a water pot is filled; the wise man becomes full of good, even if he gather it little by little.

Let a man avoid evil deeds, as a merchant, if he has few companions and carries much wealth, avoids a dangerous road; as a man who loves life avoids poison.

He who has no wound on his hand may touch poison with his hand; poison does not affect one who has no wound; nor does evil befall one who does not commit evil.

If a man offend a harmless, pure, and innocent person, the evil falls back upon that fool, like light dust thrown up against the wind.

Some people are born again; evildoers go to hell; righteous people go to heaven; those who are free from all worldly desires attain Nirvana.

Not in the sky, not in the midst of the sea, not if we enter into the clefts of the mountains, is there known a spot in the whole world where a man might be freed from an evil deed.

Not in the sky, not in the midst of the sea, not if we enter into the clefts of the mountains, is there known a spot in the whole world where death could not overcome a mortal.

Chapter x   PUNISHMENT

All men tremble at punishment, all men fear death; remember that you are like unto them, and do not kill, nor cause slaughter.

All men tremble at punishment, all men love life; remember that you are like unto them, and do not kill, nor cause slaughter.

He who, seeking his own happiness, punishes[1] beings who also long for happiness, will not find happiness after death.

He who, seeking his own happiness, does not punish beings who also long for happiness, will find happiness after death.

[1] Strikes with a stick, literally.

Do not speak harshly to anyone; those who are spoken to will answer you in the same way. Angry speech is painful: blows for blows will touch you.

If, like a shattered gong, you utter nothing, then you have reached Nirvana; anger is not known to you.

As a cowherd with his staff drives his cows into the stable, so do age and death drive the life of men.

A fool does not know what awaits him when he commits his evil deeds; but the wicked man burns by his own deeds, as if burned by fire. . . .

Chapter XII   SELF

Let each man first direct himself to what is proper, then let him teach others; thus a wise man will not suffer.

If a man make himself as he teaches others to be, then, being himself well-subdued, he may subdue others; for one's own self is difficult to subdue.

Self is the lord of self, who else could be the lord? With self well-subdued, a man finds a lord such as few can find.

The evil done by one's self, born of one's self, begotten by one's self, crushes the foolish, as a diamond breaks even a precious stone. . . .

The foolish man who scorns the instruction of the saintly, of the elect [ariya], of the virtuous, and follows a false doctrine—he bears fruit to his own destruction, like the fruits of the Katthaka reed.[1]

By one's self the evil is done, by one's self one suffers; by one's self evil is left undone; by one's self one is purified. The pure and the impure stand and fall by themselves; no one can purify another.

Let no one forget his own duty for the sake of another's, however great; let a man after he has discerned his own duty, be faithful to his duty.

Chapter XIII   THE WORLD

Do not follow the evil law! Do not live on in thoughtlessness! Do not follow false doctrine! Be not a friend of the world.

[1] A reed which dies when it has borne fruit, or is at once cut down for the sake of its fruit.

Rouse yourself! Do not be idle! Follow the law of virtue! The virtuous rest in bliss in this world and in the next.

Follow the law of virtue; do not follow that of sin. The virtuous rest in bliss in this world and in the next.

Look upon the world as you would on a bubble, look upon it as on a mirage: the king of death does not see him who thus looks down upon the world.

Come, look at this world, glittering like a royal chariot; the foolish are immersed in it, but the wise are not attached to it.

He who formerly was reckless and afterward became sober brightens up this world, like the moon when freed from clouds.

He whose evil deeds are covered by good deeds brightens up this world, like the moon when freed from clouds. . . .

Chapter XIV

THE BUDDHA—THE AWAKENED

He whose conquest cannot be conquered again, into whose conquest no one in this world enters, by what track can you lead him, the Awakened, the Omniscient, the trackless?

He whom no desire with its snares and poisons can lead astray, by what track can you lead him, the Awakened, the Omniscient, the trackless?

Even the gods envy those who are awakened and not forgetful, who are given to meditation, who are wise, and who delight in the repose of retirement from the world.

Difficult to obtain is birth in human form, difficult is the life of mortals, difficult is the hearing of the True Law, difficult is the attainment of Buddhahood.

Not to commit any sin, to do good, and to purify one's mind, that is the teaching of all the Awakened.

The Awakened call patience the highest penance, long-suffering the highest Nirvana; for he is not an anchorite who oppresses others, he is not an ascetic who insults others.

Not to blame, not to strike, to live restrained under the law, to be moderate in eating, to sleep and sit alone, and to dwell on the highest thoughts—this is the teaching of the Awakened.

There is no satisfying lusts, even by a shower of gold pieces; he who knows that lusts have a short taste and cause pain, he is wise; even in heavenly pleasures he finds no satisfaction; the disciple who is fully awakened delights only in the destruction of all desires.

Men, driven by fear, go to many a refuge—to mountains and forests, to groves and sacred trees.

But that is not a safe refuge, that is not the best refuge; a man is not delivered from all pains after having gone to that refuge.

He who takes refuge with Buddha, the Law, and the Order[1]—he who, with clear understanding, sees the Four Holy Truths: pain, the origin of pain, the destruction of pain, and the Eightfold Holy Way that leads to the quieting of pain—that is the safe refuge, that is the best refuge; having gone to that refuge, a man is delivered from all pain.

A Buddha is not easily found: he is not born everywhere. Wherever such a sage is born, that race prospers.

Happy is the birth of the Awakened, happy is the teaching of the True Law, happy is peace in the Order, happy is the devotion of those who are at peace.

He who pays homage to those who deserve homage, whether the Awakened [Buddhas] or their disciples, those who have overcome the host of evils and crossed the flood of sorrow—he who pays homage to such as have found deliverance and know no fear, his merit can never be measured by anyone.

Chapter xv   HAPPINESS

We live happily indeed, not hating those who hate us! among men who hate us we dwell free from hatred! We live happily indeed, free from ailments among the ailing! among men who are ailing we dwell free from ailments!

We live happily indeed, free from greed among the greedy! among men who are greedy let us dwell free from greed!

We live happily indeed, though we call nothing our own! We shall be like the bright gods, feeding on happiness!

[1] The "Three Jewels" of Buddhism.

Victory breeds hatred, for the conquered is unhappy. He who has given up both victory and defeat, he is contented and happy.

There is no fire like passion; there is no evil like hatred; there is no pain like this bodily existence; there is no happiness higher than peace.

Hunger is the worst of diseases, bodily demands the greatest evil; if one knows this truly, that is Nirvana, the highest happiness.

Health is the greatest of gifts, contentedness the best riches; trust is the best of relationships, Nirvana the highest happiness.

He who has tasted the sweetness of solitude and tranquillity becomes free from fear and free from sin, while he tastes the sweetness of drinking in the law.

The sight of the elect is good, to live with them is always happiness; if a man does not see fools, he will be truly happy.

He who walks in the company of fools suffers a long way; company with fools, as with an enemy, is always painful; company with the wise is happiness, like meeting with kinsfolk.

Therefore, one ought to follow the wise, the intelligent, the learned, the much-enduring, the dutiful, the elect; one ought to follow such a good and wise man, as the moon follows the path of the stars.

Chapter XVI   PLEASURE

He who gives himself to vanity, and does not give himself to meditation, forgetting the real aim of life and grasping at pleasure, will in time envy him who has exerted himself in meditation.

Let no man ever cling to what is pleasant, or to what is unpleasant. Not to see what is pleasant is pain, and it is pain to see what is unpleasant.

Let, therefore, no man be attached to anything; loss of the beloved is evil. Those who are attached to nothing, and hate nothing, have no fetters.

From pleasure comes grief, from pleasure comes fear; he who is free from pleasure knows neither grief nor fear.

From affection comes grief, from affection comes fear;

he who is free from affection knows neither grief nor fear.

From lust comes grief, from lust comes fear; he who is free from lust knows neither grief nor fear.

From desire comes grief, from desire comes fear; he who is free from desire knows neither grief nor fear.

From craving comes grief, from craving comes fear; he who is free from craving knows neither grief nor fear.

He who possesses virtue and intelligence, who is just, speaks the truth, and does his own business, him the world will hold dear.

He in whom a desire for the Ineffable has sprung up, who in his mind is satisfied, and whose thoughts are not bewildered by desires, he is called one who is headed upstream.

Kinsmen, friends, and lovers salute a man who has been long away and returns safe from afar.

In like manner, his good works receive him who has done good and has gone from this world to the other—as kinsmen receive a friend on his return.

Chapter XVII   ANGER

Let a man leave anger, let him forsake pride, let him overcome all bondage! No sufferings befall the man who is not attached to name-and-form,[1] and who calls nothing his own.

He who holds back rising anger like a rolling chariot, him I call a real driver; other people are but holding the reins.

Let a man overcome anger by love, let him overcome evil by good; let him overcome the greedy by liberality, the liar by truth!

Speak the truth; do not yield to anger; give, if you are asked, even though it be a little: by these three steps you will come near the gods.

The sages who injure no one, and who always control their body—they will go to the unchangeable place where, if they have gone, they will suffer no more.

Those who are ever watchful, who study day and night,

[1] *Nama-rupa*, the universe as composed of distinguishable things, the phenomenal world.

and who strive after Nirvana, their passions will come to an end. . . .

Beware of bodily anger, and control your body! Leave the sins of the body, and with your body practice virtue!

Beware of the anger of the tongue, and control your tongue! Leave the sins of the tongue, and practice virtue with your tongue!

Beware of the anger of the mind, and control your mind! Leave the sins of the mind, and practice virtue with your mind!

The wise who control their body, who control their tongue; the wise who control their mind, are indeed well-controlled. . . .

Chapter XVIII   IMPURITY

Make yourself an island, work hard, be wise! When your impurities are blown away, and you are free from guilt, you will enter into the heavenly world of the elect. . . .

Let a wise man blow off the impurities of himself, as a smith blows off the impurities of silver, one by one, little by little, and from moment to moment. . . .

The fault of others is easily perceived, but that of one's self is difficult to perceive; a man winnows his neighbor's faults like chaff, but his own fault he hides, as a cheat hides an unlucky cast of the die.

If a man looks after the faults of others and is always inclined to be offended, his own passions will grow, and he is far from the destruction of passion. . . .

Chapter XX   THE WAY

The best of paths is the Eightfold; the best of truths the Four Sayings;[1] the best of virtues passionlessness; the best of men he who has eyes to see.

This is the path, there is no other that leads to the purifying of the mind. Go on this path! This will confuse Mara the tempter.

If you go on this way, you will make an end of pain—the way preached by me, when I had understood the removal of the thorns in the flesh.

You yourself must make an effort. The Tathagatas

[1] The Four Noble Truths.

(Buddhas) are only preachers. The thoughtful who enter the way are freed from the bondage of Mara.

All created things perish—he who knows and sees this is at peace though in a world of pain; this is the way to purity.

All created things are grief and pain—he who knows and sees this is at peace though in a world of pain; this is the way that leads to purity.

All forms are unreal—he who knows and sees this is at peace though in a world of pain; this is the way that leads to purity.

He who does not rouse himself when it is time to rise, who, though young and strong, is full of sloth, whose will and thought are weak, that lazy and idle man never finds the way to wisdom.

Watching his speech, well-restrained in mind, let a man never commit any wrong with his body! Let a man but keep these three roads of action clear, and he will achieve the way which is taught by the wise.

Through zeal knowledge is gained, through lack of zeal knowledge is lost; let a man who knows this two-fold path of gain and loss thus place himself that knowledge may grow.

Cut down the whole forest of desires, not a tree only! Danger comes out of the forest of desires. When you have cut down both the forest of desires and its undergrowth, then, bhikshus, you will be rid of the forest and of desires!

So long as the desire of man toward women, even the smallest, is not destroyed, so long is his mind in bondage, as the calf that drinks milk is to its mother.

Cut out the love of self, like an autumn lotus with your hand! Cherish the road to peace. Nirvana has been shown by the Blessed One.

"Here I shall dwell in the rain, here in winter and summer"—thus the fool thinks, and does not think of death.

Death comes and carries off that man, boastful of his children and flocks, his mind distracted, as a flood carries off a sleeping village.

Sons are no help, nor a father, nor relatives; there is no help from kinsfolk for one whom death has seized.

A wise and virtuous man who knows the meaning of this should quickly clear the way that leads to Nirvana.

Chapter XXI   MISCELLANEOUS

If by leaving a small pleasure one sees a great pleasure, let a wise man leave the small pleasure and look to the great.

He who, by causing pain to others, wishes to obtain pleasure for himself, he, entangled in the bonds of hatred, will never be free from hatred.

What ought to be done is neglected, what ought not to be done is done; the desires of unruly, thoughtless people are always increasing.

But they whose whole watchfulness is always directed to their body, who do not follow what ought not to be done, and who steadfastly do what ought to be done, the desires of such watchful and wise people will come to an end. . . .

The disciples of Gautama are always well awake, and their thoughts day and night are always set on the Buddha.

The disciples of Gautama are always well awake, and their thoughts day and night are always set on the Law.

The disciples of Gautama are always well awake, and their thoughts day and night are always set on the Order.

The disciples of Gautama are always well awake, and their thoughts day and night are always set on their body.

The disciples of Gautama are always well awake, and their mind day and night always delights in compassion.

The disciples of Gautama are always well awake, and their mind day and night always delights in meditation. . . .

Chapter XXIII   THE ELEPHANT

This mind of mine went formerly wandering about as it liked, as it listed, as it pleased; but I shall now hold it in firmly, as the rider who wields the hook holds in the furious elephant.

Be not thoughtless, watch your thoughts! Draw yourself out of the evil way, like an elephant sunk in mud.

If a man find a prudent companion who walks with him, is wise, and lives soberly, it is well to walk with him, overcoming all dangers, happy, but considerate.

If a man find no prudent companion who walks with him, is wise, and lives soberly, let him walk alone, like a king who has left his conquered country behind—like an elephant in the forest.

It is better to live alone; there is no companionship with a fool; let a man walk alone, let him commit no sin, having few wishes, like an elephant in the forest.

If the occasion arises, friends are pleasant; enjoyment is pleasant, whatever be the cause; a good deed is pleasant in the hour of death; the giving up of all grief is pleasant.

Pleasant in the world is the state of a mother, pleasant the state of a father, pleasant the state of an ascetic, pleasant the state of a brahmana.[1]

Pleasant is virtue lasting to old age, pleasant is a faith firmly rooted; pleasant is attainment of intelligence, pleasant is avoiding of sins.

Chapter XXIV   THIRST

The thirst[2] of a thoughtless man grows like a creeper; he runs from life to life, like a monkey seeking fruit in the forest.

Whomsoever this fierce poisonous thirst overcomes, in this world his sufferings increase like the abounding Birana grass.

But from him who overcomes this fierce thirst, difficult to be conquered in this world, sufferings fall off, like water drops from a lotus leaf.

This salutary counsel I give you: "Do ye, as many as are here assembled, dig up the root of thirst, as he who wants the sweet-scented Usira root must dig up the Birana grass, that Mara, the tempter, may not crush you again and again, as the stream crushes the reeds." . . .

He who, having got rid of the jungle of lust, gives himself over to lust, and who, when free from the jungle, runs to the jungle, look at that man—though free, he runs into bondage!

Wise people do not call that a strong fetter which is made of iron, wood, or hemp; passionately strong is the care for precious stones and rings, for sons and a wife.

That fetter wise people call strong which drags down, yields, but is difficult to undo; after having cut this at last,

[1] In this meaning, usually spelled "Brahmin."
[2] I.e., craving. The word is *tanha*.

people leave the world, free from cares; and leaving the pleasures of sense behind.

Those who are slaves to passions follow the stream of desires, as a spider runs down the web which he has made himself; when they have cut this, at last, wise people go onward, free from cares, leaving all pain behind.

Give up what is before, give up what is behind, give up what is between, when you go to the other shore of existence; if your mind is altogether free, you will not again enter into birth and decay.

If a man delights in quieting doubts, and, always reflecting, dwells on what is not pleasurable, he certainly will remove, nay, he will cut the fetter of Mara.

He who has reached the consummation, who does not fear, who is without thirst and without sin; he has broken all the thorns of life—this will be his last body.

He who is without thirst and without attachment, who understands the sayings and their interpretation, who knows the order of letters (those which are before and which are after), he has received his last body, he is called the great sage, the great man.

"I have conquered all, I know all, in all conditions of life I am free from taint; I have left all, and through the destruction of thirst I am free; having learned myself, whom should I indicate as my teacher?"

The gift of the Law exceeds all gifts; the sweetness of the Law exceeds all sweetness; the delight in the Law exceeds all delights; the extinction of thirst overcomes all pain.

Riches destroy the foolish; not those who seek the other shore; the foolish by his thirst for riches destroys himself, as he destroys others. . . .

Chapter xxv THE BHIKSHU

Restraint in the eye is good, good is restraint in the ear; in the nose restraint is good, good is restraint in the tongue.

In the body restraint is good, good is restraint in speech; in thought restraint is good, good is restraint in all things. A bhikshu, restrained in all things, is freed from all pain.

He who controls his hand, he who controls his feet, he who controls his speech, he who is well-controlled, he who delights inwardly, who is collected, who is solitary and content, him they call a bhikshu.

The bhikshu who controls his mouth, who speaks wisely and calmly, who teaches the meaning and the Law, his word is sweet.

He who dwells in the Law, delights in the Law, meditates on the Law, recollects the Law: that bhikshu will never fall away from the true Law.

Let him not overrate what he has received, nor ever envy others: a mendicant who envies others does not obtain peace of mind.

A bhikshu who, though he receives little, does not overrate what he has received, even the gods will praise him if his life is pure and if he is not slothful.

He who never identifies himself with name-and-form, and does not grieve over what is no more, he indeed is called a bhikshu.

The bhikshu who behaves with kindness, who is happy in the doctrine of Buddha, will reach the quiet place (Nirvana), and will find happiness arising from the cessation of bodily existence. . . .

The bhikshu whose body and tongue and mind are quieted, who is collected, and has rejected the baits of the world, he is called quiet.

Rouse yourself by yourself, examine yourself by yourself, thus self-protected and attentive will you live happily, O bhikshu!

For self is the lord of self, self is the refuge of self; therefore curb yourself as the merchant curbs a noble horse.

The bhikshu, full of delight, who is happy in the doctrine of Buddha, will reach the quiet place (Nirvana), and will find happiness consisting in the cessation of bodily existence.

He who, even as a young bhikshu, applies himself to the doctrine of Buddha, brightens up this world, like the moon when free from clouds.

Chapter XXVI   THE BRAHMANA

Stop the stream valiantly, drive away the desires, O brahmana! When you have understood the destruction of all that was made, you will understand that which was not made.

If the brahmana has reached the other shore in both insight, in restraint and contemplation, all bonds vanish from him who has obtained knowledge. . . .

I do not call a man a brahmana because of his origin or of his mother. He is indeed arrogant, and he is wealthy: but the poor who is free from all attachments, him I call indeed a brahmana.

Him I call indeed a brahmana who, after cutting all fetters, never trembles, is free from bonds and unshackled.

Him I call indeed a brahmana who, after cutting the strap and the thong, the rope with all that pertains to it, has destroyed all obstacles and is awakened.

Him I call indeed a brahmana who, though he has committed no offense, endures reproach, stripes, and bonds; who has endurance as his force and strength for his army.

Him I call indeed a brahmana who is free from anger, dutiful, virtuous, without appetites, who is subdued and has received his last body.

Him I call indeed a brahmana who does not cling to sensual pleasures, like water on a lotus leaf, like a mustard seed on the point of a needle.

Him I call indeed a brahmana who, even here, knows the end of his own suffering, has put down his burden and is unshackled.

Him I call indeed a brahmana whose knowledge is deep, who possesses wisdom, who knows the right way and the wrong, and has attained the highest end.

Him I call indeed a brahmana who keeps aloof both from laymen and from mendicants, who frequents no houses, and has but few desires.

Him I call indeed a brahmana who without hurting any creatures, whether feeble or strong, does not kill nor cause slaughter.

Him I call indeed a brahmana who is tolerant among the intolerant, mild among the violent, and free from greed among the greedy.

Him I call indeed a brahmana from whom anger and hatred, pride and hypocrisy, have dropped like a mustard seed from the point of a needle.

Him I call indeed a brahmana who utters true speech,

instructive and free from harshness, so that he offends no one.

Him I call indeed a brahmana who takes nothing in the world that is not given him, be it long or short, small or large, good or bad.

Him I call indeed a brahmana who fosters no desires for this world or for the next, who has no desires and is unshackled.

Him I call indeed a brahmana who has no longings, and when he has understood the truth, does not express any doubt, and who has reached the deeps of the eternal.

Him I call indeed a brahmana who in this world has risen above bondage to both good and evil; who is free from grief, from sin, and from impurity.

Him I call indeed a brahmana who is bright like the moon, pure, serene, undisturbed, and in whom all unseemly gaiety is extinct.

Him I call indeed a brahmana who has traversed this miry road, the impassible world, difficult to pass, and its vanity; who has gone through and reached the other shore, is thoughtful, steadfast, free from doubts, free from attachment, and content.

Him I call indeed a brahmana who in this world, having abandoned all desires, travels about without a home, and in whom all concupiscence is extinct.

Him I call indeed a brahmana who, having abandoned all longings, travels about without a home, and in whom all covetousness is extinct.

Him I call indeed a brahmana who, after leaving all bondage to men, has risen above all bondage to the gods, and is free from all and every bondage.

Him I call indeed a brahmana who has left what gives pleasure and what gives pain, who is cold[1] and free from all germs of renewed life—the hero who has conquered all the worlds.

Him I call indeed a brahmana who knows the destruction and the return of beings everywhere, who is free from bondage, welfaring, and awakened.

Him I call indeed a brahmana whose path the gods do not know, nor spirits, nor men, whose passions are extinct, and who is an *arhat*.

[1] I.e., free from passion.

Him I call indeed a brahmana who calls nothing his own, whether it be before, behind, or between; who is poor and free from the love of the world.

Him I call indeed a brahmana, the manly, the noble, the hero, the great sage, the conqueror, the sinless, the accomplished, the awakened.

Him I call indeed a brahmana who knows his former abodes, who sees heaven and hell, has reached the end of births, is perfect in knowledge, a sage, and whose accomplishments are all complete.

2. Songs of the Wayfarers

The following Psalms of the Brethren and Sisters (translated by Mrs. C. A. F. Rhys Davids from the Theri- and Theragatha) need little further comment. The psalms of the brethren that I have chosen are so selected and arranged that they express, in the order in which they here appear: admiring and grateful praise of the Master (a, b); delight in the wooded and mountain haunts of contemplation (c, d, e, i); joy in spiritual progress away from the world (f, g, h); the testimony of a converted bandit (j), and of a monk who has fallen into the hands of bandits (k); and the bhikkhu's attitude toward death (l). The psalm of the sisters, which comes at the end (m), tells a very dramatic and moving story.

a.

Buddha the Wake, the son of man,
Self-tamed, by inward vision rapt,
Bearing himself by ways sublime,
Glad in tranquillity of heart;
To whom men honour pay as one
Who hath transcended all we know;
To whom gods also honour yield:—
So I, an arahant, have heard—
From jungle to Nibbana come,
With every fetter left behind, ...
He goeth wheresoe'er he will,
Nor careth wheresoe'er he goes,
As lotus born within a lake,
By water nowise is defiled,

But groweth fragrant, beautiful;
So is the Buddha in this world,
Born in the world and dwelling there,
But by the world nowise defiled,
E'en as the lily by the lake.

b.

O thou of perfect form and beauty rare,
Of fairest parts and lovely to behold,
Exalted One! thy colour like fine gold,
Thou valiant spirit, with the dazzling teeth,
Whose body shows the features that betray
The man of perfectly adjusted parts,
Yea, all the traits that mark the Super-Man;
Thou with the eyes so clear, thy countenance
So fair, broad, straight, majestic, thou dost shine
As doth the sun, the centre thou of all
The chosen band of brethren gathered round:
Thou bhikkhu noble of aspect, whose skin
Resembleth gold, say, what is friar's life
To thee with presence so supremely fair?
A prince thou dost deserve to be, a Bull
Drawing the chariot of the world's empire;
Lord of the earth from end to end foursquare,
A conqueror, of Jambudipa chief. . . .

c.

Well-roofed and pleasant is my little hut,
And screened from winds:—Rain at thy will, thou god!
My heart is well composed, my heart is free,
And ardent is my mood. Now rain, god! rain.

d.

The burdened earth is sprinkled by the rain,
The winds blow cool, the lightnings roam on high.
Eased and allayed th' obsessions of the mind,
And in my heart the spirit's mastery.

e.

The lightning's flash e'en in the rocky cave,
Smiting Vebhara's crest and Pandava,[1]

[1] These are two hill peaks rising above Rajagaha.

And, in the mountain-bosom hid, a child
Of that incomparable Master sits
Ardent in contemplative ecstasy.

f.

All passion have I put away, and all
Ill will for ever have I rooted out;
Illusion utterly has passed from me;
Cool am I now. Gone out all fire within.

g.

All longings as to this or other life
Have I put far from me, as one who hath
Beta'en himself to truth, whose heart's at peace,
Who, self-subdued, in all things undefiled,
Discerns the world's incessant ebb and flow.

h.

Burnt up in me is all that doth defile,
And rooted out all life's continuance;
Slain utterly the cycle of re-birth:
Now is there no more coming back to be.

i.

Those upland glades delightful to the soul,
Where the kareri[2] spreads its wildering wreaths,
Where sound the trumpet-calls of elephants:
Those are the braes wherein my soul delights.
Those rocky heights with hue of dark blue clouds,
Where lies embosomed many a shining tarn
of crystal-clear, cool waters, and whose slopes
the "herds of Indra"[3] cover and bedeck:
Those are the braes wherein my soul delights.
Like serried battlements of blue-black cloud,
Like pinnacles on stately castle built,
Re-echoing to the cries of jungle folk:
Those are the braes wherein my soul delights.
Fair uplands rain-refreshed, and resonant

[2] Mrs. Rhys Davids thinks that this probably means the musk rose tree.
[3] I.e., rain clouds.

With crested creatures' cries antiphonal
Lone heights where silent Rishis[4] oft resort:
Those are the braes wherein my soul delights.

Here is enough for me who fain would dwell
in meditation rapt, mindful, and tense.
Here is enough for me, who fain would seek
The highest good, a brother filled with zeal.
Here is enough for me, who fain would dwell
In happy ease, a brother filled with zeal.
Here is enough for me who give myself
To studious toil, so am I filled with zeal.
Clad with the azure bloom of flax, blue-flecked
As sky in autumn; quick with crowds
Of all their varied winged populace:
Such are the braes wherein my soul delights.
Free from the crowds of citizens below,
But thronged with flocks of many winged things,
The home of herding creatures of the wild:
Such are the braes wherein my soul delights.
Crags where clear waters lie, a rocky world,
Haunted by black-faced apes and timid deer,
Where 'neath bright blossoms run the silver streams:
Such are the braes wherein my soul delights.
For that which brings me exquisite delight
Is not the strains of string and pipe and drum,
But when, with intellect well poised, intent,
I gain the perfect vision of the Norm.[5]

j.

Innocens! such the name I bear,
While Noxious in the past was I;
To-day most truly am I named,
For now I hurt not any man.

Once an obnoxious bandit I,
Known by my name of Finger-wreathed,
Till toiling 'mid the awful flood,
I refuge in the Buddha found.
Once were my hands imbrued with blood;

[4] Hermit saints.
[5] Mrs. Rhys Davids uses this word for *dhamma,* "the Doctrine."

Known was my name as Finger-wreathed.
O see the Refuge I have found,
With every craving rooted out!
Me who had wrought such direful deeds,
Fast going to my place of doom,
Me all that doing's aftermath
Hath touched e'en here—and freed from debt
Now take I my allotted share.
'Tis a fool's part heedless to waste his life:—
Such are the folk who will not understand.
He who is wise doth foster earnestness
As he were watching o'er his chiefest wealth.
Give not yourselves to wastage in your lives,
Nor be familiar with delights of sense.
He who doth strenuously meditate,
His shall it be to win the bliss supreme.

O welcome this that came nor came amiss!
O goodly was the counsel given to me!
'Mong divers doctrines mooted among men,
Of all 'twas sure the Best I sought and found.
O welcome this that came nor came amiss!
O goodly was the counsel given to me!
The threefold wisdom have I made mine own,
And all the Buddha's ordinance is done.

Deep in the wild beneath some forest tree,
Or in the mountain cave, is't here, is't there,
So have I stood and let my throbbing heart
Transported beat. Happy I seek my rest,
Happy I rise, happy I pass the day,
Escaped from snare of evil—ah! behold
The Master's sweet compassion shown to me! . . . .

k.

Bandit Chief

Of all the lot whom we, for god or pelf,
Have smitten in our time, there's not been one
But hath shown fear, trembled and clamoured sore.
But thou, who'rt not affrighted, nay, whose face
Shows brighter bloom, why dost thou not lament,
When such a fearsome peril threatens thee?

Adhimutta

No misery of mind, O chief, is there
For him who hath no wants. All fear have I
Transcended, since the fetters were destroyed.
By death of that which leadeth to rebirth,
The truths are seen e'en as they really are,
And hence in death there lies no fear for me;
'Tis as a laying down the load I bore. . . .
So hath the mighty Sage declared to us.
And he who knows that things are even so,
As by the Buddha it is taught, no more
Would he take hold of any form of birth
Than he would grasp a red-hot iron ball.
Comes not to me the thought: " 'Tis I have been,"
Nor comes the thought: "What shall I next become?"
Thoughts, deeds and words are no persisting [soul],[6]
Therefore what ground for lamentations here?
To him who seeth, as it really is,
The pure and simple causal rise of things,
The pure and simple sequence of our acts: —
To such an one can come no fear, O chief.
That all this world is like the forest grass
And brushwood [no man's property]:—when one
By wisdom seeth this, finds naught that's "Mine,"
Thinking: " 'Tis not for me," he grieveth not.
This body irketh me; no seeker I
To live. This mortal frame will broken be,
And ne'er another from it be reborn.
Your business with my body, come, that do
E'en as ye will! and not on that account
Will hatred or affection rise in me.

The young men marvelled at his words, and thrilled
With awe, casting away their knives they said:
What are your honour's practices, or who
Is teacher to you? Of whose ordinance
A member, have you gained this grieflessness?

[6] This refers to the doctrine that man has no substantial soul; there
is only the continuity of karma. See below, p. 85 *ff*.

Adhimutta

My teacher is the conqueror knowing all
And seeing all, the Master infinite
In pity, all the world's physician, he.
And he it is by whom these truths are taught,
Norm to Nibbana leading unsurpassed.
Within his rule I've won this grieflessness.

Now when the robbers heard the well-spoke utterance of
  the sage,
They laid aside their knives, their arms, and some forsook
  that trade,
And some besought that they might leave the world for
  holy life. . . .

l.

Since I went forth from home to homeless life,
Ne'er have I harboured conscious wish or plan
Un-ariyan or linked with enmity.
Ne'er mine the quest, all this long interval;—
"Let's smite our fellow-creatures, let us slay,
Let them be brought to pain and misery."
Nay, love I do avow, made infinite,
Well trained, by orderly progression grown,
Even as by the Buddha it is taught.
With all am I a friend, comrade to all,
And to all creatures kind and merciful;
A heart of amity I cultivate,
And ever in good will is my delight.
A heart that cannot drift or fluctuate
I make my joy; the sentiments sublime
That evil men do shun I cultivate.

Whoso hath won to stage of ecstasy
Beyond attention's range of flitting sense,
He, follower of the Enlightened One Supreme,
To ariyan silence straightway doth attain.
E'en as a mountain crag unshaken stands
Sure-based, a brother with illusions gone
Like very mountain stands unwavering.

The man of blameless life, who ever seeks
For what is pure, doth deem some trifling fault,
That is no heavier than the tip of hair,
Weighty as [burden of the gravid] cloud.
E'en as a border city guarded well
Within, without, so guard ye well yourselves.
See that the moment[7] pass not vainly by.

With thought of death I dally not, nor yet
Delight in living. I await the hour
Like any hireling who hath done his task.
With thought of death I dally not, nor yet
Delight in living. I await the hour
With mind discerning and with heedfulness.
The Master hath my fealty and my love,
And all the Buddha's bidding hath been done.
Low have I laid the heavy load I bore,
Cause for rebirth is found in me no more.
The Good for which I bade the world farewell,
And left the home to lead the homeless life,
That highest Good have I accomplished,
And every bond and fetter is destroyed.

Work out your good with zeal and earnestness!
This is my [last] commandment unto you.
For lo! now shall I wholly pass away,
To me comes absolute enfranchisement.

m.

In Jivaka's pleasant woodland walked Subha
The bhikkhuni. A gallant met her there
And barred the way. To him thus spake Subha.

"What have I done to offend thee, that thus in my path thou
    comest?
No man, O friend, it beseemeth to touch a Sister in Orders.
So hath my Master ordained in the precepts we honour
    and follow:
So hath the Welcome One taught in the training wherein
    they have trained me,
Purified discipline holy. Why standest thou blocking my
    pathway?
[7] Any unique spiritual opportunity.

Me pure, thou impure of heart; me passionless, thou of
    vile passions;
Me who as to the whole of me freed am in spirit and
    blameless,
Me whence comes it that thou dost hinder, standing ob-
    noxious?"

"Young art thou, maiden, and faultless—what seekest *thou*
    in the holy life?
Cast off that yellow-hued raiment and come! in the blos-
    soming woodland
Seek we our pleasure. Filled with the incense of blossoms
    the trees waft
Sweetness. See, the spring's at the prime, the season of
    happiness!
Come with me then to the flowering woodland, and seek
    we our pleasure.
Sweet overhead is the sough of the blossoming crests of the
    forest
Swayed by the Wind-gods. But on thou goest alone in the
    jungle,
Lost in its depths, how wilt thou find aught to delight or
    content thee? . . .

I would live but to serve thee, an thou would'st abide in
    the woodland.
Dearer and sweeter to me than art thou in the world is no
    creature,
Thou with the languid and slow-moving eyes of an elf of
    the forest.
If thou willst list to me, come where the joys of the
    sheltered life wait thee;
Dwell in a house of verandas and terraces, handmaidens
    serving thee.
Robe thyself in delicate gear of Benares, don garlands, use
    unguents.
Ornaments many and divers I give to thee, fashioned with
    precious stones,
Gold work and pearls. And thou shalt mount on a couch
    fair and sumptuous,
Carved in sandalwood, fragrant with essences, spread with
    new pillows,

Coverlets fleecy and soft, and decked with immaculate
canopies." . . .

"What now to thee, in this carrion-filled, grave-filling car-
case so fragile
Seen by thee, seemeth to warrant the doctrine thou speak-
est, infatuate?"

"Eyes hast thou like the gazelle's, like an elf's in the heart
of the mountains——
'Tis those eyes of thee, sight of which feedeth the depth of
my passion.
Shrined in thy dazzling, immaculate face as in calyx of
lotus,
'Tis those eyes of thee, sight of which feedeth the strength
of my passion.
Though thou be far from me, how could I ever forget thee,
O maiden,
Thee of the long-drawn eyelashes, thee of the eyes so
miraculous?
Dearer to me than those orbs is naught, O thou witching-
eyed fairy!" . . .

"O thou art blind! thou chasest a sham, deluded by puppet
shows
Seen in the midst of the crowd; thou deemest of value and
genuine
Conjurer's trickwork, trees all of gold that we see in our
dreaming.
What is this eye but a little ball lodged in the fork of a
hollow tree,
Bubble of film, anointed with tear-brine, exuding slime-
drops,
Compost wrought in the shape of an eye of manifold
aspects?"
Forthwith the maiden so lovely tore out her eye and gave it
him:
"Here, then! take thou thine eye!" Nor sinned she, her
heart unobstructed.
Straightway the lust in him ceased and he her pardon imploring:
"O that thou mightest recover thy sight, thou maid pure and
holy!

Never again will I dare to offend thee after this fashion.
Sore hast thou smitten my sin; blazing flames have I clasped
    to my bosom;
Poisonous snake have I handled—but O! be thou heal'd
    and forgive me!"
Freed from molesting, the bhikkhuni went on her way to
    the Buddha,
Chief of th' Awakened. There in his presence, seeing those
    features
Born of uttermost merit, straightway her sight was restored
    to her.

PART III: The Spirit of Theravada Buddhism

Introduction

The major lands in which Theravada Buddhism[1] prevails are
Ceylon, Burma, and Thailand. From the viewpoint of its
thinkers they are simply preserving in its essential purity the
Buddhism taught by the Master and practiced, as well as they
were able to practice it, by the early generations of his followers. For this reason, in the eyes of Theravada Buddhists no
line of division can be drawn between the scriptures given
above and those included in the present section; all might properly be linked together as disclosing the authentic and orthodox
position of their religion from the beginning. And it is true
that most of the documents from which we shall now select are
the same as those which have been drawn upon in Part I, and
the others are perhaps equally ancient.

However, it is possible that as Buddhism passed from its
earliest form into that which has since prevailed in the Theravada countries there has been at work at least a selection, an
emphasis, and a tendency toward a more extreme interpretation than that of the Buddha on several important points.
Happily, we do not need to decide whether this is actually the
case or not. Our purpose in the following group of passages is
to bring out vividly the characteristic emphases that reveal the
spirit of Theravada Buddhism, as we find them presented in
the scriptures which, through the centuries, have been influential in the Theravada countries. In any case, we shall discover

[1] For the division between Theravada and Mahayana Buddhism, see
above, p. 23.

significant contrasts from the Mahayana ideas soon to be expounded.

It must be remembered, of course, that in all these groups of selections we are dealing with ideas that became guides to the thought and experience of the spiritual leaders in the geographical areas where Buddhism spread. We are not dealing with the religion practiced by the masses of the people. Such religion, in the Buddhist countries as in others, reflects an amalgam of the teachings of the respected leaders with popular superstitions which come down from the hoary past and which vary greatly from country to country.

The vital area of continuity between Theravada and original Buddhism lies mainly in the earnest, hopeful, and self-sufficient humanism that is so constantly displayed in the *Dhammapada* and the *Psalms*. Pain and unhappiness constitute the great problem of life; the Master has found the essential solution to that problem by discovering the basic cause of suffering and how it can be brought under control, but neither he nor anyone else can magically save his fellows; our responsibility therefore is resolutely to follow him out of the entanglements of the world into the freedom of the homeless life, to find thus for ourselves the salvation that he has pioneered and to set an inspiring example to those who as yet are too lethargic for such a step. When the Theravada Buddhist speaks the three vows: "I take my refuge in the Buddha; I take my refuge in the Dhamma; I take my refuge in the Sangha," it is in this context that his dedication to these "Three Jewels" is to be understood. By the Buddha he means the human Gautama who first achieved enlightenment and has shown the way to the peace and joy of Nirvana; upon him he looks gratefully as his beloved Master and trusted teacher. By the Dhamma he means the essential doctrines about suffering, its cause and cure, that were taught by the Master and have been handed down for the disciples' guidance—at first by word of mouth and since embodied in the Canon of the "Three Baskets." By the Sangha he means the community of monks, established by Gautama and given its regulations during his lifetime; it is now the representative on earth of his aggressive zeal in pursuit of the conditions of true well-being, and the custodian of his teaching. If he is not yet ready to embark on the homeless life himself he will look to the monks as his spiritual guides, since they embody more of the ideal of resolute self-purification which he accepts, and he will hope by good moral conduct and the accumulation of merit to be reborn in a form less handicapped by torpor and worldliness than he is at present.

The selections I have picked will reveal this continuity, but they will also emphasize certain doctrines in which Theravada Buddhism, as interpreted by many influential thinkers, adopts an extreme position, uncompromisingly rejecting ideas that give comfort and security to the religion of the masses and which, in philosophic form, have been defended by the theologies of Hinduism. These include the doctrines about Nirvana and about the radical transitoriness of all things. Popular religion, in almost all ages and countries, has longed for a blissful and peaceful existence after death, and has been eager to believe in some Beneficent Power in dependence upon which assurance of such final freedom from pain and insecurity can be gained; Hinduism has justified such longings by its conviction that there is a changeless *atman* which is the true self of each individual and that ultimately it is one with Brahman, the transcendent source of all reality.

So far as the doctrine of Nirvana is concerned, the Buddha seems clearly to have taught that Nirvana is a state which is the natural and inevitable result of the extinction of craving. And among the forms of craving which must be rooted out is the longing for continued separate existence, in this life and the next. Did he go beyond this, and positively teach that this state involves the dissolution of conscious awareness as such, in its possibly universal as well as its obviously individual form? Or was he agnostic on this point? Or was he perhaps convinced, as the result of his own experience, of the reality of such a universal awareness freed from the painful fluctuations of separate and transitory forms of consciousness, but felt it wiser not to share this conviction with his disciples, lest they be beguiled by comforting hopes of immortality instead of aggressively concentrating on the needed task of destroying, through self-understanding, whatever forms of craving still lurk in their make-up? We do not need to decide, but it is clear that many Theravada thinkers insist without qualification on the more extreme position. They hold that the Buddha himself, for example, entered Nirvana at the time of his enlightenment (a state in which he was still in the realm of earthly existence but no longer subject to its determining causes), and at his death he passed into "Paranirvana," which means utter extinction—no longer participating in any describable form of existence nor, indeed, of non-existence.

This doctrine of Nirvana is naturally allied with a belief in the radical impermanence of all things. Buddha clearly rejected the Upanishadic concept of a substantial and unchanging *atman*, convinced that neither experience nor reason supports such a concept. He was also sure that the quest for liberation from the sources of evil requires a thoroughly dynamic interpretation of personality, emphasizing, as constituting its core, continuity of moral growth toward liberated integrity rather than any supposed metaphysical self-identity. He likewise held a correspondingly dynamic conception of the physical world. Did he go beyond this, and teach that all things, including any state of a living personality, have nothing but momentary existence, the only temporal continuity being provided by the causal law according to which one momentary entity succeeds another? Again we do not need to decide, but many of his Theravada followers do not shrink from this conclusion.[2] What we call a personality is just an individual stream of becoming; a cross-section of it at any given moment is an aggregate of the five *skandhas*, which (as long as it continues) are in unstable and unceasing interaction with each other. These five are (1) the body (which is not dualistically separated from the mental factors in Eastern psychology), (2) feelings, (3) ideas, (4) volitions, and (5) conscious awareness or pure sensation. They are held together in this shifting interaction by a force called *prapti;* at death they are dissolved and the aggregate which they have formed is no longer capable of persisting. Many Theravada thinkers apply this concept of momentariness not only to psychological states but also to all entities in the physical world.

It is evident that this radical rejection of every form of stability in the universe might be so interpreted as to threaten the moral optimism and spiritual goals that lie at the very heart of Buddhism as a religion. This consequence is guarded against by the significance given in Theravada thought—and here it clearly follows the Master—to the causal laws which provide the real continuity through time that no school of Buddhism means to deny, especially the laws governing the accumulation of karma and its passing from one form of individual existence to its successor, and the laws reflected in the twelvefold series of "conditioned origination." This latter concept attempts to show in detail how the basic factors which make the experience of living beings the kind of affair that it is are causally interrelated. Among other things, it shows how suffering is

[2] There are important differences among the Theravada schools on these matters. What has just been said applies especially to the influential Sautrantika school.

conditioned on craving and craving on ignorance; it thus provides a framework justifying the basic Buddhist faith that through concentrated self-understanding craving and the misery that arises from it can be destroyed.

The following selections, after illustrating and clarifying the Theravada orientation, conclude by bringing to a focus its major contrast with the Mahayana religious ideal which will be presented in Part IV.

1. The Zenaka Story of Buddha's Birth and Early Life

As happened with other religious founders, stories grew up in early Buddhist history about Gautama's birth and early life.[1] These are called Jataka tales. One of the most popular among them, in the Theravada countries and especially in Burma, is the Zenaka (in Burmese "Dzanecka") story. It reveals in an interesting way several Theravada emphases. I give the story as it is summarized by Bishop Paul Bigandet from his own translation from the Burmese. The narrator is Buddha himself.

In the country of Mitila there reigned a king named Dzanecka, who had two sons called Arita Dzanecka and Paula Dzanecka. After a long and prosperous reign he passed to another existence. Arita Dzanecka, having celebrated his father's obsequies and made the usual purifications, ascended the throne. He confirmed his younger brother in the situation of commander-in-chief, which he had hitherto held.

On a certain day a vile courtier, by a false report, awakened in the king's breast sentiments of jealousy and suspicion against his brother's fidelity. The innocent prince was cast into a dungeon; but in the virtue of his innocence he found means to make his escape, went to a part of the country where he had powerful supporters, and soon found himself in a condition to bid defiance to his brother. The king assembled his troops; a battle ensued, in which the king was slain, and Paula Dzanecka ascended the throne.

The queen, who was with child, on hearing the news of such a disaster, went to the treasury, took some ornaments

[1] Including his previous existences, which to believers in transmigration are naturally of great interest.

of the purest gold and the most valuable precious stones, and placed the whole in a basket. She then spread out rice so as to cover the treasure, and extended an old and dirty cloth over the opening of the basket. Putting on the dress of one of the meanest women, she went out of the town, carrying the basket over her head. She left the city through the southern gate and passed into the country without being noticed by the guards.

Having gone to a certain distance from the place, the queen did not know which way to direct her steps. She sat in a dzeat[1] during the heat of the day. Whilst in the dzeat she thought of the country of Tsampa, where some of her relatives lived, and resolved to go thither. She began to make inquiries of the people that were passing by respecting the route she would have to follow.

During this time the attention of a Nat[2] was suddenly attracted by the inspiration of Phralaong, who was in the queen's womb, to the sad position his mother was in. He, leaving forthwith his blissful seat, assumed the appearance of an old man guiding a carriage along the road. He came close to the dzeat and invited the queen to ascend his carriage, assuring her that he would convey her safely to Tsampa. The offer was accepted. As the queen was far advanced with child, she had some difficulty in getting into the conveyance, when that portion of the earth which she was standing upon suddenly swelled and rose to the level of the carriage. The queen stepped into the chariot and they departed. During the night they arrived at a beautiful place close to the neighbourhood of Tsampa. The queen alighted in a dzeat. Her celestial guide bade her to wait until daybreak before she ventured into the city, and returned to the seat of Tawadeintha.

During that very night a famous pounha,[3] attended by five hundred of his disciples, had left the town at a late hour, to take a walk by moonlight and enjoy the cool of the night and a bath in the river. Pamaouka, for such is the name of the pounha, came by chance to the very place where the queen was seated. His disciples continued their walk and went on the bank of the river. She appeared full

---

[1] A resthouse, usually for religious pilgrims.
[2] Supernatural spirit, godling.
[3] Priestly official.

of youth and beauty. But by the virtue of Phralaong the pounha knew that she was in the family way, and that the child she bore was a Phralaong. Pamaouka alone approached close to the queen and entreated her to entertain no fear whatever; that he looked upon her as his sister. The queen related to him all the particulars of her misfortune. The great pounha, moved with compassion, resolved to become her supporter and protector. At the same time he recommended her to say that he was her brother, and when his disciples should come back, to shed tears in token of the tender emotion she felt at meeting with him. Everything having been arranged, Pamaouka called his disciples, told them how happy he was at having found his sister, from whom he had parted many years ago. Meanwhile he directed them to take her to his house, and recommended her to the special care of his wife. As for him, he would be back soon after having performed the usual ablutions. The queen was welcome in the pounha's house, and treated with the greatest care and tenderest affection. A little while after she was delivered of a beautiful child, resembling a statue of gold. They gave him the name of Dzanecka.

Having reached the years of boyhood, he was one day playing with boys of his own age, when, by way of teasing, they called him the son of the widow. These keen tauntings made him urge his mother to reveal to him the name of his father. It was then that he knew the author of his birth. Pamaouka taught him all the sciences known in those days, such as medicine, mathematics, etc. At the age of sixteen years young Dzanecka had completed all his studies.

Dzanecka resolved to devote himself to trade, and acquire thereby ample means to reconquer one day the throne of his ancestors. With a part of the treasure his mother had brought with her, he was in a position to fit out a ship in company with several other merchants. He resolved to sail for a place called Caumawatoura. He had scarcely been at sea two days when a mighty storm came on. The vessel, after having held out some time against the roaring and raging billows, at last gave way, and was broken in pieces. All the crew and passengers, amounting to seven hundred, miserably perished in the sea, without making the least effort to save themselves. Our Phralaong, on the contrary, seizing the extremity of a log of wood, swam with all his

strength, resolved to struggle to the last against adversity.
Mighty were his efforts for several days. At last a daughter
of Nats, whose duty it was to watch over the sea, saw his
generous and courageous behaviour, took pity on him, and
came to his assistance. There followed a sort of dialogue
between her and Dzanecka. The latter displayed his un-
daunted courage and firm purpose. The former admired
the more his determined resolution. She resolved to save
him from the dangerous position. Taking him in her arms,
she carried him, according to his wishes, to the country of
Mitila, in the garden of mango-trees, and placed him on
the very table-stone where his ancestors were wont to enjoy themselves with a numerous retinue. Phralaong immediately fell asleep. The daughter of Nats, having
enjoined the Nat, guardian of the place, to watch over the
prince, returned to her blissful seat.

On the very day that the vessel was wrecked the ruler
of Mitila died, leaving one daughter, named Thiwalee.
Previous to his giving up the ghost and ascending to the
seat of Nats, the king had ordered his ministers into his
presence, and enjoined on them to select for the husband
of his daughter a man remarkable for the beauty and
strength of his body, as well as by the acuteness and penetration of his mind. He was to be able to bend and unbend
an enormous bow, a feat which the united efforts of a
thousand soldiers could scarcely achieve, and find the place
where he had concealed sixteen golden cups. On the
seventh day after his death, the ministers and pounhas
began to deliberate among themselves about the choice of
a match worthy of the princess. Several competitors offered
themselves for the hand of Thiwalee, but they were all
rejected. At last, not knowing what to do, they resolved to
leave to chance the solution of the difficulty. They sent
out a charmed chariot, convinced that by the virtue inherent in it they would find out the fortunate man whose
destinies were to be united to those of the princess. The
chariot was sent out attended by soldiers, musicians,
pounhas, and noblemen. It came straight forward to the
mango-trees garden, and stopped by the side of the table-
stone Phralaong was sleeping upon. The pounhas, on
inspecting the hands and feet of the stranger, saw un-
mistakable signs foreshowing his elevation to the royal

dignity. They awakened him by the sound of musical instruments, saluted him king, and begged of him to put on the royal dress, mount on the chariot, and proceed triumphantly to the royal city. He entered the palace through the eastern gate. Having been informed of the king's last intentions, he forthwith bent and unbent the bow, found out the sixteen golden cups, and was duly united to the beautiful and youthful Thiwalee. All the people showed signs of the greatest rejoicings; the rich made him all sorts of offerings; the pounhas in white costume, holding the sacred white shell, adorned with flowers and filled with water, with their bodies bent forward, poured respectfully the water, imploring blessings on the new monarch.

When the rejoicings were over, the king rewarded the pounha Pamaouka, who had been as a father to him during his exile. He applied himself to do as much good as he could in relieving the poor, and promoting the welfare of all. He delighted in mentioning to his courtiers his misfortune, and the great efforts he had made to extricate himself from difficulties. He praised the reward which attended generous efforts, and exhorted them never to flinch under difficulties, but always to exhibit a strong and unconquerable resolution under all trials, because it must sooner or later be crowned with success.

During the seven thousand years that he reigned over Mitila with the queen Thiwalee, he faithfully practised the observances of the law, governed justly, fed the Rahans[4] and Pitzega-buddhas,[5] and gave abundant alms to the poor.

On the tenth month Thiwalee was delivered of a son, whom they called Digaout. On a certain day, the king, having received from his gardener some mangoes full of flavour and beauty, wished to go to the garden to see the tree that yielded such delicious fruits. When he arrived at the place, he saw two mango-trees, one with a luxuriant foliage, but without fruits, the other loaded with fruits. The monarch approached the tree, riding his elephant, and plucked some mangoes, which he ate and found delicious. Thence he proceeded further to inspect the other parts of the extensive garden. The courtiers and the people that followed plucked fruits from the same tree, and did it with

[4] Arahats.
[5] "Dedicated spiritual seekers," is the meaning in this context.

such eagerness that they left neither fruits nor leaves on the tree.

On his return the king was surprised to see the fruitful tree destitute of both leaves and fruits, whilst the barren one had a beautiful appearance. The monarch, after a lengthened dialogue with his courtiers, concluded as follows: "The riches of this world are never without enemies; he who possesses them resembles the fruitful mango-tree. We must look out for goods that excite neither envy, jealousy, nor other passions. The Rahans and Pitzega-buddhas alone possess such riches. I will take a lesson from the barren mango-tree. That I may cut off and eradicate the troubles, vexations, and anxieties of life, I will renounce everything and embrace the profession of Rahan."

With this idea strongly impressed on his mind, Dzanecka came back to his palace. He forthwith sent for the general of his troops, and directed him to place a strong guard in front of his apartment, and allow no one for four consecutive months to come into his presence, not even the queen, but only him who would bring his daily meal. He gave orders to his ministers to judge with impartiality, agreeably to the law. Having thus arranged everything, he withdrew alone to the upper apartment of his palace. Here follows a stanza in praise of the prince, who had separated from his queen, concubines, and all the pleasures and honours attending royalty.

Dzanecka alone began to meditate on the happiness of the life of pounhas and Pitzega-buddhas; he admired their poor diet, their zeal in practising the observances of the law, their earnest longings after the happiness of Neibban,[6] their disengagement from the ties of passions, the state of inward peace and fixity which their souls enjoyed. In his enthusiasm he venerated them with a holy fervour, called them his masters and preceptors, and exclaimed: "Who will teach me to imitate their lives, and help me to become similar to them?" In ten stanzas Dzanecka reviews successively all that had belonged to him, his capital with its stately edifices, fine gates, the three walls and ditches, the beautiful and fertile country of Wintzearitz, the palace with its lofty domes and massive towers, the beautifully orna-

[6] Nirvana.

mented throne, the rich and magnificent royal dresses, the royal garden and tank, the elephants, horses, and chariots, the soldiers, the pounhas, the princes, his queen and concubines. He then concludes each stanza with the following words: "When shall I leave all these things, become poor, put on the humble habit of Rahans, and follow the same mode of a perfectly retired life?" With these and similar reflections Dzanecka endeavoured to sunder one after the other many threads of passion, to pull down successively the branches of the impure tree, until he could give a final stroke to the roots.

At the conclusion of four months' retirement, Dzanecka sent for a faithful servant, and directed him to procure for him the various articles of the dress of a Rahan. He had his head and beard shaved; put on the cherished habit, and placing a staff in his hand walked out of his apartments, and directed his course towards the gate, with the dignified deportment of a Rahan of sixty years profession.

Queen Thiwalee was tired of having been so long deprived of her husband's company. She summoned seven hundred of the handsomest damsels of the palace to go with her to the king, and by the efforts of their united charms entrap him in the net of passion and prevail upon him to come back to their society. When they ascended the stair-case, they met with Dzanecka in his new attire. None recognised him; but all paid him due reverence as some holy personage that had come to give instructions to the king. Having reached the apartment and seen the royal dress set aside, and the beautiful and long black hairs laid on one of the sofas, the queen and her attendants soon understood the sad and heart-rending intimation which these objects were designed to convey. She ran in all haste with all her retinue down the stairs and overtook the new Rahan at the moment he was crossing the outer gate of the palace. Every means that could be devised to make impression on the king's heart were resorted to by the queen and the damsels, in order to prevail upon him to forego his resolution. Tears, cries, wailings, striking of the breast, display of the most graceful and seducing forms, supplications, entreaties, were all used in vain; the new Rahan, unmoved and firm, continued his course, protesting that passions and concupiscence were dead in him, and that what could be said or done to engage him to change his resolution was in vain. During his progress towards the solitude of Himawonta, he was comforted and encouraged by the advice of two Rathees,[7] who from their solitude flew through the air to witness the beautiful struggle between passions and virtue, and help him not to flinch before the repeated obstacles the queen put in his way, to retard, impede, and prevent the execution of his holy design. The names of these two instructors were Narada and Migadzein; they were clothed in the skins of panthers. They instructed him in the duties of his new calling, and exhorted him to root out of his heart with perseverance all passions, and in particular concupiscence and pride.

Comforted with such timely instructions, the new Rahan felt himself more than ever fixed in his resolution. On his way to the solitude, Dzanecka arrived one evening at the gates of a town called Daunu. He passed the night under a tree, at a distance from the queen and the crowd that followed her. On the morning he entered the town, and went, as usual, along the streets to beg his food. He happened to stop for a while at the shop of a man that was fabricating arrows. Dzanecka, seeing the workman shutting one eye and looking with the other to see if the shaft of the arrow was straight, asked him the reason of his doing so, as he would see better with both eyes than with one. The workman told him that it was not always good that each object in this world should have a match. "Should I," said he, "look on this shaft with both eyes, my sight, distracted by several objects, could not perceive the defects of the wood, etc., but by looking on it with only one eye the least irregularity is easily detected. When we have a work to perform, if there be two opposite wills in us, it cannot be regularly made. You have put on the habit of Rahan; you have apparently renounced the world; how is it that you are followed by such a large retinue of women and other attendants? It is impossible to attend well to the duties of your profession, and at the same time keep such a company." This cutting remark made a deep impression on Dzanecka. He had gone over a little distance, when he met a number of little girls playing together. One of them had a silver bangle on each hand, with one of gold on the

[7] Solitary recluses.

right hand. When she agitated the right hand, the two bangles hitting each other produced a sound. Dzanecka, willing to try the wit of the little creature, asked her the reason why the movement of one hand produced a sound, whilst that of the other did not. She replied, "My left hand, that has but one bangle, is the image of the Rahans who ought to be alone. In this world, when an object has its match, some collision and noise inevitably result. How is it that you, who have put on the habit of Rahan, allow yourself to be followed by that woman who is still full of freshness and beauty? Is she your wife or sister? Even should she be only your sister, it is not good that she should be with you. It is dangerous for Rahans to keep the company of women."

This sharp lecture, from the mouth of a little girl, produced a deep impression on our Rahan. He left the city. A large forest was in the vicinity: he resolved to part company with the queen at once. At the entrance he stopped awhile, and paused for a moment. There, on a sudden, stretching his arm, he broke the small branch of a tree, and showing it to Thiwalee he said, "Princess, you see this small branch; it can never be reunited to the stem it has been taken from. In like manner, it is impossible that I should ever go back with you." On hearing the fatal words the queen fainted. All her attendants crowded round her, to afford her some relief. Dzanecka himself, in the tumult and confusion that was going on, stole away with rapidity and disappeared into the forest. The queen was then carried back to Daunu by her attendants, whence they all returned to Mitila. Alone in the solitude, Phralaong enjoyed the sweets of perfect contemplation during a period of three thousand years. Thiwalee, on her part, resolved to renounce the world and follow the example of her husband. She became a Rahaness, in one of the royal gardens, during the same period of years, and subsequently migrated to one of the seats of Brahmas, called Brahma-parithitsa.

At the conclusion of the narrative Buddha added: "Manimegala, the daughter of Nats, who saved me in the midst of the sea, is now my beloved fair disciple of the left, Oopalawon. The little girl who gave me such a wholesome instruction, at the gate of the town of Daunu, is now Kema, my fair disciple of the right. The Rathee Narada has since become my great disciple Thariputra,[8] whose wisdom is second only to my own. The other Rathee Migadzein is now my disciple Maukalan, whose power for displaying wonders yields only to mine. The arrow-maker has since become Ananda, my faithful and dutiful attendant. Queen Thiwalee has become the Princess Yathaudara.[9] As to Prince Dzanecka, he is now the Phra who is before you and addresses you, who is perfectly acquainted with all the laws and principles, and who is the teacher of men, Nats, and Brahmas."

2. The Fire Sermon

The Buddha taught, in his "Middle Way," that the body's functions should be respected so far as health requires, but that concern for them should never be allowed to obstruct single-minded progress toward liberation. The famous Fire Sermon in the Maha-Vagga, expresses in vivid form one characteristic emphasis of Theravada Buddhism—on the need of turning away in utter aversion from everything in our nature which is on fire with craving, so that we may achieve the "coolness" of Nirvana.

This naturally leads to the selection "On Health of Mind."[10] How does one turn away from the bodily and mental functions that are on fire? By refusing to identify one's self with them; by identifying instead with the unchanging reality that is discovered by renouncing them. Thus one achieves true health of mind, whatever happens to the body because of sickness, old age, or any other physical change.

Then the Blessed One having dwelt in Uruvela as long as he wished, proceeded on his wanderings in the direction of Gaya Head, accompanied by a great congregation of priests, a thousand in number, who had all of them aforetime been monks with matted hair. And there in Gaya, on Gaya Head, the Blessed One dwelt, together with the thousand priests.

And there the Blessed One addressed the priests:—

"All things, O priests, are on fire. And what, O priests, are all these things which are on fire?

[8] In Sanskrit, Sariputra.
[9] In Sanskrit, Yasodhara (Gotama's wife).
[10] From the Samyutta-Nikaya, *op. cit.*

"The eye, O priests, is on fire; forms are on fire; eye-consciousness[11] is on fire; impressions received by the eye are on fire; and whatever sensation, pleasant, unpleasant, or indifferent, originates in dependence on impressions received by the eye, that also is on fire.

"And with what are these on fire?

"With the fire of passion, say I, with the fire of hatred, with the fire of infatuation; with birth, old age, death, sorrow, lamentation, misery, grief, and despair are they on fire.

"The ear is on fire; sounds are on fire; . . . the nose is on fire; odors are on fire; . . . the tongue is on fire; tastes are on fire; . . . the body is on fire; things tangible are on fire; . . . the mind is on fire; ideas are on fire; . . . mind-consciousness is on fire; impressions received by the mind are on fire; and whatever sensation, pleasant, unpleasant, or indifferent, originates in dependence on impressions received by the mind, that also is on fire.

"And with what are these on fire?

"With the fire of passion, say I, with the fire of hatred, with the fire of infatuation; with birth, old age, death, sorrow, lamentation, misery, grief, and despair are they on fire.

"Perceiving this, O priests, the learned and noble disciple conceives an aversion for the eye, conceives an aversion for forms, conceives an aversion for eye-consciousness, conceives an aversion for the impressions received by the eye; and whatever sensation, pleasant, unpleasant, or indifferent, originates in dependence on impressions received by the eye, for that also he conceives an aversion. Conceives an aversion for the ear, conceives an aversion for sounds, . . . conceives an aversion for the nose, conceives an aversion for odors, . . . conceives an aversion for the tongue, conceives an aversion for tastes, . . . conceives an aversion for the body, conceives an aversion for things tangible, . . . conceives an aversion for the mind, conceives an aversion for ideas, conceives an aversion for mind-consciousness, conceives an aversion for the impressions received by the mind; and whatever sensation, pleasant, unpleasant, or indifferent, originates in dependence on

[11] That part of the mind which sees through the eye; faculty of vision.

impressions received by the mind, for this also he conceives an aversion. And in conceiving this aversion, he becomes divested of passion, and by the absence of passion he becomes free, and when he is free he becomes aware that he is free; and he knows that rebirth is exhausted, that he has lived the holy life, that he has done what it behooved him to do, and that he is no more for this world." . . .

3. On Health of Mind

The householder Nakulapita came to Sariputta, saluted him, and sat down at one side. As he was seated there Sariputta said to him, "Your senses are calmed, householder, the colour of your face is pure and clean. Have you heard a discourse on the doctrine from the Lord face to face with him to-day?"

"How else could it be, reverend one? I have just now been sprinkled by the Lord with the nectar of a discourse on the doctrine."

"And in what way have you been sprinkled by the Lord with the nectar of a discourse on the doctrine?"

"Well, reverend one, I went to the Lord, saluted him, and sat down at one side. As I sat there I said to the Lord, 'I am decrepit, Lord, old, aged, advanced in years and life: I have reached my span of life, ill in body and constantly ailing. Only occasionally, Lord, do I see the Lord and the worshipful monks. May the Lord exhort me, may the Lord instruct me, so that it may long be for my welfare and happiness.'

"Thereat the Lord said to me, 'Even so, householder, even so, householder, ill is your body, advanced in life and overcome with age. For one who bears this body about, and who should claim even a moment's good health, what is that but folly? Therefore, householder, you should thus train yourself: "Though I am ill in body my mind shall not be ill." Even so should you train yourself.' Even thus did the Lord sprinkle me with the nectar of a discourse on the doctrine."

"But, householder, did it not occur to you to question the Lord further, asking in what respect one is ill in body and ill in mind, or in what respect one is ill in body and not ill in mind?"

"We would come a long way, reverend one, to understand from the reverend Sariputta the meaning of that saying."

"Then, listen, householder, reflect on it well, I will speak."

"Even so," the householder Nakulapita replied.

The reverend Sariputta said: "How, householder, is one ill in body and ill in mind? Herein an unlearned common person, who does not perceive the noble ones, who is unskilled and untrained in the noble doctrine, who does not perceive good men, who is unskilled and untrained in the doctrine of good men, looks upon his body as his self, thinking that his self consists of body or that his body is in his self or that his self is in his body, being possessed by the thought, 'I am body, body is mine.' The body of one possessed by this thought changes and becomes otherwise, and through the change and alteration of his body grief, lamentation, pain, dejection, and despair arise.

"He looks upon feeling as his self, thinking that his self consists of feeling. . . .

"He looks upon perception as his self. . . .

"He looks upon the aggregates (the mental and other activities) as his self. . . .

"He looks upon consciousness as his self. . . .

"The consciousness of one possessed by this thought changes and becomes otherwise, and through the change and alteration of consciousness grief, lamentation, pain, dejection, and despair arise. Even so, householder, is one ill in body and ill in mind.

"And how, householder, is one ill in body and not ill in mind? Herein a learned noble disciple, who perceives the noble ones, who is skilled and well-trained in the noble doctrine, does not look upon his body as his self, not thinking that his self consists of his body, nor that his body is in his self, nor that his self is in his body, not being possessed by the thought, 'I am body, body is mine.' The body of one not possessed by this thought changes and becomes otherwise, but through the change and alteration of his body grief, lamentation, pain, dejection, and despair do not arise.

"He does not look upon feeling as his self, not thinking

that his self consists of feeling. . . .

"He does not look upon perception as his self. . . .

"He does not look upon the aggregates as his self. . . .

"He does not look upon consciousness as his self, not thinking that his self consists of consciousness, nor that consciousness is in his self, nor that his self is in consciousness, and he is not possessed by the thought, 'I am consciousness, consciousness is mine.' The consciousness of one not possessed by this thought changes and becomes otherwise, but through the change and alteration of his consciousness grief, lamentation, pain, dejection, and despair do not arise. Even so, householder, is one ill in body but not ill in mind."

4. What Is Gained by Abandoning the World and Becoming a Monk?

A question raised by many Westerners who become acquainted with the life of the Buddhist monks was also raised in India in the early days of Buddhism: What values, significant for this life and verifiable to others, are attained by those who renounce the world? Buddha's reported answer to this question is charmingly presented in the following selection from the Sammanaphala Suttanta. *The reader will especially note the emphasis on the cumulative importance of the values portrayed.*

[Word has been brought to King Agatasattu that Gautama is lodging nearby.]

"The Blessed One, Sire, the Arahat, the all-awakened one, is now lodging in our Mango Grove, with a great company of the brethren, with twelve hundred and fifty brethren. And this is the good report that has been noised abroad as to Gotama the Blessed One: 'An Arahat, fully awakened, is the exalted one, abounding in wisdom and goodness, happy, with knowledge of the worlds, unsurpassed as a guide to mortals willing to be led, the teacher of gods and men, a blessed Buddha.' Let your Majesty pay a visit to him. It may well be that, on calling upon him, your heart, Sire, shall find peace."

"Then, friend Givaka, have the riding-elephants made ready."

"Very good, Sire!" said Givaka the physician in assent to the words of the king. And he had five hundred she-elephants made ready, and the state elephant the king was wont to ride, and had word brought to the king: "The elephants, Sire, are caparisoned. Do now what seemeth to you meet." Then the king had five hundred of his women mounted on the she-elephants, one on each; and himself mounted the state elephant; and he went forth, the attendants bearing torches, in royal pomp, from Ragagaha to Givaka the physician's Mango Grove.

And the king, when close upon the Mango Grove, was seized with a sudden fear and consternation, and the hairs on his body stood erect. And, anxious and excited, he said to Givaka: "You are playing me no tricks, Givaka? You are not deceiving me? You are not betraying me to my foes? How can it be that there should be no sound at all, not a sneeze nor a cough, in so large an assembly of the brethren, among twelve hundred and fifty of the brethren?"

"Fear not, O king. I play no trick, neither deceive you; nor would I betray you to the foe. Go on, O king, go straight on: There, in the pavilion hall, the lamps are burning."

Then the king went on, on his elephant as far as the path was passable for elephants, and then on foot, to the door of the pavilion; and then said to Givaka: "But where, Givaka, is the Blessed One?"

"That is he, O king, sitting against the middle pillar, and facing the east, with the brethren around him."

Then the king went up, and stood respectfully on one side. And as he stood there and looked on the assembly, seated in perfect silence, calm as a clear lake, he broke out: "Would that my son, Udayi Bhadda, might have such calm as this assembly of the brethren now has!" . . .

Then the king bowed to the Blessed One, and stretching forth his joined palms in salutation to the Order took his seat aside, and said to the Blessed One: "I would fain question the Blessed One on a certain matter, if he give me opportunity to set forth the question."

"Ask, O king, whatsoever you desire."

"There are, Sir, a number of ordinary crafts:—mahouts,

horsemen, charioteers, archers, standard bearers, camp marshals, camp followers, high military officers of royal birth, military scouts, men brave as elephants, champions, heroes, warriors in buckskin, home-born slaves, cooks, barbers, bath attendants, confectioners, garland-makers, washermen, weavers, basket-makers, potters, arithmeticians, accountants, and whatsoever others of like kind there may be. All these enjoy, in this very world, the visible fruits of their craft. They maintain themselves, and their parents and children and friends, in happiness and comfort. They keep up gifts, the object of which is gain on high, to recluses and Brahmans—gifts that lead to rebirth in heaven, that redound to happiness, and have bliss as their result. Can you, Sir, declare to me any such immediate fruit, visible in this very world, of the life of a recluse?" . . .

"I can, O king. And to that end I would fain put a question to you. Answer it as you may think most fit.

"Now what do you think, O king. Suppose among the people of your household there were a slave who does work for you, rises up in the morning before you do and retires earlier to rest, who is keen to carry out your pleasure, anxious to make himself agreeable in what he does and says, a man who watches your every look. Suppose he should think, 'Strange is it and wonderful, this issue of meritorious deeds, this result of merit! Here is this king of Magadha, Agatasattu, the son of the Videha princess—he is a man, and so am I. But the king lives in the full enjoyment and possession of the five pleasures of sense—a very god, methinks—and here am I a slave, working for him, rising before him and retiring earlier to rest, keen to carry out his pleasure, anxious to make myself agreeable in deed and word, watching his very looks. Would that I were like him, that I too might earn merit. Why should not I have my hair and beard shaved off, and don the yellow robes, and going forth from the household state, renounce the world?' And suppose, after a time, he should do so. And having been admitted into an Order, suppose he should dwell restrained in act and word and thought, content with mere food and shelter, delighting in solitude. And suppose your people should tell you of this, saying: 'If it please your majesty, do you know that such a one, formerly your slave, who worked for you, and so on (all as before) has now donned the yellow robes, and has been admitted into an Order, and dwells restrained, content with mere food and shelter, delighting in solitude?' Would you then say: 'Let the man come back; let him become a slave again, and work for me'?"

"Nay, Lord, rather should we greet him with reverence and rise up from our seat out of deference towards him, and press him to be seated. And we should have robes and a bowl, and a lodging place, and medicine for the sick—all the requisites of a recluse—made ready, and beg him to accept of them. And we should order watch and ward and guard to be kept for him according to the law."

"But what do you think, O king. That being so, is there, or is there not, some fruit, visible in this world, of the life of a recluse?"

"Certainly, Lord, that is so."

"This then, O king, is the first kind of the fruit, visible in this world, which I maintained to arise from the life of a recluse."

"Can you, Lord, show me any other fruit, visible in this world, of the life of a recluse?" . . .

"I can, O king. Give ear therefore, O king, and give good heed, and I will speak.

"Suppose, O king, there appears in the world one who has won the truth, an Arahat, a fully awakened one, abounding in wisdom and goodness, happy, who knows all worlds, unsurpassed as a guide to mortals willing to be led, a teacher for gods and men, a Blessed One, a Buddha. He, by himself, thoroughly knows and sees, as it were, face to face this universe, —including the worlds above of the gods, the Brahmas, and the Maras, and the world below with its recluses and Brahmans, its princes and peoples— and having known it, he makes his knowledge known to others. The truth, lovely in its origin, lovely in its progress, lovely in its consummation, doth he proclaim, both in the spirit and in the letter, the higher life doth he make known, in all its fullness and in all its purity.

"A householder or one of his children, or a man of inferior birth in any class listens to that truth; and on hearing it he has faith in the Tathagata (the one who has found the truth); and when he is possessed of that faith, he considers thus within himself:

" 'Full of hindrances is household life, a path for the dust of passion. Free as the air is the life of him who has renounced all worldly things. How difficult is it for the man who dwells at home to live the higher life in all its fullness, in all its purity, in all its bright perfection! Let me then cut off my hair and beard, let me clothe myself in the orange-coloured robes, and let me go forth from the household life into the homeless state.'

"Then, before long, forsaking his portion of wealth, be it great or small, forsaking his circle of relatives, be they many or be they few, he cuts off his hair and beard, he clothes himself in the orange-coloured robes, and he goes forth from the household life into the homeless state.

"When he has thus become a recluse, he lives self-restrained by that restraint that should be binding on a recluse. Uprightness is his delight, and he sees danger in the least of those things he should avoid. He adopts, and trains himself in, the precepts. He encompasses himself with good deeds in act and word. Pure are his means of livelihood, good is his conduct, guarded the door of his senses. Mindful and self-possessed he is altogether happy.

"And how, O king, is his conduct good?

"In this, O king, that the Bhikshu, putting away the killing of living things, holds aloof from the destruction of life. The cudgel and the sword he has laid aside, and ashamed of roughness, and full of mercy, he dwells compassionate and kind to all creatures that have life.

"This is part of the goodness that he has. . . .

"And how, O king, is the Bhikshu mindful and self-possessed?

"In this matter, O king, the Bhikshu in going forth or in coming back keeps clearly before his mind's eye [all that is wrapt up therein—the immediate object of the act itself, its ethical significance, whether or not it is conducive to the high aim set before him, and the real facts underlying the mere phenomenon of the outward act]. And so also in looking forward, or in looking round; in stretching forth his arm, or in drawing it in again; in eating or drinking, in masticating or swallowing, in obeying the calls of nature, in going or standing or sitting, in sleeping or waking, in speaking or in being still, he keeps himself aware of all it really means. Thus is it, O king, that the Bhikshu becomes mindful and self-possessed.

"And how, O king, is the Bhikshu content?

"In this matter, O king, the Bhikshu is satisfied with sufficient robes to cherish his body, with sufficient food to keep his stomach going. Whithersoever he may go forth, these he takes with him as he goes—just as a bird with his wings, O king, whithersoever he may fly, carries his wings with him as he flies. Thus is it, O king, that the Bhikshu becomes content.

"Then, master of this so excellent body of moral precepts, gifted with this so excellent self-restraint as to the senses, endowed with this so excellent mindfulness and self-possession, filled with this so excellent content, he chooses some lonely spot to rest at on his way—in the woods, at the foot of a tree, on a hill side, in a mountain glen, in a rocky cave, in a charnel place, or on a heap of straw in the open field. And returning thither after his round for alms he seats himself, when his meal is done, cross-legged, keeping his body erect, and his intelligence alert, intent.

"Putting away the hankering after the world, he remains with a heart that hankers not, and purifies his mind of lusts. Putting away the corruption of the wish to injure, he remains with a heart free from ill-temper, and purifies his mind of malevolence. Putting away torpor of heart and mind, keeping his ideas alight,[1] mindful and self-possessed, he purifies his mind of weakness and of sloth. Putting away flurry and worry, he remains free from fretfulness, and with heart serene within, he purifies himself of irritability and vexation of spirit. Putting away wavering, he remains as one passed beyond perplexity; and no longer in suspense as to what is good, he purifies his mind of doubt. . . .

"O king, the Bhikshu, so long as these five hindrances are not put away within him, looks upon himself as in debt, diseased, in prison, in slavery, lost on a desert road. But when these five hindrances have been put away within him, he looks upon himself as freed from debt, rid of disease, out of jail, a free man, and secure;

"And gladness springs up within him on his realising that, and joy arises to him thus gladdened, and so rejoicing

[1] Probably, "free from confusion."

all his frame becomes at ease, and being thus at ease he is filled with a sense of peace, and in that peace his heart is stayed. . . .

"With his heart thus serene [etc., as before], he directs and bends down his mind to the knowledge of the fall and rise of beings. With the pure Heavenly Eye,[2] surpassing that of men, he sees beings as they pass away from one form of existence and take shape in another; he recognises the mean and the noble, the well favoured and the ill favoured, the happy and the wretched, passing away according to their deeds: 'Such and such beings, my brethren, in act and word and thought, revilers of the noble ones, holding to wrong views, acquiring for themselves that karma which results from wrong views, they, on the dissolution of the body, after death, are reborn in some unhappy state of suffering or woe. But such and such beings, my brethren, well doers in act and word and thought, not revilers of the noble ones, holding to right views, acquiring for themselves that karma that results from right views, they, on the dissolution of the body, after death, are reborn in some happy state in heaven.' Thus with the pure Heavenly Eye, surpassing that of men, he sees beings as they pass away from one state of existence, and take form in another; he recognises the mean and the noble, the well favoured and the ill favoured, the happy and the wretched, passing away according to their deeds.

"Just, O king, as if there were a house with an upper terrace on it in the midst of a place where four roads meet, and a man standing thereon, and with eyes to see, should watch men entering a house, and coming forth out of it, and walking hither and thither along the street, and seated in the square in the midst. Then he would know: 'Those men are entering a house, and those are leaving it, and those are walking to and fro in the street, and those are seated in the square in the midst.'

"This, O king, is an immediate fruit of the life of a recluse, visible in this world, and higher and sweeter than the last.

"With his heart thus serene [etc., as before], he directs and bends down his mind to the knowledge of the destruc-

---

[2] One of the stages of supernormal vision recognized in Buddhist thought.

tion of the Deadly Floods.[8] He knows as it really is: 'This is pain.' He knows as it really is: 'This is the origin of pain.' He knows as it really is: 'This is the cessation of pain.' He knows as it really is: 'This is the path that leads to the cessation of pain.' He knows as they really are: 'These are the Deadly Floods.' He knows as it really is: 'This is the path that leads to the cessation of the Deadly Floods.' To him, thus knowing, thus seeing, the heart is set free from the deadly taint of lusts, is set free from the deadly taint of becomings, is set free from the deadly taint of ignorance. In him, thus set free, there arises the knowledge of his emancipation, and he knows: 'Rebirth has been destroyed. The higher life has been fulfilled. What had to be done has been accomplished. After this present life there will be no beyond!'

"Just, O king, as if in a mountain fastness there were a pool of water, clear, translucent, and serene; and a man, standing on the bank, and with eyes to see, should perceive the oysters and the shells, the gravel and the pebbles and the shoals of fish, as they move about or lie within it: he would know: 'This pool is clear, transparent, and serene, and there within it are the oysters and the shells, and the sand and gravel, and the shoals of fish are moving about or lying still.'

"This, O king, is an immediate fruit of the life of a recluse, visible in this world, and higher and sweeter than the last. And there is no fruit of the life of a recluse, visible in this world, that is higher and sweeter than this."

And when he had thus spoken, Agatasattu the king said to the Blessed One: "Most excellent, Lord, most excellent! Just as if a man were to set up that which has been thrown down, or were to reveal that which is hidden away, or were to point out the right road to him who has gone astray, or were to bring a lamp into the darkness so that those who have eyes could see external forms—just even so, Lord, has the truth been made known to me, in many a figure, by the Blessed One. And now I betake myself, Lord, to the Blessed One as my refuge, to the Truth, and to the Order. May the Blessed One accept me as a disciple, as one who, from this day forth, as long as life endures, has taken his

[8] The three moral taints enumerated later in the paragraph. The taint of "becomings" is the hankering after continued sensuous existence.

refuge in them. Sin has overcome me, Lord, weak and foolish and wrong that I am, in that, for the sake of sovereignty, I put to death my father, that righteous man, that righteous king! May the Blessed One accept it of me, Lord, that do so acknowledge it as a sin, to the end that in future I may restrain myself."

"Verily, O king, it was sin that overcame you in acting thus. But inasmuch as you look upon it as sin, and confess it according to what is right, we accept your confession as to that. For that, O king, is custom in the discipline of the noble ones,[4] that whosoever looks upon his fault as a fault, and rightfully confesses it, shall attain to self-restraint in future."

When he had thus spoken, Agatasattu the king said to the Blessed One: "Now, Lord, we would fain go. We are busy, and there is much to do."

"Do, O king, whatever seemeth to thee fit."

Then Agatasattu the king, pleased and delighted with the words of the Blessed One, arose from his seat, and bowed to the Blessed One, and keeping him on the right hand as he passed him, departed thence. . . .

5. The Duties of the Theravada Layman

Thus far in this section our attention has been centered on the ideas dominating the minds of those who were ready to renounce the world of ordinary social activities to seek the goal of Nirvana as quickly as possible.

But the Theravada layman must not be forgotten, especially since we shall wish later to catch a glimpse of the role of the layman in Mahayana Buddhism. How is he expected to conduct his life, so as to express appropriately his less strenuous commitment but none the less sincere acceptance of the Buddhist way? By what moral and social principles should he be guided?

The following selection, taken from the Sigalovada Suttanta, *gives an interesting and instructive answer to this question. It also shows how Buddha, like other great religious teachers, often found it wise to give ethical meaning to primitive customs and ceremonies instead of trying to do away with them.*

[4] Probably, the arahats.

Thus have I heard: The Exalted One was once staying near Rajagaha in the Bamboo Wood at the Squirrels' Feeding Ground.

Now at this time young Sigala, a householder's son, rising betimes, went forth from Rajagaha, and with wet hair and wet garments and clasped hands uplifted, paid worship to the several quarters of earth and sky:—to the east, south, west, and north, to the nadir and the zenith.

And the Exalted One early that morning dressed himself, took bowl and robe and entered Rajagaha seeking alms. Now he saw young Sigala worshipping and spoke to him thus:

"Why, young householder, do you, rising betimes and leaving Rajagaha, with wet hair and raiment, worship the several quarters of earth and sky?"

"Sir, my father, when he was a-dying, said to me: Dear son, you should worship the quarters of earth and sky. So I, sir, honouring my father's word, reverencing, revering, holding it sacred, rise betimes and, leaving Rajagaha, worship on this wise."

"But in the religion of an Ariyan, young householder, the six quarters should not be worshipped thus."

"How then, sir, in the religion of an Ariyan, should the six quarters be worshipped?

"It would be an excellent thing, sir, if the Exalted One would so teach me the doctrine according to which, in the religion of an Ariyan, the six quarters should be worshipped."

"Hear then, young householder, give ear to my words and I will speak. . . .

[After discussing various vices and temptations against which one must be on guard, the Buddha continued]:

"How, O young householder, does the Ariyan disciple serve the six quarters? The following should be looked upon as the six quarters:—parents as the east, teachers as the south, wife and children as the west, friends and companions as the north, servants and work people as the nadir, religious teachers and brahmins as the zenith.

"In five ways a child should minister to his parents as the eastern quarter:—'Once supported by them I will now be their support; I will perform duties incumbent on them;

I will keep up the lineage and tradition of my family; I will make myself worthy of my heritage.'

"In five ways parents thus ministered to, as the eastern quarter, by their child, show their love for him:—they restrain him from vice, they exhort him to virtue, they train him to a profession, they contract a suitable marriage for him, and in due time they hand over his inheritance.

"Thus is this eastern quarter protected by him and made safe and secure.

"In five ways should pupils minister to their teachers as the southern quarter: by rising [from their seat, in salutation], by waiting upon them, by eagerness to learn, by personal service, and by attention when receiving their teaching.

"And in five ways do teachers, thus ministered to as the southern quarter by their pupils, love their pupil:—they train him in that wherein he has been well trained; they make him hold fast that which is well held; they thoroughly instruct him in the lore of every art; they speak well of him among his friends and companions. They provide for his safety in every quarter.

"Thus is this southern quarter protected by him and made safe and secure.

"In five ways should a wife as western quarter be ministered to by her husband:—by respect, by courtesy, by faithfulness, by handing over authority to her, by providing her with adornment.

"In these five ways does the wife, ministered to by her husband as the western quarter, love him:—her duties are well performed, by hospitality to the kin of both, by faithfulness, by watching over the goods he brings, and by skill and industry in discharging all her business.

"Thus is this western quarter protected by him and made safe and secure.

"In five ways should a clansman minister to his friends and familiars as the northern quarter:—by generosity, courtesy and benevolence, by treating them as he treats himself, and by being as good as his word.

"In these five ways thus ministered to as the northern quarter, his friends and familiars love him:—they protect him when he is off his guard, and on such occasions guard his property; they become a refuge in danger, they do not

forsake him in his troubles, and they show consideration for his family.

"Thus is the northern quarter by him protected and made safe and secure.

"In five ways does an Ariyan master minister to his servants and employees as the nadir:—by assigning them work according to their strength; by supplying them with food and wages; by tending them in sickness; by sharing with them unusual delicacies; by granting leave at times.

"In these ways ministered to by their master, servants and employees love their master in five ways:—they rise before him, they lie down to rest after him; they are content with what is given to them; they do their work well; and they carry about his praise and good fame.

"Thus is the nadir by him protected and made safe and secure.

"In five ways should the clansman minister to recluses and brahmins as the zenith:—by affection in act and speech and mind; by keeping open house to them, by supplying their temporal needs.

"Thus ministered to as the zenith, recluses and brahmins show their love for the clansman in six ways:—they restrain him from evil, they exhort him to good, they love him with kindly thoughts; they teach him what he has not heard, they correct and purify what he has heard, they reveal to him the way to heaven.

"Thus by him is the zenith protected and made safe and secure." . . .

When the Exalted One had thus spoken, Sigala the young householder said. . . . "Even so hath the Truth been manifested by the Exalted One in many ways. And I, even I, do go to him as my refuge, and to the Truth and to the Order. May the Exalted One receive me as his lay-disciple, as one who has taken his refuge in him from this day forth as long as life endures."

6. What Is Nirvana?

The Theravada concept of Nirvana is succinctly presented in these selections, taken largely from the Samyutta-Nikaya *and the* Questions of King Milinda.

Nirvana is, and is realized through the conquest of craving,

*though its nature is beyond the possibility of description by
any analogies derived from the world of ordinary experience.
Entrance into it by any person means the dissolution of all
the elements whose composition makes him the existent entity
he now is. Since the Buddha has entered Nirvana, these con-
clusions apply to him. We can assuredly know that he was
real, however, by the teaching which has come down from
him and which we too can follow.*

A wanderer who ate rose-apples spoke thus to the venerable Sariputta:

"Reverend Sariputta, it is said: 'Nirvana, Nirvana.' Now,
what, your reverence, is Nirvana?"

"Whatever, your reverence, is the extinction of passion,
of aversion, of confusion, this is called Nirvana."

"Is there a way, your reverence, is there a course for the
realization of this Nirvana?"

"There is, your reverence."

"What is it, your reverence?"

"This ariyan eightfold way itself is for the realization
of Nirvana; that is to say, right view, right thought, right
speech, right action, right mode of livelihood, right en-
deavour, right mindfulness, right concentration."

"Goodly, your reverence, is the way, goodly the course
for the realization of this Nirvana. But for certain it needs
diligence." . . .

"Ananda, when Sariputta attained final Nirvana did he
take with him either the body of moral habit, of concentration, of wisdom, of freedom, of the knowledge and insight
of freedom?"

"No, Lord." . . .

"Have I not aforetime, Ananda, pointed out that in all
that is dear and beloved there is the nature of diversity,
separation, and alteration? That one could say in reference
to what has been born, has become, is compounded and
liable to dissolution: 'O let not that be dissolved'—this
situation does not exist. As, Ananda, one of the larger
boughs of a great, stable, and pithy tree might rot away, so
out of the great, stable, and pithy Order of monks, Sariputta has attained final Nirvana. Wherefore, Ananda, dwell
having self for island, self for refuge and no other refuge;

having Dhamma for island, Dhamma for refuge and no other refuge. And how does one do this?

"As to this, Ananda, a monk lives contemplating the body in the body, ardent, clearly comprehending it and mindful of it; likewise the feelings in the feelings, the mind in the mind, and mental states in mental states, so as to control the coveting and dejection in the world."[1] . . .

"There is, monks, an unborn, not become, not made, uncompounded, and were it not, monks, for this unborn, not become, not made, uncompounded, no escape could be shown here for what is born, has become, is made, is compounded. But because there is, monks, an unborn, not become, not made, uncompounded, therefore an escape can be shown for what is born, has become, is made, is compounded." . . .

"Revered Nagasena, things produced of karma are seen in the world, things produced of cause are seen, things produced of nature are seen. Tell me what in the world is born not of karma, not of cause, not of nature."

"These two, sire, in the world are born not of karma, not of cause, not of nature. Which two? Ether, sire, and Nirvana."

"Do not, revered Nagasena, corrupt the Conqueror's words and answer the question ignorantly."

"What did I say, sire, that you speak thus to me?"

"Revered Nagasena, what you said about ether—that it is born not of karma nor of cause nor of nature—is right. But with many a hundred reasons did the Lord, revered Nagasena, point out to disciples the Way to the realization of Nirvana—and then you speak thus: 'Nirvana is born of no cause.' "

"It is true, sire, that with many a hundred reasons did the Lord point out to disciples the Way to the realization of Nirvana; but he did not point out a cause for the production of Nirvana."

"Here we, revered Nagasena, are entering from darkness into greater darkness, from a jungle into a deeper jungle, from a thicket into a denser thicket, inasmuch as there is indeed a cause for the realization of Nirvana, but no cause

[1] I.e., understanding each of these things for what it is, and refusing to identify oneself with it.

for the production of that thing. If, revered Nagasena, there is a cause for the realization of Nirvana, well then, one would also require a cause for the production of Nirvana. For inasmuch, revered Nagasena, as there is a child's father, for that reason one would also require a father of the father; as there is a pupil's teacher, for that reason one would also require a teacher of the teacher; as there is a seed for a sprout, for that reason, one would also require a seed for the seed. Even so, revered Nagasena, if there is a cause for the realization of Nirvana, for that reason one would also require a cause for the production of Nirvana. Because there is a top to a tree or a creeper, for this reason there is also a middle, also the root. Even so, revered Nagasena, if there is a cause for the realization of Nirvana, for that reason one would also require a cause for the production of Nirvana."

"Nirvana, sire, is not to be produced; therefore a cause for Nirvana being produced is not pointed out."

"Please, revered Nagasena, giving me a reason, convince me by means of the reason, so that I may know: There is a cause for the realization of Nirvana; there is no cause for the production of Nirvana."

"Well then, sire, attend carefully, listen closely, and I will tell the reason as to this. Would a man, sire, with his natural strength be able to go from here up a high Himalayan mountain?"

"Yes, revered Nagasena."

"But would that man, sire, with his natural strength be able to bring a high Himalayan mountain here?"

"Certainly not, revered sir."

"Even so, sire, it is possible to point out the Way for the realization of Nirvana, but impossible to show a cause for the production of Nirvana. Would it be possible, sire, for a man who, with his natural strength, has crossed over the great sea in a boat to reach the farther shore?"

"Yes, revered sir."

"But would it be possible, sire, for that man, with his natural strength, to bring the farther shore of the great sea here?"

"Certainly not, revered sir."

"Even so, sire, it is possible to point out the Way to the realization of Nirvana, but impossible to show a cause for the production of Nirvana. For what reason? It is because of the uncompounded nature of the thing."

"Revered Nagasena, is Nirvana uncompounded?"

"Yes, sire, Nirvana is uncompounded; it is made by nothing at all. Sire, one cannot say of Nirvana that it arises or that it does not arise or that it is to be produced or that it is past or future or present, or that it is cognizable by the eye, ear, nose, tongue or body."

"If revered Nagasena, Nirvana neither arises nor does not arise and so on, as you say, well then, revered Nagasena, you indicate Nirvana as a thing that is not; Nirvana is not."

"Sire, Nirvana is; Nirvana is cognizable by mind; an ariyan disciple, faring along rightly with a mind that is purified, lofty, straight, without obstructions, without temporal desires, sees Nirvana."

"But what, revered sir, is that Nirvana like that can be illustrated by similes? Convince me with reasons according to which a thing that is can be illustrated by similes."

"Is there, sire, what is called wind?"

"Yes, revered sir."

"Please, sire, show the wind by its colour or configuration or as thin or thick or long or short."

"But it is not possible, revered Nagasena, for the wind to be shown; for the wind cannot be grasped in the hand or touched; but yet there is the wind."

"If, sire, it is not possible for the wind to be shown, well then, there is no wind."

"I, revered Nagasena, know that there is wind; I am convinced of it, but I am not able to show the wind."

"Even so, sire, there is Nirvana; but it is not possible to show Nirvana by colour or configuration."

"Very good, revered Nagasena, well shown is the simile, well seen the reason; thus it is and I accept it as you say: There is Nirvana."

7. The Nirvana of the Buddha

"If a fire were blazing in front of you, Vaccha, would you know that it was?"

"Yes, good Gotama."

"And would you know the reason for its blazing?"

"Yes, because it had a supply of grass and sticks."

"And would you know if it were to be put out?"

"Yes, good Gotama."

"And on its being put out, would you know the direction the fire had gone to from here—east, west, north, south?"

"This question does not apply, good Gotama. For the fire blazed because it had a supply of grass and sticks; but when it had consumed this and had no other fuel, then, being without fuel, it is reckoned as gone out."

"Even so, Vaccha, that material shape, that feeling, perception, those impulses, that consciousness by which one, in defining the Tathagata, might define him—all have been got rid of by the Tathagata, cut off at the root, made like a palm-tree stump that can come to no further existence in the future. Freed from reckoning by material shape, feeling, perception, the impulses, consciousness, is the Tathagata; he is deep, immeasurable, unfathomable, as is the great ocean. 'Arises' does not apply, nor does 'does not arise,' nor 'both arises and does not arise,' nor 'neither arises nor does not arise'." . . .

Since a Tathagata, even when actually present, is incomprehensible, it is inept to say of him—of the Uttermost Person, the Supernal Person, the Attainer of the Supernal —that after dying the Tathagata is, or is not, or both is and is not, or neither is nor is not. . . .

The king said: "Did you, revered Nagasena, see the Buddha?"

"No, sire."

"Then did your teachers see the Buddha?"

"No, sire."

"Well, then, revered Nagasena, there is not a Buddha."

"But have you, sire, seen the Himalayan river Uha?"

"No, revered sir."

"Then did your father ever see it?"

"No, revered sir."

"Well then, sire, there is not a river Uha."

"There is, revered sir. Even if neither my father nor I have seen it, there is the river Uha all the same."

"Even so, sire, even if neither my teachers nor I have seen the Lord, there is the Lord all the same."

"Very good, revered Nagasena. But is the Buddha pre-eminent?"

"Yes, sire."

"But how do you know, revered Nagasena, when you have not seen him in the past, that the Buddha is pre-eminent?"

"What do you think about this, sire? Could those who have not already seen the great ocean know that it is so mighty, deep, immeasurable, unfathomable, that although these five great rivers—the Ganges, Jumna, Aciravati, Sarabhu, and the Mahi—flow into it constantly and continually, yet is neither its emptiness nor its fulness affected thereby?"

"Yes, they could know that, revered sir."

"Even so, sire, having seen great disciples who have attained Nirvana, I know that the Lord is pre-eminent."

"Very good, revered Nagasena. Is it then possible to know this?"

"Once upon a time, sire, the Elder named Tissa was a teacher of writing. Many years have passed since he died. How is it that he is known?"

"By his writing, revered sir."

"Even so, sire, he who sees Dhamma sees the Lord; for Dhamma, sire, was taught by the Lord."

"Very good, revered Nagasena. Have you seen Dhamma?"

"Sire, disciples are to conduct themselves for as long as life lasts with the Buddha as guide, with the Buddha as designation."

"Very good, revered Nagasena. But is there a Buddha?"

"Yes, sire, there is a Buddha."

"But is it possible, revered Nagasena, to point to the Buddha as being either here or there?"

"Sire, the Lord has attained Nirvana in the Nirvana-element that has no groups of existence[1] still remaining. It is not possible to point to the Lord as being either here or there."

"Make a simile."

"What do you think about this, sire? When some flame in a great burning mass of fire goes out, is it possible to point to the flame as being either here or there?"

[1] Factors composing an existent entity.

"No, revered sir. That flame has ceased to be, it has disappeared."

"Even so, sire, the Lord has attained Nirvana in the Nirvana-element that has no groups of existence still remaining. The Lord has gone home. It is not possible to point to him as being here or there. But it is possible, sire, to point to the Lord by means of the Dhamma-body; for Dhamma, sire, was taught by the Lord."

"Very good, revered Nagasena."

8. Crossing the Ford

This selection, condensed from the Majjhima-Nikaya, *is of interest on four accounts.*

A metaphor that became popular in all schools of Buddhism is here employed; the path to salvation is like crossing a turbulent stream and reaching safety on the farther shore. The important difference between various levels of spiritual commitment and attainment is insisted upon, from the arahats who are already liberated down to the weak and dependent "young calf," tottering after its mother. But ultimate salvation is promised for all who respond to the truth, however feebly. And although Buddhism makes no claim to the exclusive possession of the truth, it finds it necessary to warn aspirants against spiritual teachers who are unskilled—who lack the wise competence to guide them across the stream that is possessed by the Buddha.

Thus have I heard: At one time the Lord was staying among the Vajjis at Ukkacela on the banks of the river Ganges. While he was there, the Lord addressed the monks, saying: "Monks." "Revered One," these monks answered the Lord in assent.

"Once upon a time, monks, an incompetent herdsman of Magadha in the last month of the rains at harvest time, without considering either the hither or the farther bank of the river Ganges, drove his cattle across to the farther bank in Suvideha at a place where there was no ford. Then, monks, the cattle, huddled together in the middle of the stream of the river Ganges, got into difficulties and misfortune there. Even so, monks, whoever think they should listen to and put their trust in those recluses and brahmans who are unskilled about this world, the world beyond, Mara's realm, what is not Mara's realm, Death's realm, what is not Death's realm, that will be for a long time for their woe and anguish.

"Once upon a time, monks, a competent herdsman of Magadha in the last month of the rains at harvest time, having considered both the hither and the farther bank of the river Ganges, drove his cattle across to the farther bank in Suvideha at a place where there was a ford. First of all he drove across those bulls who were the sires and leaders of the herd, next the sturdy bullocks and young steers, then the half-grown bull-calves and heifers, and then the weaker calves. All cut across the stream of the Ganges and went safely beyond. At that time there was a young new-born calf which, by following the lowing of its mother, also cut across the stream of the Ganges and went safely beyond. Even so, monks, whoever think they should listen to and put their faith in those recluses and brahmans who are skilled about this world, the world beyond, Mara's realm, what is not Mara's realm, Death's realm, what is not Death's realm, that will be for a long time for their welfare and happiness.

"Monks, like unto those bulls who were the sires and leaders of the herd and who, having cut across the stream of the Ganges, went safely beyond, are those monks who are arahats, the outflows extinguished, who have lived the life, done what was to be done, laid down the burden, attained their own goal, the fetters of becoming utterly extinguished, freed by perfect gnosis. For these, having cut across Mara's stream, have gone safely beyond.

"Monks, like unto those sturdy bullocks and young steers who, having cut across the stream of the Ganges, went safely beyond, are those monks who, by utterly extinguishing the five fetters binding to this lower [shore], are of spontaneous uprising, and being ones who attain Nirvana there, are not liable to return from that world. For these also, having cut across Mara's stream, will go safely beyond.

"Monks, like those half-grown bull-calves and heifers who, having cut across the stream of the Ganges, went safely beyond, are those monks who, by utterly extinguishing the three fetters, by reducing passion, aversion and confusion, are once-returners who, having come back again to this world once only, will make an end of suffering. For these also, having cut across Mara's stream, will go safely beyond.

"Monks, like unto those weaker calves who, having cut across the stream of the Ganges, went safely beyond, are those monks who, by utterly extinguishing the three fetters, are stream-winners, not liable for a sorrowful state, assured, bound for awakening. For these also, having cut across Mara's stream, will go safely beyond.

"Monks, like unto that young new-born calf which, by following the lowing of its mother, also cut across the stream of the Ganges and went safely beyond, are those monks who are striving for Dhamma, striving for faith. For these also, having cut across Mara's stream, will go safely beyond.

"Now I, monks, am skilled about this world, the world beyond, Mara's realm, what is not Mara's realm, Death's realm, and what is not Death's realm. For those who think they should listen to me and place faith in me there will be welfare and happiness for a long time."

Thus spoke the Lord; the Well-farer having said this, the Teacher then spoke thus:

"This world, the world beyond, are well explained by the one who knows,
And what is accessible by Mara and what is not accessible by Death.
By the Buddha, comprehending, thoroughly knowing every world,
Opened is the door of the Deathless for reaching Nirvana-security.
Cut across is the stream of the Malign One, shattered, destroyed;
Let there be abundant rapture, monks, let security be reached."

9. Is the Buddha Equally Compassionate Toward All?

These two selections are included mainly because they give, by anticipation, the answer of Theravada Buddhism to questions that troubled the Mahayana thinkers, and which the latter

believed it possible to answer only by the distinctive develop-
ments that will be portrayed in the three following parts.

Is this hierarchy of varied levels of spiritual attainment,
with Buddha's special concern for the arahats and the fact that
they push on to liberation ahead of the rest of us, consistent
with his equal compassion toward all living creatures? And
does the arahat not show himself a selfish person, in forsaking
ordinary social relationships and responsibilities so that, by
the freedom from distraction of the homeless life, he can enter
Nirvana by himself?

We shall wish to keep clearly in mind the answers which the
Buddha is reported to have made to these questions, as we
pass to the scriptures of Mayayana Buddhism.

A village headman spoke thus to the Lord:

"Is a Tathagata compassionate towards all living, breath-
ing creatures?"

"Yes, headman," answered the Lord.

"But does the Lord teach Dhamma in full to some, but
not likewise to others?"

"Now, what do you think, headman? Suppose a farmer
had three fields, one excellent, one mediocre, and one poor
with bad soil. When he wanted to sow the seed, which
field would he sow first?"

"He would sow the excellent one, then the mediocre
one. When he had done that, he might or might not sow
the poor one with the bad soil. And why? Because it might
do if only for cattle-fodder."

"In the same way, headman, my monks and nuns are
like the excellent field. It is to these that I teach Dhamma
that is lovely at the beginning, lovely in the middle and
lovely at the ending, with the spirit and the letter, and to
whom I make known the Brahma-faring[1] completely fulfilled, utterly pure. And why? It is these that dwell with me
for light, me for shelter, me for stronghold, me for refuge.

"Then my men and women lay followers are like the
mediocre field. To these too I teach Dhamma . . . and
make known the Brahma-faring completely fulfilled, utterly
pure. For they dwell with me for light, me for shelter, me
for stronghold, me for refuge.

"Then recluses, Brahmins and wanderers of other sects

[1] Way to the spiritual goal.

than mine are like the poor field with the bad soil. To these too I teach Dhamma . . . and make known the Brahma-faring completely fulfilled, utterly pure. And why? Because if they were to understand even a single sentence, that would be a happiness and a blessing for them for a long time."

10. Is Adopting the Way of the Monk a Selfish Act?

The Brahmin Sangarava spoke thus to the Lord:

"Let me tell you, good Gotama, that Brahmins offer sacrifice and get others to do so. All these are following a course of merit, due to sacrifice, that benefits many people. But whoever from this or that family has gone forth from home into homelessness, he tames but one self, calms but one self, makes but one self attain final Nirvana. Thus, due to his going forth, he is following a course of merit that benefits only one person."

"Well, Brahmin, I will ask you a question in return. What do you think? A Tathagata arises here in the world, an Arahat, a perfect Buddha, endowed with knowledge and right conduct, well-farer, knower of the world(s), incomparable charioteer of men to be tamed, teacher of devas and mankind, a Buddha, a Lord. He speaks thus: 'Come, this is the Way, this is the course I have followed until, having realized by my own super-knowledge the matchless plunge into the Brahma-faring, I have made it known. Come you too, follow likewise, so that you also, having realized by your own super-knowledge the matchless plunge into the Brahma-faring, may abide in it.' It is thus that the Teacher himself teaches Dhamma, and others follow for the sake of Suchness.[1] And moreover these number many hundreds, many thousands, many hundreds of thousands. So, as this is the case, do you think that the course of merit that is due to going forth benefits one person or many?"

"As this is the case, good Gotama, the course of merit that is due to going forth benefits many persons."

[1] The essence of truth and reality.

Book Two

BUDDHIST THOUGHT THROUGH

LATER CENTURIES

PART IV: The Mahayana Religious Ideal

Introduction

As the selections of the preceding group reveal, Theravada
Buddhism is continuous with the Buddhism of the early disciples in emphasizing the necessity of renouncing the world
and aggressively pursuing the path of self-conquest, irrespec-
tive of how many other people are prepared to follow one's
lead in taking such a step. Its spiritual ideal is symbolized by
the *arahat*—the individual who in self-sufficient homelessness
has overcome the power of *tanha*, thrown aside the fetters
which bind him to the cycle of birth and death, and has thus
gained the unutterable peace of Nirvana—the assurance that
he has accomplished what it behooved him to accomplish, and
that for him the weary series of rebirths has been brought to
an end. For others, he has also done the greatest thing that
could be done. He has set them an inspiring example of one
who boldly explores ahead and he has shown them the way
to the spiritual goal; when they are ready, in understanding,
aspiration, and determination, they will follow.

One who has known Buddhism only in its early and Theravada forms will be greatly puzzled when he reads the description given by Anesaki, the great historian of religion in Japan,
of Buddhism as it was introduced to that island country in
the sixth and seventh centuries A.D. Anesaki's words are as
follows:

"Whatever the Western critics may say, the influence Buddhism exerted everywhere lay in its practice of love and equality, which was an outcome of its fundamental teaching of the unity of all beings, and of its ideal of supreme enlightenment (Bodhi) to be attained by all. This Bodhi amounts to realizing, in the spirit and in life, the basic unity of existence, the spiritual communion pervading the whole universe. This was exemplified by the person of Buddha, not only in his teaching of all-oneness but in his life of all-embracing charity. Those united in the faith in Buddha and his teaching form a close community of spiritual fellowship, in which the truth of oneness is embodied and the life of charity is practised. . . .

"Now the Buddhism brought over to Japan was a developed form of this religion, demonstrated artistically in ceremonies and supported by a system of idealistic philosophy.

"The central idea in Buddhist teaching is the gospel of universal salvation based on the idea of the fundamental oneness of all beings. There are in the world, Buddhism teaches, manifold existences and innumerable beings, and each of these individuals deems himself to be a separate being and behaves accordingly. But in reality they make up one family, there is one continuity throughout, and this oneness is to be realized in the attainment of Buddhahood on the part of each and all, in the full realization of the universal communion. Individuals may purify themselves and thereby escape the miseries of sinful existence, yet the salvation of anyone is imperfect so long as and so far as there remain any who have not realized the universal spiritual communion, i.e., who are not saved. To save oneself by saving others is the gospel of universal salvation taught by Buddhism."*

Here is disclosed a quite different ideal of spiritual perfection—emphasizing as central a sense of loving unity with all men and women however imperfect they at present may be, expressed in a tender and consuming eagerness to help them achieve the goal of salvation too, and in a realization that because of one's compassionate concern for them one's own enjoyment of spiritual peace cannot be perfect as long as salvation has not been universally won. And yet, what Anesaki says is strictly true—only it is true because the Buddhism introduced into Japan was not Theravada Buddhism but Mahayana Buddhism in its fully developed form. What is the essence of this altered Mahayana viewpoint in religion? How did the

* M. Anesaki, History of Japanese Religion, pp. 53-54.

change in the direction of such a novel spiritual ideal come about? How shall we understand the concepts in which it is expressed and the doctrines through which it is interpreted?

These questions cannot be answered very adequately or confidently. They trench on that deep area in human experience which only a man of comprehensive saintliness who has lived through all the varied nuances of spiritual struggle and insight of which man is capable could fully understand or explain. But a few hints can, I hope, clarify the process sufficiently so that the reader may follow the selections in this section and appreciate what they hold in store for him.

All Buddhists look back upon their great Master as the living embodiment, in his rich and radiant personality, of the spiritual ideal which they seek to realize. But when the Theravada Buddhists do this what they primarily see is the man who left behind entanglement in worldly interests, who resolutely purged himself of all attachments and obstructions, and who pioneered the way of escape from the suffering involved in transitory forms of existence. His entrance into the blissful peace of Nirvana was the natural effect of his achievement of complete detachment in this fashion; it could not be affected by the degree to which others might be moved to follow his lead. In fact, he might even have decided not to share his insight with others or to help them reach the goal that he had found. "Whether the perfect man tells or does not tell his disciples the truth, he is and remains the same. How is this possible? Because the perfect man has denied and cut out from the roots the illusion which defiles, which sows repeated existences, which breeds pain, which produces life, old age, and death."[1] When the Mahayana Buddhists look back upon their Master, however, what they primarily see is the princely heir of pomp, luxury, and power who gave these up not merely for his own peace but in pity for suffering mankind—for the sake of the truth that might save all—and the Buddha who upon attaining enlightenment refused to hug his great discovery to himself but devoted the rest of his life to sharing with others the way to enduring happiness that he had found. And they are confident that this loving dedication and devoted sharing were involved in the very realization of enlightenment—if he had not shown this sense of compassionate oneness with others, that would prove that he was still caught in the web of self-seeking *tanha* and had not achieved

[1] Quoted in O. Neumann, *Die Reden Gotama Buddhas*, I, 516.

the love which is the culminating mark of true spiritual perfection. The basic conviction of Mahayana at this point is the conviction beautifully expressed in John G. Whittier's little poem "The Meeting":

> He findeth not who seeks his own;
> The soul is lost that's saved alone.

In the distinctively Mahayana sutras (not recognized as authentic by Theravada historians) Buddha is presented as expounding typical Mahayana doctrines; among the most influential of them are the *Diamond Sutra,* the *Lankavatara Sutra,* the *Lotus of the Perfect Law,* the *Surangama Sutra,* the *Sukhavati-Vyuha Sutra,* and the *Awakening of Faith.*

How did the Mahayana thinkers deal with the fact that many obviously early sutras taught a religious ideal and a conception of salvation quite different from the one they had come to accept? Some, of course, did not concern themselves with this question. But others frankly confronted the problem posed by these sutras, and did so in a very natural and revealing way. This way is developed especially in the *Lotus of the Perfect Law;* according to it, Buddha taught to each group of his disciples at each stage of their development the highest truths that they were able to grasp. The Theravada teachings were adapted to the needs of those who had made some progress and had gained partial insight, but the Mahayana doctrines could only be revealed later to those who had reached the point where they could understand and follow them. The main purpose of some of the Mahayana parables is to explain and justify this idea. In the parable of the "burning house,"[1] the householder realizes that his small boys, who are at play in the building, unaware of danger, will be overwhelmed by the fire if he does not entice them to run out of the house to the gate at once. He has a present of incomparable value to give them, but they do not appreciate its worth and would not be attracted by it. So he must call to each of them that he has for him the trinket that would be most appealing to a child of his years and his degree of understanding. He does so and all are lured away from danger. Was he deceiving them in doing this?

So with the Buddha in relation to his followers. He has salvation to give, after the Mahayana ideal, but he leads the

[1] See below, p. 142.

immature Sravakas[2] and Pratyekabuddhas[3] toward it by teaching them the highest form of realization that they can as yet apprehend. In the tradition of Zen Buddhism in China and Japan this concept is carried to the extreme, as we shall later observe.

Now, this Mahayana ideal not only became theoretically clarified in doctrinal formulations but was also concretely embodied, especially in the cosmic Buddha Amitabha and in the compassionate Bodhisattvas. Amitabha is mythically portrayed as having gained Buddhahood on the express condition that all mortals who call sincerely upon his name will be received at death in his Western paradise, where they can continue the process of liberation under far happier and more encouraging auspices than would be the case if they remained tied to the wheel of bodily existence on earth. And this idea reveals the important fact that Buddha, now, is not thought of as identical with the historic Gautama who lived and died some hundreds of years ago. That individual was one incarnation of a transcendent cosmic reality, the Buddha-nature, which is working in all ages and in innumerable worlds for the salvation of all sentient beings. Amitabha is one celestial exemplification of Buddhahood, thus conceived.

A Bodhisattva is one who, having attained the goal of purification and emancipation, refuses to enter Nirvana, out of devoted love for those who still remain behind and a consuming zeal to help them. He postpones his own entrance into perfect bliss because his sense of spiritual oneness with others leads him to prefer to wait with them and lovingly serve them until all are ready to enter together. In Anesaki's words, he feels that his own salvation would be imperfect, and even impossible, as long as any living beings remain unsaved.

Among the particular doctrines which are profoundly affected by the adoption of this Mahayana ideal is the doctrine of the nature of Nirvana and what is meant by entering it. The last selection in this section, from the *Lankavatara Sutra*, deals with this theme.

[2] "Hearers"—those who listen to preaching but lack spiritual initiative.
[3] "Separate Buddha"—one who wins enlightenment only for himself, independently of others.

1. Hymn to the Buddha of Infinite Compassion and Wisdom

The devotional attitude of Mahayana Buddhism, which pervades all Mahayana thought and experience, is beautifully revealed in the following verses from the Satapancasatka *of Matrceta, who probably lived in the second century* A.D.

All the faults can never in any way be in him;
All the virtues are in every way in him established.

To go to him for refuge, to praise and honour him,
To abide in his religion, that is fit for those with sense. . . .

Homage to the Self-Existent! Wonderful his many works,
Virtues potent and abundant, which refuse to be defined.

Any worldly thing one might compare can be damaged or obstructed,
Time and place set limits to it, to surpass it is not hard.

How can there be a likeness to your virtues, untouched by foe or obstacle,
Everlasting, unlimited, and which cannot be surpassed? . . .

This form of yours, calm yet lovely, brilliant without dazzling,
Soft but mighty—whom would it not entrance?

Whether one has seen it a hundred times, or beholds it for the first time,
Your form gives the same pleasure to the eye. . . .

Without distinction all this world was bound to the defilements,
That you might free it you were long in bondage to compassion.

Which shall I praise first, you or the great compassion, by which

For so long you were held in Samsara, although you well
  knew its faults?

It was your compassion, given free course, which made
  you pass your time
Among the crowds, when the happiness of seclusion
  suited you so much better. . . .

Your birth gives joy to people, and your growth delights
  them;
While you are there they benefit, on your departure they
  feel lost.

To praise you takes all guilt away, to recollect you lifts
  up the heart,
To seek you brings understanding, to comprehend you
  purity. . . .

An island you are to those swept along by the flood, a
  shelter to the stricken,
A refuge to those terrified by becoming, the resource of
  those who desire release. . . .

No matter by whom or where or how provoked,
Never do you transgress your own fair path of conduct.

Other men do not as much study the welfare of those
  who mean them well,
As you study that of those who seek your harm.

To an enemy intent on ill you are a good friend intent on
  good.
To one who constantly seeks for faults you respond by
  seeking for virtues. . . .

Those who wish to benefit beings, and who are compassionate,
What can they do wherein you have not led the way?

Out of pity for the world you have promoted the good
  Dharma for a long time,
Many worthy disciples able to help the triple world[1] have
  you raised . . .

What steadfastness! What conduct! What form! What
  virtues!
In a Buddha's dharmas there is nothing that is not wonderful.

[1] The worlds of the past, present, and future.

2. The Bodhisattva's Vow of Universal Redemption

In these selections, from various sutras, the Mahayana answer to the questions raised in the last two selections of Part III is presented. The Bodhisattva has transcended the state in which he is concerned for his own salvation; he is committed to the eternal weal of all living beings, and will not rest until he has led them all to the goal. On attaining enlightenment he does not leave the world behind and enter Nirvana by himself; he remains in the world, appearing like an ordinary person, but devoting his compassionate skill to the aid of others. He shares and bears the burden of their sufferings, in loving union with them, instead of merely giving others an example of a person who has overcome the causes of suffering for himself.

The Lord: "What do you think, Sariputra, does it occur to any of the Disciples and Pratyekabuddhas to think that 'after we have known full enlightenment, we should lead all beings to Nirvana, into the realm of Nirvana which leaves nothing behind'?"

Sariputra: "No indeed, O Lord."

The Lord: "One should therefore know that this wisdom of the Disciples and Pratyekabuddhas bears no comparison with the wisdom of a Bodhisattva. What do you think, Sariputra, does it occur to any of the Disciples and Pratyekabuddhas that 'after I have practised the six perfections, have brought beings to maturity, have purified the Buddhafield, have fully gained the ten powers of a Tathagata, his four grounds of self-confidence, the four analytical knowledges and the eighteen special dharmas of a Buddha, after I have known full enlightenment, I shall lead countless beings to Nirvana'?"

Sariputra: "No, O Lord."

The Lord: "But such are the intentions of a Bodhisattva. A glowworm, or some other luminous animal, does not think that its light could illuminate the Continent of Jambudvipa, or radiate over it. Just so, the Disciples and Pratyekabuddhas do not think that they should, after winning full enlightenment, lead all beings to Nirvana. But the sun, when it has risen, radiates its light over the whole of

Jambudvipa. Just so a Bodhisattva, after he has accomplished the practices which lead to the full enlightenment of Buddhahood, leads countless beings to Nirvana."

The Lord: "Suppose, Subhuti, that there was a most excellent hero, very vigorous, of high social position, handsome, attractive and most fair to behold, of many virtues, in possession of all the finest virtues, of those virtues which spring from the very height of sovereignty, morality, learning, renunciation, and so on. He is judicious, able to express himself, to formulate his views clearly, to substantiate his claims; one who always knows the suitable time, place, and situation for everything. In archery he has gone as far as one can go, he is successful in warding off all manner of attack, most skilled in all arts, and foremost, through his fine achievements, in all crafts. . . . He is versed in all the treatises, has many friends, is wealthy, strong of body, with large limbs, with all his faculties complete, generous to all, dear and pleasant to many. Any work he might undertake he manages to complete, he speaks methodically, shares his great riches with the many, honours what should be honoured, reveres what should be revered, worships what should be worshipped. Would such a person, Subhuti, feel ever-increasing joy and zest?"

Subhuti: "He would, O Lord."

The Lord: "Now suppose, further, that this person, so greatly accomplished, should have taken his family with him on a journey, his mother and father, his sons and daughters. By some circumstance they find themselves in a great, wild forest. The foolish ones among them would feel fright, terror, and hair-raising fear. He, however, would fearlessly say to his family: 'Do not be afraid! I shall soon take you safely and securely out of this terrible and frightening forest. I shall soon set you free!' If then more and more hostile and inimical forces should rise up against him in that forest, would this heroic man decide to abandon his family, and to take himself alone out of that terrible and frightening forest—he who is not one to draw back, who is endowed with all the force of firmness and vigour, who is wise, exceedingly tender and compassionate, courageous and a master of many resources?"

Subhuti: "No, O Lord. For that person, who does not

abandon his family, has at his disposal powerful resources, both within and without. On his side forces will arise in that wild forest which are quite a match for the hostile and inimical forces, and they will stand up for him and protect him. Those enemies and adversaries of his, who look for a weak spot, who seek for a weak spot, will not gain any hold over him. He is competent to deal with the situation, and is able, unhurt and uninjured, soon to take out of that forest, both his family and himself, and securely and safely will they reach a village, city, or market town."

The Lord: "Just so, Subhuti, is it with a Bodhisattva who is full of pity and concerned with the welfare of all beings, who dwells in friendliness, compassion, sympathetic joy, and evenmindedness.

"Although the son of Jina[1] has penetrated to this immut-
able true nature of dharmas,
Yet he appears like one of those who are blinded by ignorance, subject as he is to birth, and so on. That is truly
wonderful.

It is through his compassionate skill in means for others
that he is tied to the world,
And that, though he has attained the state of a saint, yet
he appears to be in the state of an ordinary person.

He has gone beyond all that is worldly, yet he has not
moved out of the world;
In the world he pursues his course for the world's weal, un-
stained by worldly taints.

As a lotus flower, though it grows in water, is not polluted
by the water,
So he, though born in the world, is not polluted by worldly
dharmas.

Like a fire, his mind constantly blazes up into good works
for others;
At the same time he always remains merged in the calm of
the trances and formless attainments.[2]

Through the power of his previous penetration (into reality), and because he has left all discrimination behind,

[1] "Conqueror."
[2] Insights and indescribable realizations.

He again exerts no effort when he brings living things to
maturity.

He knows exactly who is to be educated, how, and by what
means,
Whether by his teaching, his physical appearance, his practices, or his bearing.

Without turning towards anything, always unobstructed in
his wisdom,
He goes along, in the world of living beings, boundless as
space, acting for the weal of beings.

When a Bodhisattva has reached this position, he is like
the Tathagatas,
Insofar as he is in the world for the sake of saving beings.

But as a grain of sand compares with the earth, or a puddle
in a cow's footprint with the ocean,
So great still is the distance of the Bodhisattvas from the
Buddha."

A Bodhisattva resolves: I take upon myself the burden
of all suffering, I am resolved to do so, I will endure it. I
do not turn or run away, do not tremble, am not terrified,
nor afraid, do not turn back or despond.

And why? At all costs I must bear the burdens of all
beings. In that I do not follow my own inclinations. I have
made the vow to save all beings. All beings I must set free.
The whole world of living beings I must rescue, from the
terrors of birth, of old age, of sickness, of death and rebirth,
of all kinds of moral offence, of all states of woe, of the
whole cycle of birth-and-death, of the jungle of false views,
of the loss of wholesome dharmas, of the concomitants of
ignorance, —from all these terrors I must rescue all beings.
. . . I walk so that the kingdom of unsurpassed cognition
is built up for all beings. My endeavours do not merely aim
at my own deliverance. For with the help of the boat of the
thought of all-knowledge, I must rescue all these beings
from the stream of Samsara, which is so difficult to cross;
I must pull them back from the great precipice, I must free
them from all calamities, I must ferry them across the
stream of Samsara. I myself must grapple with the whole
mass of suffering of all beings. To the limit of my endurance

I will experience in all the states of woe, found in any world system, all the abodes of suffering. And I must not cheat all beings out of my store of merit. I am resolved to abide in each single state of woe for numberless aeons; and so I will help all beings to freedom, in all the states of woe that may be found in any world system whatsoever.

And why? Because it is surely better that I alone should be in pain than that all these beings should fall into the states of woe. There I must give myself away as a pawn through which the whole world is redeemed from the terrors of the hells, of animal birth, of the world of Yama[3]; and with this my own body I must experience, for the sake of all beings, the whole mass of all painful feelings. And on behalf of all beings I give surety for all beings, and in doing so I speak truthfully, am trustworthy, and do not go back on my word. I must not abandon all beings.

And why? There has arisen in me the will to win all-knowledge, with all beings for its object, that is to say, for the purpose of setting free the entire world of beings. And I have not set out for the supreme enlightenment from a desire for delights, not because I hope to experience the delights of the five sense-qualities, or because I wish to indulge in the pleasures of the senses. And I do not pursue the course of a Bodhisattva in order to achieve the array of delights that can be found in the various worlds of sense-desire.

And why? Truly no delights are all these delights of the world. All this indulging in the pleasures of the senses belongs to the sphere of Mara.

3. The Path of Light and Love

The following passages show how the Bodhisattva ideal, once it became fully accepted, transformed and permeated the Mahayanist's attitude toward the entire quest for enlightenment and liberation. He wants to overcome cravings and obstructions which block the path to spiritual realization, not to achieve his own perfection but for the sake of a deeper oneness with others, and for the greater power to serve them—even those who are his enemies—that such realization will bring.

[1] The god of death.

The passages are taken from the Bodhicharyavatara *of Santideva, who lived about 600 A.D. In philosophy, Santideva was a follower of the great thinker Nagarjuna, to whom we shall be introduced in the next part.*

Reverently bowing before the Blessed Ones, their Sons, the Body of the Law, and all the worshipful ones, I will briefly set forth in accordance with Holy Writ the way whereby the sons of the Blessed Ones enter the godly life. Nothing new will be told here, nor have I skill in writing of books; therefore I have done this work to hallow my own thought, not designing it for the welfare of others. By it the holy impulse within me to frame righteousness is strengthened; but if a fellow-creature should see it, this my book will fulfil another end likewise.

This brief estate, which once gotten is a means to all the aims of mankind, is exceeding hard to win; if one use it not for wholesome reflection, how shall it ever come again to his lot? As in the night, amidst the gross darkness of the clouds, the lightning shows for an instant its radiance, so by the grace of the Enlightened it may hap that the mind of man turn for an instant to holy works. Thus righteousness is feeble, and the power of evil is constant, mighty, and dire; by what righteousness could it be overcome, if there were not the Thought of Enlightenment? Pondering through many aeons, the Supreme Saints have found this blessing, whereby a swelling joy sweeps in sweetness down the boundless waters of mankind. They who would escape the hundreds of life's sorrows, who would end the anguish of living creatures, and who would taste hundreds of deep delights, must never surrender the Thought of Enlightenment. . . .

Eager to escape sorrow, men rush into sorrow; from desire of happiness they blindly slay their own happiness, enemies to themselves; they hunger for happiness and suffer manifold pains; whence shall come one so kind as he who can satisfy them with all manner of happiness, allay all their pains, and shatter their delusion—whence such a friend, and whence such a holy deed? He who repays good deed with good deed is praised; what shall be said of the Son of Enlightenment, who does kindness unsought? . . .

In reward for all this righteousness that I have won by my works, I would fain become a soother of all the sorrows of all creatures. May I be a balm to the sick, their healer and servitor, until sickness come never again; may I quench with rains of food and drink the anguish of hunger and thirst; may I be in the famine of the ages' end their drink and meat; may I become an unfailing store for the poor, and serve them with manifold things for their need. My own being and my pleasures, all my righteousness in the past, present, and future, I surrender indifferently, that all creatures may win through to their end. The stillness lies in surrender of all things, and my spirit is fain for the stillness; if I must surrender all, it is best to give it for fellow-creatures. I yield myself to all living things to deal with me as they list; they may smite or revile me for ever, bestrew me with dust, play with my body, laugh and wanton; I have given them my body, why shall I care? Let them make me do whatever works bring them pleasure; but may never mishap befall any of them by reason of me. . . .

This day my birth is fruitful, my human life a blessing; this day have I been born in the race of the Enlightened, now am I their son. And henceforth mine is the task of them who work worthily of their race, lest any blemish fall upon this stainless stock. This thought of Enlightenment has arisen within me I know not how, even as a gem might be gotten by a blind man from a dunghill; it is an elixir made to destroy death in the world, an unfailing treasure to relieve the world's poverty, a supreme balm to allay the world's sickness, a tree under which may rest all creatures wearied with wandering over life's paths, a bridge open to all wayfarers for passing over hard ways, a moon of thought arising to cool the fever of the world's sin, a great sun driving away the gloom of the world's ignorance, a fresh butter created by the churning of the milk of the Good Law. For the caravan of beings who wander through life's paths hungering to taste of happiness this banquet of bliss is prepared, that will satisfy all creatures coming to it. I summon to-day the world to the estate of Enlightenment, and meanwhile to happiness; may gods, demons, and other beings rejoice in the presence of all the Saviours!

Ah, when I vowed to deliver all beings within the

bounds of space in its ten points[1] from the passions, I myself had not won deliverance from the passions. Knowing not my own measure, I spoke like a madman. My foes, desire, hate, and their kindred, are handless and footless, they are neither valiant nor cunning; how can they have enslaved me? But they dwell in my spirit, and there at their ease smite me. Then I will never turn back from smiting the passions. I will grapple with them, will wrathfully make war on them all except the passion that makes for the destruction of the passions. Though my bowels ooze out and my head fall off, I will nowise abase myself before my foes the passions. An enemy, though driven away, may establish himself in another spot, whence he may return with gathered powers; but such is not the way of the enemy passion. Where can this dweller in my spirit go when I cast him out; where can he stand, to labour for my destruction? It is only that I—fool that I am—make no effort; the miserable passions are to be overcome by the vision of wisdom. . . .

Let me not despair that the Enlightenment will come to me; for the Blessed One, the speaker of truth, has revealed this truth, that they who by force of striving have gained hard-won supreme Enlightenment have been erstwhile gnats, gadflies, flies, and worms. Now I am a man by birth, able to know good and evil: why shall I not win the Enlightenment by following the rule of the All-knowing? If I am afraid when I think that I must give my hand or foot, it is because in my heedlessness I confound things of great and of small weight. I may be cleft, pierced, burnt, split open many and many a time for countless millions of aeons, and never win the Enlightenment. But this pain that wins me the Enlightenment is of brief term; it is like the pain of cutting out a buried arrow to heal its smart. All physicians restore health by painful courses; then to undo much suffering let us bear a little. But even this fitting course the Great Physician has not enjoined upon us; he heals them that are grievously sick by tender treatment. . . .

The body is made happy by righteous works, the spirit by knowledge; what can vex the compassionate one who remains in embodied life only for the welfare of others? Annulling his former sins, amassing oceans of righteousness,

[1] North, northeast, east, etc.; zenith and nadir.

by the power of his thought of Enlightenment he travels more swiftly than the Disciples. Having thus in the thought of Enlightenment a chariot that removes all vexation and weariness, travelling from happiness to happiness, who that is wise will despair? . . .

Passion is overcome only by him who has won through stillness of spirit the perfect vision. Knowing this, I must first seek for stillness; it comes through the contentment that is regardless of the world. What creature of a day should cling to other frail beings, when he can never again through thousands of births behold his beloved? . . .

Trees are not disdainful, and ask for no toilsome wooing; fain would I consort with those sweet companions! Fain would I dwell in some deserted sanctuary, beneath a tree or in caves, that I might walk without heed, looking never behind! Fain would I abide in nature's own spacious and lordless lands, a homeless wanderer free of will, my sole wealth a clay bowl, my cloak profitless to robbers, fearless and careless of my body! Fain would I go to my home the graveyard, and compare with other skeletons my own frail body! For this my body will become so foul that the very jackals will not approach it because of its stench. The bony members born with this corporeal frame will fall asunder from it, much more so my friends. Alone man is born, alone he dies; no other has a share in his sorrows. What avail friends, but to bar his way? As a wayfarer takes a brief lodging, so he that is travelling through the way of existence finds in each birth but a passing rest.

It is well for a man to depart to the forest ere the four bearers carry him away amidst the laments of his folk. Free from commerce and hindrance, possessing naught but his body, he has no grief at the hour of death, for already he has died to the world; no neighbours are there to vex him or disturb his remembrance of the Enlightened and like thoughts. Then I will ever woo sweet solitude, untroubled dayspring of bliss, stilling all unrest. Released from all other thoughts, with mind utterly set upon my own spirit, I will strive to centre and control my spirit. . . .

Mark how fortune brings endless misfortune by the miseries of winning it, guarding it, and losing it; men's thoughts cling altogether to their riches, so that they have not a moment to free themselves from the sorrows of life.

Thus they who are possessed by desire suffer much and enjoy little, as the ox that drags a cart gets but a morsel of grass. For the sake of this morsel of enjoyment, which falls easily to the beast's lot, man, blinded by his destiny, wastes this brief fortune, that is so hard to win.[2] For all time lasts the struggle for the welfare of the mean body that is doomed to depart and fall into hell, and even a millionth part of this labour would win the rank of the Enlightened. Greater is the pain of them that are possessed by desire than the pain of the way of holiness, and no Enlightenment comes to them. Neither sword, nor poison, nor fire, nor a fall into abysses, nor foemen may be compared to the desires, if we bear in mind the agonies of hell and the like. Then shrink from the desires, and learn delight in solitude, in the peaceful woodlands void of strife and toil. Happy are they who are fanned by the sweet silent breezes of the forest, as they walk upon the pleasant rock-floors broad as in a palace and cooled by the moonbeams' sandal ointment, and take thought for the weal of their fellow-creatures! Dwelling anywhere for what time they will, in deserted sanctuary or cave or beneath the trees, saved from the weariness of winning and guarding possessions, they wander fancy-free at pleasure. Indra himself can hardly win the bliss of contentment that is enjoyed by him who wanders homeless at his own free will and unattached to aught.

By pondering in such wise upon the excellences of solitude a man stills vain imaginations and strengthens his thought of Enlightenment. First he will diligently foster the thought that his fellow-creatures are the same as himself. "All have the same sorrows, the same joys as I, and I must guard them like myself. The body, manifold of parts in its division of members, must be preserved as a whole; and so likewise this manifold universe has its sorrow and its joy in common. Although my pain may bring no hurt to other bodies, nevertheless it is a pain to me, which I cannot bear because of the love of self; and though I cannot in myself feel the pain of another, it is a pain to him which he cannot bear because of love of self. I must destroy the pain of another as though it were my own, because it is a pain; I must show kindness to others, for they are creatures as I am myself. . . . Then, as I would guard myself from evil repute, so

[2] Being born in this life as a human being.

I will frame a spirit of helpfulness and tenderness towards others."

By constant use the idea of an "I" attaches itself to foreign drops of seed and blood, although the thing exists not. Then why should I not conceive my fellow's body as my own self? That my body is foreign to me is not hard to see. I will think of myself as a sinner, of others as oceans of virtue; I will cease to live as self, and will take as my self my fellow-creatures. We love our hands and other limbs, as members of the body; then why not love other living beings, as members of the universe? By constant use man comes to imagine that his body, which has no self-being, is a "self"; why then should he not conceive his "self" to lie in his fellows also? Thus in doing service to others pride, admiration, and desire of reward find no place, for thereby we satisfy the wants of our own self. Then, as thou wouldst guard thyself against suffering and sorrow, so exercise the spirit of helpfulness and tenderness towards the world. . . .

Make thyself a spy for the service of others, and whatso-ever thou seest in thy body's work that is good for thy fellows, perform it so that it may be conveyed to them. Be thou jealous of thine own self when thou seest that it is at ease and thy fellow in distress, that it is in high estate and he is brought low, that it is at rest and he is at labour. . . .

So I have surrendered my body indifferently for the weal of the world; it is but as an instrument of work that I still bear it, with all its guilt. Enough then of worldly ways! I follow in the path of the wise, remembering the Discourse upon Heedfulness[3] and putting away sloth. To overcome the power of darkness I centre my thought, drawing the spirit away from vain paths and fixing it straightly upon its stay. . . .

Alas, how lamentable is the estate of them that are borne down in the floods of affliction, and in their sore distress see not how sad their plight is, like one who should again and again come forth from the waters of his bath and cast him-self into fire, and so in their sore trouble deem themselves to be in happy estate! As thus they live in sport that knows not of age and dissolution, dire afflictions will come upon them, with death in their forefront. Then when will the day come when I may bring peace to them that are tortured in

[3] Chapter II of the *Dhammapada*. See above, p. 54.

the fire of sorrow by my ministrations of sweetness born from the rain-clouds of my righteousness, and when I may reverently declare to the souls who imagine a real world that all is void, and righteousness is gathered by looking beyond the Veiled Truth?[4]

4. Famous Mahayana Parables: Burning House, Prodigal Son, Rain Cloud

As indicated in the introduction to this section, the main purpose of some of the most popular and frequently quoted Mahayana parables was to meet the objection that according to the ancient sutras Buddha taught Theravada doctrine rather than the Mahayana ideal. This purpose is present in each of the following parables, although the point of major emphasis varies. The "burning house" develops the thought that although the Buddha had a far more wonderful truth to give to those who could understand it, he was not deceiving the minds of the beginners by teaching them Theravada ideas. Such teaching was all they could receive and it would lead them in the right direction. In the "prodigal son" it is the fear and distrust of the immature seekers that must gradually and patiently be overcome by the loving Buddha-Father, in order that they may become able fully to respond to his love and share in his compassionate service of others. The "rain cloud" is a beautiful hymn to the grace of the Buddha that gently spreads over all the world and is able to meet the need of every parched living soul, whatever that need may be.

These parables are taken from the Lotus of·the Wonderful Law. *This sutra provides the basis for the distinctive ·philosophy of the Ti'en T'ai School of Chinese Buddhism and the Nichiren School in Japan.*

"The dull, who delight in petty rules,
Who are greedily attached to mortality,
Who have not, under countless Buddhas,
Walked the profound and mystic Way,
Who are harassed by all the sufferings—
To these I (at first) preach Nirvana.
[4] The truth hidden in the phenomenal realm.

Such is the expedient I employ
To lead them to Buddha-wisdom.
Not yet could I say to them,
'You all shall attain to Buddhahood,'
For the time had not yet arrived.
But now the very time has come
And I must preach the Great Vehicle." . . .

"Have I not before said that the Buddhas, the World-honoured Ones, with a variety of reasonings, parables and terms, preach the Law as may be expedient, with the aim of final Perfect Enlightenment? All their teachings are for the purpose of transforming [their disciples into] bodhisattvas. But Sariputra! Let me again in a parable make this meaning still more clear, for intelligent people, through a parable, reach understanding."

Parable of the Burning House

"Sariputra! Suppose, in a [certain] kingdom, city, or town, there is a great elder, old and worn, of boundless wealth, and possessing many fields, houses, slaves, and servants. His house is spacious and large, but it has only one door, and many people dwell in it, one hundred, two hundred, or even five hundred in number. Its halls and chambers are decayed and old, its walls crumbling down, the bases of its pillars rotten, the beams and roof-trees toppling and dangerous. On every side, at the same moment, fire suddenly starts and the house is in conflagration. The boys of the elder, say ten, twenty, or even thirty, are in the dwelling. The elder, on seeing this conflagration spring up on every side, is greatly startled and reflects thus: 'Though I am able to get safely out of the gate of this burning house, yet my boys in the burning house are pleasurably absorbed in amusements without apprehension, knowledge, surprise, or fear. Though the fire is pressing upon them and pain and suffering are instant, they do not mind or fear and have no impulse to escape.'

"Sariputra! This elder ponders thus: 'I am strong in my body and arms. Shall I get them out of the house by means of a flower-vessel, or a bench, or a table?' Again he ponders: 'This house has only one gate, which moreover is narrow and small. My children are young, knowing nothing as yet, and attached to their place of play; perchance they will fall into the fire and be burnt. I must speak to them on this dreadful matter [warning them] that the house is burning, and that they must come out instantly lest they are burnt and injured by the fire.' Having reflected thus, according to his thoughts, he calls to his children: 'Come out quickly, all of you!'

"Though their father, in his pity, lures and admonishes with kind words, yet the children, joyfully absorbed in their play, are unwilling to believe him and have neither surprise nor fear, nor any mind to escape; moreover, they do not know what is the fire [he means], or what the house, and what he means by being lost, but only run hither and thither in play, no more than glancing at their father. Then the elder reflects thus: 'This house is burning in a great conflagration. If I and my children do not get out at once, we shall certainly be burnt up by it. Let me now, by some expedient, cause my children to escape this disaster.' Knowing that to which each of his children is predisposed, and all the various attractive playthings and curiosities to which their natures will joyfully respond, the father tells them, saying: '[Here are] rare and precious things for your amusement—if you do not [come] and get them, you will be sorry for it afterwards. So many goat-carts, deer-carts, and bullock-carts are now outside the gate to play with. All of you come quickly out of this burning house, and I will give you whatever you want.' Thereupon the children, hearing of the attractive playthings mentioned by their father, and because they suit their wishes, every one eagerly, each pushing the other, and racing one against another, comes rushing out of the burning house.

"Then the elder, seeing that his children have safely escaped and are all in the square, sits down in the open, no longer embarrassed, but with a mind at ease and ecstatic with joy. Then each of the children says to the father: 'Father! Please now give us those playthings you promised us—goat-carts, deer-carts, and bullock-carts.' Sariputra! Then the elder gives to his children equally each a great cart, lofty and spacious, adorned with all the precious things, surrounded with railed seats, hung with bells on its four sides, and covered with curtains, splendidly decorated also with various rare and precious things, draped with strings of precious stones, hung with garlands of flowers, thickly spread with beautiful mats, and supplied with rosy pillows. It is yoked with white bullocks of pure [white] skin, of handsome appearance, and of great muscular power, which walk with even steps, and with the speed of the wind, and also it has many servants and followers to guard them. Wherefore? Because this great elder is of boundless wealth and all his various storehouses are full to overflowing. So he reflects thus: 'My possessions being boundless, I must not give my children inferior small carts. All these children are my sons, whom I love without partiality. Having such great carts made of the seven precious things, infinite in number, I should with equal mind bestow them on each one without discrimination. Wherefore? Because, were I to give them to the whole nation, these things of mine would not run short—how much less so to my children! Meanwhile, each of the children rides on his great cart, having received that which he had never before had and never expected to have.'

"Sariputra! What is your opinion? Has that elder, in [only] giving great carts of the precious substances to his children equally, been in any way guilty of falsehood?"

"No, World-honoured One!" says Sariputra. "That elder only caused his children to escape the disaster of fire and preserved their bodies alive—he committed no falsity. Why? He thus preserved their bodies alive, and in addition gave them the playthings they obtained; moreover, it was by his expedient that he saved them from that burning house! World-honoured One! Even if that elder did not give them one of the smallest carts, still he is not false. Wherefore? Because that elder from the first formed this intention, 'I will, by an expedient, cause my children to escape.' For this reason he is not false. How much less so seeing that, knowing his own boundless wealth and desiring to benefit his children, he gives them great carts equally!"

"Good! Good!" replies the Buddha to Sariputra. "It is even as you say. Sariputra! The Tathagata is also like this, for he is the Father of all worlds, who has forever entirely ended all fear, despondency, distress, ignorance, and enveloping darkness, and has perfected boundless knowledge, strength, and fearlessness. He is possessed of great supernatural power and wisdom-power, has completely attained the Paramitas[1] of adaptability and wisdom, and is the greatly merciful and greatly compassionate, ever tireless, ever seeking the good, and benefiting all beings. He is born in this triple world, the old decayed burning house, to save all living creatures from the fires of birth, age, disease, death, grief, suffering, foolishness, darkness, and the Three Poisons,[2] and teach them to obtain Perfect Enlightenment. He sees how all living creatures are scorched by the fires of birth, age, disease, death, grief, and sorrow, and suffer all kinds of distress by reason of the five desires and the greed of gain; and how, by reason of the attachments of desire and its pursuits, they now endure much suffering and hereafter will suffer in hell, or as animals or hungry spirits. Even if they are born in a heaven, or amongst men, there are all kinds of sufferings, such as the bitter straits of poverty, the bitterness of parting from loved ones, the bitterness of association with the detestable. Absorbed in these things, all living creatures rejoice and take their pleasure, while they neither apprehend, nor perceive, are neither alarmed, nor fear, and are without satiety, never seeking to escape, but, in the burning house of this triple world are running to and fro, and although they will meet with great suffering, count it not as cause for anxiety.

"Sariputra! The Buddha, having seen this, reflects thus: 'I am the Father of all creatures and must snatch them from suffering and give them the bliss of the infinite, boundless Buddha-wisdom for them to play with.'

"Sariputra! The Tathagata again reflects thus: 'If I only use supernatural power and wisdom, casting aside every tactful method, and extend to all living creatures the wisdom, power, and fearlessness of the Tathagata, the living creatures cannot by this method be saved. Wherefore? As long as all these creatures have not escaped birth, age, disease, death, grief, and suffering, but are being burnt in the burning house of the triple world, how can they understand the Buddha-wisdom?'

"Sariputra! Even as that elder, though with strength in body and arms, yet does not use it, but only by diligent tact, resolutely saves his children from the calamity of the

---

[1] "Ideal perfections" or virtues.
[2] Sensual longing, ignorance, desire for continued separate existence.

burning house, and then gives each of them great carts adorned with precious things, so is it with the Tathagata. Though he has power and fearlessness, he does not use them, but only by his wise tact does he remove and save all living creatures from the burning house of the triple world, preaching the Three-Vehicles, viz. the Sravaka,[3] Pratyekabuddha, and Buddha vehicles. And thus he speaks to them: 'Ye all! Delight not to dwell in the burning house of the triple world. Do not hanker after its crude forms, sounds, odours, flavours, and contacts. For if, through hankering, ye beget a love of it, then ye will be burnt by it. Get ye out with haste from the triple world and take to the Three-Vehicles, viz. the Sravaka, Pratyekabuddha, and Buddha Vehicles. 1 now give you my pledge for this, and it will never prove false. Be only diligent and zealous!' By these expedients does the Tathagata lure all creatures forth, and again speaks thus: 'Know ye! All these Three-Vehicles are praised by sages: in them you will be free and independent, without wanting to rely on aught else. Riding in these Three-Vehicles, by means of perfect faculties, powers, perceptions, ways, concentrations, emancipations, and samadhis,[4] ye will, as a matter of course, be happy and gain infinite peace and joy.'

"Sariputra! If there are living beings who have a spirit of wisdom within and, following the Buddha, the World-honoured One, hear the Law, receive it in faith, and zealously make progress, desiring speedily to escape from the triple world and seeking Nirvana for themselves—this [type] is called the Sravaka-Vehicle, just as some of those children come out of the burning house for the sake of a goat-cart. If there are living beings who, following the Buddha, the World-honoured One, hear the Law, receive it in faith, and zealously make progress, seeking self-gained Wisdom, taking pleasure in becoming good and calm, and deeply versed in the causes and reasons of the laws—this type is called the Pratyekabuddha-Vehicle, just as some of those children come out of the burning house for the sake of a deer-cart. If there are living beings who, following the Buddha, the World-honoured One, hear the Law, receive it in faith, diligently practise and zealously

[3] See the following paragraph. Cf. above, p. 127.
[4] Ecstatic contemplation or meditation.

advance, seeking the Complete Wisdom, Buddha-Wisdom, the Natural Wisdom, the Masterless Wisdom, and Tathagata knowledge, powers, and fearlessness, who take pity on and comfort innumerable creatures, benefit devas and men, and save all beings—this type is called the Great Vehicle. Because bodhisattvas seek this vehicle, they are named mahasattvas. They are like those children who come out of the burning house for the sake of a bullock-cart.

"Sariputra! Just as that elder, seeing his children get out of the burning house safely to a place free from fear, and pondering on his immeasurable wealth, gives each of his children a great cart, so also is it with the Tathagata. Being the Father of all living creatures, if he sees infinite thousands of kotis[5] of creatures, by the teaching of the Buddha, escape from the suffering of the triple world, from fearful and perilous paths, and gain the joys of Nirvana, the Tathagata then reflects thus: 'I possess infinite, boundless wisdom, power, fearlessness, and other Law-treasuries of Buddhas. All these living creatures are my children to whom I will equally give the Great Vehicle, so that none will gain an individual Nirvana, but all gain Nirvana by the same Nirvana as the Tathagata. All these living creatures who escape the triple world are given the playthings of Buddhas, viz. concentrations, emancipations, and so forth, all of the same pattern and of one kind, praised by sages and able to produce pure, supreme pleasure.

"Sariputra! Even as that elder at first attracted his children by the three carts, and afterwards gave them only a great cart magnificently adorned with precious things and supremely comfortable, yet that elder is not guilty of falsehood, so also is it with the Tathagata; there is no falsehood in first preaching Three-Vehicles to attract all living creatures and afterwards in saving them by the Great Vehicle only. Wherefore? Because the Tathagata possesses infinite wisdom, power, fearlessness, and the treasury of the laws, and is able to give all living creatures the Great Vehicle Law; but not all are able to receive it. Sariputra! For this reason know that Buddhas, by their adaptability, in the One Buddha-Vehicle define and expound the Three." . . .

[5] Huge numbers.

Though Buddhas, the World-honoured,
Convert by expedient methods,
Yet the living they convert
Are indeed all bodhisattvas.
To such as are of little wit,
Deeply attached to desire and passion,
The Buddha, for their sake,
Preaches the Truth about Suffering,
And all the living joyfully
Attain the unprecedented.
    The Buddha's Truth about Suffering,
Is real without distinction.
Those living beings who
Know not the root of suffering,
Cling to the cause of suffering,
Unable to leave it a moment.
Again, for the sake of these,
He preaches the Truth with tact (saying):
"The cause of all suffering
Is rooted in desire."
If desire be extinguished,
Suffering has no foothold.
To annihilate suffering
Is called the Third Truth.
For the sake of the Truth of Extinction,
To cultivate oneself in the Way,
Forsaking all ties to suffering,
This is called Emancipation.
From what then have these people
Attained Emancipation?
Merely to depart from the false
They call Emancipation;
But in truth that is not yet
Complete Emancipation.
    So Buddha declares: "These people
Have not reached real extinction;
Because these people have not yet
Gained the Supreme Way,
I am unwilling to declare
That they have attained extinction.
I am the King of the Law,
Absolute in regard to the Law,

For comforting all creatures
I appear in the world.
    "Sariputra! This,
My final Seal of the Law,
Because of my desire to benefit
All the world, is now announced;
Wherever you may wander,
Do not carelessly proclaim it.
If there be hearers who joyfully
Receive it with deep obeisance,
You may know those people
Are Avinivartaniyah.[6]
If there be any who receive
This Sutra-Law in faith,
These people must already
Have seen Buddhas of past times,
Revered and worshipped them
And listened to this Law.
If there be any who are able
To believe in your preaching,
They must formerly have seen me,
And also have seen you,
And these bhikshu-monks,
As well as these bodhisattvas.
    "This Law-Flower Sutra
Is addressed to the truly wise;
Men shallow of knowledge hearing it,
Go astray, not understanding.
All the Sravakas,
And Pratyekabuddhas,
Cannot by their powers
Attain unto this Sutra.
Sariputra!
Even you, into this Sutra
Enter only by faith,
Much more must the other Sravakas.
The other Sravakas,
By believing the Buddha's words,
Obediently follow this Sutra,
Not by wisdom they have of their own."

[6] Such as never return to the realm of mortal existence.

The Prodigal Son and the Seeking Father

"It is like a youth who, on attaining manhood, leaves his father and runs away. For long he dwells in some other country, ten, twenty, or fifty years. The older he grows, the more needy he becomes. Roaming about in all directions to seek clothing and food, he gradually wanders along till he unexpectedly approaches his native country. From the first the father searched for his son, but in vain, and meanwhile has settled in a certain city. His home becomes very rich; his goods and treasures are incalculable; gold, silver, lapis lazuli, corals, amber, crystal, and other gems so increase that his treasuries overflow; many others and slaves has he, retainers and attendants, and countless elephants, horses, carriages, animals to ride, and kine and sheep. His revenues and investments spread to other countries, and his traders and customers are many in the extreme.

"At this time, the poor son, wandering through village after village, and passing through countries and cities, at last reached the city where his father has settled. Always has the father been thinking of his son, yet, though he has been parted from him over fifty years, he has never spoken of the matter to any one, only pondering over it within himself and cherishing regret in his heart, as he reflects: 'Old and worn, I own much wealth; gold, silver, and jewels, granaries and treasuries overflowing; but I have no son. Some day my end will come and my wealth be scattered and lost, for there is no one to whom I can leave it.' Thus does he often think of his son, and earnestly repeats this reflection: 'If I could only get back my son and commit my wealth to him, how contented and happy should I be, with never a further anxiety!'

"World-honoured One! Meanwhile the poor son, hired for wages here and there, unexpectedly arrives at his father's house. Standing by the gate, he sees from afar his father seated on a lion-couch, his feet on a jewelled footstool, revered and surrounded by brahmanas, kshatriyas,[1] and citizens, and with strings of pearls, worth thousands and myraids, adorning his body; attendants and young slaves with white chowries wait upon him right and left; he is covered by a rich canopy from which hang streamers of

[1] Members of the second highest caste.

flowers; perfume is sprinkled on the earth, all kinds of famous flowers are scattered around, and precious things are placed in rows for his acceptance or rejection. Such is his glory, and the honour of his dignity. The poor son, seeing his father possessed of such great power, is seized with fear, regretting that he has come to this place, and secretly reflects thus: 'This must be a king, or some one of royal rank; it is no place for me to obtain anything for the hire of my labour. I had better go to some poor hamlet, where there is a place for letting out my labour, and food and clothing are easier to get. If I tarry here long, I may suffer oppression and forced service.'

"Having reflected thus, he hastens away. Meanwhile, the rich elder on his lion-seat has recognized his son at first sight, and with great joy in his heart has also reflected: 'Now I have some one to whom my treasuries of wealth are to be made over. Always have I been thinking of this my son, with no means of seeing him; but suddenly he himself has come and my longing is satisfied. Though worn with years, I yearn for him as of old.'

"Instantly he dispatches his attendants to pursue him quickly and fetch him back. Thereupon the messengers hasten forth to seize him. The poor son, surprised and scared, loudly cries his complaint: 'I have committed no offence against you; why should I be arrested?' The messengers all the more hasten to lay hold of him and compel him to go back. Thereupon, the poor son, thinking within himself that though he is innocent yet he will be imprisoned, and that now he will surely die, is all the more terrified; he faints away and falls prostrate on the ground. The father, seeing this from afar, sends word to the messengers: 'I have no need for this man. Do not bring him by force. Sprinkle cold water on his face to restore him to consciousness and do not speak to him any further.' Wherefore? The father, knowing that his son's disposition is inferior, knowing that his own lordly position has caused distress to his son, yet convinced that he is his son, tactfully does not say to others: 'This is my son.'

"A messenger says to the son: 'I now set you free; go wherever you will.' The poor son is delighted, thus obtaining the unexpected. He rises from the ground and goes to a poor hamlet in search of food and clothing. Then the elder, desiring to attract his son, sets up a device. Secretly he sends two men, doleful and shabby in appearance, saying—'You go and visit that place and gently say to the poor man—"There is a place for you to work here; you will be given double wages." If the poor man agrees, bring him back and give him work. If he asks what work you wish him to do, then you may say to him—"We will hire you for scavenging, and we both also will work along with you".' Then the two messengers go in search of the poor son and, having found him, place before him the above proposal. Thereupon the poor son, having received his wages beforehand, joins with them in removing a dirt-heap.

"His father, beholding the son, is struck with compassion for, and wonder at, him. Another day he sees at a distance, through a window, his son's figure, gaunt, lean, and doleful, filthy and unclean with dirt and dust; thereupon he takes off his strings of jewels, his soft attire, and ornaments, and puts on a coarse, torn, and dirty garment, smears his body with dust, takes a dust-hod in his right hand, and with an appearance fear-inspiring says to the labourers: 'Get on with your work, don't be lazy.' By such a device he gets near to his son, to whom he afterwards says: 'Aye, my man, you stay and work here, do not go again elsewhere; I will increase your wages; give whatever you need, bowls, utensils, rice, wheat-flour, salt, vinegar, and so on; have no hesitation; besides, there is an old and worn-out servant whom you shall be given if you need him. Be at ease in your mind; I am, as it were, your father; do not be worried again. Wherefore? I am old and advanced in years, but you are young and vigorous; all the time you have been working, you have never been deceitful, lazy, angry or grumbling; I have never seen you, like the other labourers, with such vices as these. From this time forth you shall be as my own begotten son.'

"Thereupon the elder gives him a new name and calls him a son. The poor son, though he rejoices at this happening, still thinks of himself as a humble hireling. For this reason, during twenty years he continues to be employed in scavenging. After this period, there grows mutual confidence between them, and he goes in and out and is at his ease, though his abode is still the original place.

"World-honoured One! Then the elder becomes ill and,

knowing that he will die before long, says to the poor son: 'Now I possess abundance of gold, silver, and precious things, and my granaries and treasuries are full to over-flowing. The quantities of these things, and the amounts which should be received and given, I want you to under-stand in detail. Such is my mind, and you must agree to this my wish. Wherefore? Because, now, I and you are of the same mind. Be increasingly careful so that there be no waste.'

"The poor son accepts his instruction and commands, and becomes acquainted with all the goods, gold, silver, and precious things, as well as all the granaries and treas-uries, but has no idea of expecting to inherit so much as a meal, while his abode is still the original place and he is yet unable to abandon his sense of inferiority.

"After a short time has again passed, the father, know-ing that his son's ideas have gradually been enlarged, his aspirations developed, and that he despises his previous state of mind, on seeing that his own end is approaching, commands his son to come, and gathers together his rela-tives, and the kings, ministers, kshatriyas, and citizens. When they are all assembled, he thereupon addresses them saying: 'Now, gentlemen, this is my son, begotten by me. It is over fifty years since, from a certain city, he left me and ran away to endure loneliness and misery. His former name was so-and-so and my name was so-and-so. At that time in that city I sought him sorrowfully. Suddenly in this place I met and regained him. This is really my son and I am really his father. Now all the wealth which I possess entirely belongs to my son, and all my previous disburse-ments and receipts are known by this son.'

"World-honoured One! When the poor son heard these words of his father, great was his joy at such unexpected news, and thus he thought: 'Without any mind for, or effort on my part, these treasures now come of themselves to me.'

"World-honoured One! The very rich elder is the Tathagata, and we are all as the Buddha's sons. The Tathagata has always declared that we are his sons. World-honoured One! Because of the three sufferings, in the midst of births and deaths we have borne all kinds of torments, being deluded and ignorant and enjoying our attachment to trifles. To-day the World-honoured One has caused us to ponder over and remove the dirt of all diverting discussions of inferior things. In these we have hitherto been diligent to make progress, and have got, as it were, a day's pay for our effort to reach Nirvana. Obtaining this, we greatly rejoiced and were contented, saying to ourselves: 'For our diligence and progress in the Buddha-law, what we have received is ample.' But the World-honoured One, knowing beforehand that our minds were attached to low desires and took delight in inferior things, let us go our own way, and did not discriminate for us, saying: 'You shall yet have possession of the treasure of Tathagata-knowledge.' The World-honoured One, in his tactfulness, told of the Tathagata-wisdom; but we, though following the Buddha and receiving a day's wage of Nirvana, deemed this a sufficient gain, never having a mind to seek after the Great Vehicle. We, also, have declared and expounded the Tathagata-wisdom to bodhisattvas, but in regard to this Great Vehicle we have never had a longing for it. Wherefore? The Buddha, knowing that our minds delighted in inferior things, by his tactfulness taught according to our capacity, but still we did not perceive that we were really Buddha-sons.

"Now we have just realized that the World-honoured One does not grudge even the Buddha-wisdom. Wherefore? From of old we are really sons of Buddha, but have only taken pleasure in minor matters; if we had had a mind to take pleasure in the Great, the Buddha would have preached the Great Vehicle Law to us. At length, in this Sutra, he preaches only the One Vehicle; and though formerly, in the presence of bodhisattvas, he spoke disparagingly of sravakas who were pleased with minor matters, yet the Buddha had in reality been instructing them in the Great Vehicle. Therefore we say that though we had no mind to hope or expect it, yet now the Great Treasure of the King of the Law has of itself come to us, and such things as Buddha-sons should obtain, we have all obtained."

The Rain Cloud

"Know, Kasyapa!
It is like unto a great cloud
Rising above the world,
Covering all things everywhere—
A gracious cloud full of moisture;
Lightning-flames flash and dazzle,
Voice of thunder vibrates afar,
Bringing joy and ease to all.
The sun's rays are veiled,
And the earth is cooled;
The cloud lowers and spreads
As if it might be caught and gathered;
Its rain everywhere equally
Descends on all sides,
Streaming and pouring unstinted,
Permeating the land.
On mountains, by rivers, in valleys,
In hidden recesses, there grow
The plants, trees, and herbs;
Trees, both great and small,
The shoots of the ripening grain,
Grape vine and sugar-cane.
Fertilized are these by the rain
And abundantly enriched;
The dry ground is soaked;
Herbs and trees flourish together.
From the one water which
Issued from that cloud,
Plants, trees, thickets, forests,
According to need receive moisture.
All the various trees,
Lofty, medium, low,
Each according to its size,
Grows and develops
Roots, stalks, branches, leaves,
Blossoms and fruits in their brilliant colours;
Wherever the one rain reaches,
All become fresh and glossy.
According as their bodies, forms,

And natures are great or small,
So the enriching [rain],
Though it is one and the same,
Yet makes each of them flourish.
In like manner also the Buddha
Appears here in the World,
Like unto a great cloud
Universally covering all things;
And having appeared in the world,
He, for the sake of the living,
Discriminates and proclaims
The truth in regard to all laws.
The Great Holy World-honoured One,
Among the gods and men,
And among the other beings,
Proclaims abroad this word:
'I am the Tathagata,
The Most Honoured among men;
I appear in the world
Like unto this great cloud,
To pour enrichment on all
Parched living beings,
To free them from their misery
To attain the joy of peace,
Joy of the present world,
And joy of Nirvana.
Gods, men, and every one!
Hearken well with your mind;
Come you here to me;
Behold the Peerless Honoured One!
I am the World-honoured,
Who cannot be equalled.
To give rest to every creature,
I appear in the world,
And, to the hosts of the living,
Preach the pure Law, sweet as dew;
The one and only Law
of Deliverance and Nirvana.
With one transcendent voice
I proclaim this truth,
Ever taking the Great Vehicle
As my subject.

Upon all I ever look
Everywhere impartially,
Without distinction of persons,
Or mind of love or hate.
I have no predilections
Nor any limitations;
Ever to all beings
I preach the Law equally;
As I preach to one person,
So I preach to all.
Ever I proclaim the Law,
Engaged in naught else;
Going, coming, sitting, standing,
Never am I weary of
Pouring it copiously on the world,
Like the all-enriching rain.
On honoured and humble, high and low,
Law-keepers, and law-breakers,
Those of perfect character,
And those of imperfect,
Orthodox and heterodox,
Quick-witted and dull-witted,
Equally I rain the Law-rain
Unwearyingly'."

5. The Eternal Buddha of Countless Worlds— Parable of the Physician

One of the most dramatic and stupendous scenes in all religious literature is portrayed in this passage, also from the Lotus sutra. *In the presence of Buddhas and Bodhisattvas, brought together in conclave from countless regions of the universe, the Blessed One proclaims that he is not identical with the historical Gautama of this particular world, but that his Eternal Love reveals itself in all times and places for the blessing and weal of all creatures.*

The relation of the parable of the physician, with which the selection closes, to the preceding parables is obvious. It gives a compassionate reason for the early teaching that at his death Buddha ended his existence and became extinct.

Then says the Buddha to the Bodhisattvas and the vast Assembly:

"Listen then each of you attentively to the secret, mysterious and supernatural power of Tathagata. All the worlds of gods, men and asuras[1] declare: 'Now has Sakyamuni-Buddha, coming forth from the palace of the Sakya clan, and seated at the place of enlightenment, not far from the city of Gaya, attained to Perfect Enlightenment.' But, good sons, since I veritably became Buddha, there have passed infinite, boundless, hundreds, thousands, myraids, kotis, nayutas of kalpas.[2] For instance, suppose there were five hundred thousand myriad kotis, nayutas of numberless Three-Thousand-Great-Thousandfold-Worlds; let some one grind them to atoms, pass eastward through five hundred thousands, myriads, kotis, nayutas of numberless countries, and then drop one of those atoms; suppose he thus proceeded eastward till he had finished those atoms—what do you think, good sons, is it possible to imagine and calculate all those worlds so as to know their number?

"Good sons! Now I must clearly announce and declare to you. Suppose you take as atomized all those worlds, everywhere that an atom has been deposited, and everywhere that it has not been deposited, and count an atom as a kalpa, the time since I became the Buddha still surpasses these by hundreds, thousands, myriads, kotis, nayutas of numberless kalpas. From that time forward I have constantly been preaching and teaching in this Saha-world[3] and also leading and benefiting the living in other places in hundreds, thousands, myriads, kotis, nayutas of numberless domains. Good sons! During this time, I have spoken of the Buddha 'Burning Light' and other Buddhas, and also have told of their entering Nirvana. Thus have I tactfully described them all. Good sons! Whenever living beings came to me, I beheld with a Buddha's eyes all the faculties, keen or dull, of their faith, and so forth; and I explained to them, in stage after stage, according to their capacity and degree of salvation, my different names and the length of my lives, and moreover plainly stated that I must enter Nirvana. I also, with various expedients,

[1] Demonic powers, at war with the gods.
[2] Large numbers of ages.
[3] Our present universe, in which there is much to endure.

preached the Wonderful Law which is able to cause the living to beget a joyful heart. Good sons! Beholding the propensities of all the living towards lower things, so that they have little virtue and much vileness, to these the Tathagata declares: 'I, in my youth, left home and attained to Perfect Enlightenment.' But since I veritably became Buddha, thus have I ever been, only by my expedient methods teaching and transforming all the living, so that they may enter into Buddhahood, and thus have I made declaration.

"Good sons! All the sutras which the Tathagata preaches are for the deliverance of the living—whether they speak of himself or speak of others, whether they indicate himself or others, and whether they indicate his own affairs or those of others; whatever they say is all real, and not empty air. Wherefore? Because the Tathagata knows and sees the character of the triple world as it really is; to him there is neither birth nor death, neither going away nor coming forth; neither existence in the world nor cessation of existence; neither reality nor unreality; neither thus nor otherwise. Unlike the way the triple world beholds the triple world, the Tathagata sees clearly such things as these without mistake. Because all the living have various natures, various desires, various activities, various ideas and reasonings, so, desiring to cause them to produce the roots of goodness, the Tathagata by so many reasonings, parables, and discourses has preached his various Truths. The Buddha-deeds which he performs never fail for a moment. Thus it is, since I became Buddha, in the far distant past, that my lifetime is of numberless kalpas, forever existing and immortal.

"Good sons! The lifetime which I fulfil in following the Bodhisattva-Way is not even yet completed, but will be again twice the previous number of kalpas. But now in this unreal Nirvana, I announce that I must enter the real Nirvana. In this expedient way the Tathagata teaches all living. Wherefore? If the Buddha abides long in the world, men of little virtue—who do not cultivate the roots of goodness and are spiritually poor and mean, greedily attached to the five desires, and caught in the net of wrong reflection and false views—if they see the Tathagata constantly present and not extinct, will become puffed up and lazy, and unable to conceive the idea that it is difficult to meet a Buddha, and be unable to develop a mind of reverence for him. Therefore the Tathagata tactfully says: 'Know, Bhikshus! The appearance of a Buddha in the world is a rare occurrence.' Wherefore? In the course of countless hundreds, thousands, myriads, kotis of kalpas, some men of little virtue may happen to see a Buddha, or none may see him. For this reason I say: 'Bhikshus! A Tathagata may rarely be seen!' All these living beings, hearing such a statement, must indeed realize the thought of the difficulty of meeting a Buddha and cherish a longing and a thirst for him; thus will they cultivate the roots of goodness. Therefore the Tathagata, though he does not in reality become extinct, yet announces his extinction."

The Parable of the Physician

"Suppose, for instance, a good physician, who is wise and perspicacious, conversant with the medical art, and skilful in healing all sorts of diseases. He has many sons, say ten, twenty, even up to a hundred. Because of some matter, he goes abroad to a distant country. After his departure his sons drink his poisonous medicines, which send them into a delirium and they lie rolling on the ground. At this moment their father comes back to his home. Of the sons who drank the poison, some have lost their senses; others are still sensible and, on seeing their father approaching in the distance, they are greatly delighted, and kneeling greet him:

" 'How good it is that you are returned in safety! We, in our foolishness, have mistakenly dosed ourselves with poison. We beg that you will heal us and give us back our lives.'

"The father, seeing his sons in such distress, in accordance with his prescriptions, seeks for good herbs, perfect in colour, scent, and fine flavour, and then pounds, sifts, and mixes them and gives them to his sons to take, saying thus:

" 'This excellent medicine with colour, scent and fine flavour all perfect, do you take, and it will at once rid you of your distress so that you will have no more suffering.'

"Those amongst the sons who are sensible, seeing this excellent medicine with colour and scent both good, take it immediately and are wholly delivered from their illness. The others who have lost their senses, seeing their father come, though they are also delighted, salute him, and ask him to heal their illness, yet when he offers them the medicine, they are unwilling to take it. Wherefore? Because the poison has entered deeply, they have lost their senses, and even in regard to this medicine of excellent colour and scent they say that it is not good. The father reflects thus:

" 'Alas! for these sons, afflicted by this poison, and their minds all unbalanced! Though they are glad to see me and implore for healing, yet they are unwilling to take such excellent medicine as this. Now I must arrange an expedient plan so that they will take this medicine.'

"Then he says to them: 'Know, all of you, that I am now worn out with old age and that the time of my death has arrived. This excellent medicine I now leave here. You may take it and have no fear of not being better.' After thus admonishing them, he departs again for another country and sends a messenger back to inform them: 'Your father is dead.' And now, when these sons hear that their father is dead, their minds are greatly distressed and they thus reflect: 'If our father were alive, he would have pity on us, and we should be saved and preserved. But now he has left us and died in a distant country.'

"Deeming themselves orphans with no one to rely on, continuous grief brings them to their senses; they recognize the colour, scent, and excellent flavour of the medicine, and thereupon take it, when their poisoning is entirely relieved. Their father, hearing that the sons are recovered, seeks an opportunity and returns, showing himself to them all.

"Good sons! What is your opinion? Are there any who could say that this good physician has committed the sin of falsehood?"

6. What Is Nirvana? (Mahayana View)

With the adoption of the Bodhisattva ideal, there arose a serious problem about Nirvana, and one influential form of the Mahayana answer to it is explained in the following passages from the Lankavatara Sutra. *A fuller philosophical elaboration of this type of answer is given in the* Mahayana Method of Cessation and Contemplation, *the basic manual of the Ti'en T'ai School of Chinese Buddhism.*

Of course, the philosophers who place unqualified trust in analytic reason cannot be expected to understand the truth of Nirvana, but how about the Theravada notion that it is the state which one enters, by oneself, when he has overcome the fetters which block the path to liberation? If this is the true concept of Nirvana then the Bodhisattva, who most deserves the bliss of perfect attainment, never enjoys it, because he turns back and shares the suffering of those still caught in the stream of life and death, in loving concern for their salvation. The answer is that if this concept is retained then, indeed, for the Buddhas and Bodhisattvas there is no Nirvana. But as the Bodhisattva goes through the various stages leading toward Tathagatahood he comes to realize that the essential meaning of Nirvana is not this—it rather stands for the true state of spiritual perfection. Now the Theravadin has not clearly understood that state. Rightly conceived, it is one in which the particularities of ordinary experience and the illusory distinctions of the discriminating mind are left behind; and the religious aspect of this is that it is a state in which compassionate oneness with others has transcended all thoughts of oneself as a separately distinguishable entity. Thus the perfected Bodhisattva becomes aware that just by being a Bodhisattva he is already in Nirvana as it is truly understood. For him Nirvana and Samsara are not two different realms. Nothing is outside Nirvana.

Paradoxically put, the spiritual insight here is that to renounce Nirvana for oneself, in love for others, is to find oneself in Nirvana, in its real meaning.

At that time, Mahamati the Bodhisattva-Mahasattva said this to the Blessed One: "Nirvana, Nirvana, is talked of by the Blessed One; what does this term designate? What is the Nirvana that is discriminated by all the philosophers?"

Said the Blessed One: "Mahamati, listen well and reflect well within yourself; I will tell you."

"Certainly, Blessed One," said Mahamati the Bodhisattva-Manhasattva, and gave ear to the Blessed One.

The Blessed One said this to him: "As to such Nirvanas as are discriminated by the philosophers, there are really

none in existence. Some philosophers conceive Nirvana to
be found where a system of analytic reasoning no more
operates, owing to the cessation of the Skandhas, Dhatus,[1]
and Ayatanas,[2] or to indifference to the objective world, or
to the recognition that all things are impermanent; or
where there is no recollection of the past and present, just
as when a lamp is extinguished, or when a seed is burnt,
or when a fire goes out, because then there is the cessation
of all the substrate—which is explained by the philosophers
as the non-rising of discrimination. But, Mahamati, Nirvana does not consist in mere annihilation. . . .

"Some, seeing that time is a creator and that the rise of
the world depends on time, conceive that Nirvana consists in recognising this fact. Again Mahamati, some conceive that all things and Nirvana are not to be distinguished
one from the other.

"All these views of Nirvana, severally advanced by the
philosophers with their reasonings, are not in accord with
logic, nor are they acceptable to the wise. Mahamati, they
all conceive Nirvana dualistically and in a causal connection. By these discriminations, Mahamati, all philosophers
imagine Nirvana, but there is nothing rising, nothing disappearing here [and there is no room for discrimination].
Mahamati, each philosopher relying on his own text-book
from which he draws his understanding and intelligence,
examines [the subject] and sins against [the truth], because [the truth] is not such as is imagined by him; [his
reasoning] ends in setting the mind to wandering about
and becoming confused, so that Nirvana is not to be found
anywhere.

"Again, Mahamati, there are others who, roaring with
their all-knowledge as a lion roars, explain Nirvana in the
following wise: that is, Nirvana is where it is recognised
that there is nothing but what is seen of the Mind itself;
where there is no attachment to external objects, existent
or non-existent; where, getting rid of the four propositions,
there is an insight into the abode of reality as it is; where,
recognising the nature of the mind in itself, one does not
cherish the dualism of discrimination; where grasped and
grasping are no more obtainable; . . . where the stages of

[1] Modes of consciousness.
[2] Sources of cognition.

Bodhisattvahood are passed one after another until the stage of Tathagatahood is attained, in which all the samadhis beginning with the Mayopama [Maya-like] are realised, and the Citta, Manas, and Manovijnana[3] are put away. Nirvana is the realm of self-realisation attained by noble wisdom, which is free from the discrimination of eternality and extinction, existence and non-existence."

Again Mahamati the Bodhisattva-Mahasattva said this to the Blessed One: "Pray tell me, Blessed One, about the state of perfect tranquillisation and its further development as attained by all the Bodhisattvas, Sravakas, and Pratyekabuddhas; for when this further development is thoroughly understood by myself and other Bodhisattva-Mahasattvas, all may be saved from being confounded by the happiness which comes from the attainment of perfect tranquillisation and also from falling into the confused state of mind of the Sravakas, Pratyekabuddhas, and philosophers."

Said the Blessed One: "Then listen well and reflect well within yourself; I will tell you."

"Certainly, Blessed One," said Mahamati the Bodhisattva-Mahasattva, and gave ear to the Blessed One.

The Blessed One said this to him: "Those Bodhisattva-Mahasattvas who have reached the sixth stage, as well as all the Sravakas and Pratyekabuddhas, attain perfect tranquillisation. At the seventh stage, the Bodhisattva-Mahasattvas, giving up the view of a separate essence as subsisting in all things, attain perfect tranquillisation in every minute of their mental lives, which is not, however, the case with the Sravakas and Pratyekabuddhas; for with them karma is still being produced, and in their attainment of perfect tranquillisation there is a trace [of dualism], of grasped and grasping. Therefore, they do not attain the perfect tranquillisation in every minute of their mental lives which is possible at the seventh stage. . . .

"At the seventh stage, Mahamati, the Bodhisattva properly examines into the nature of the Citta, Manas, and Manovijnana; he examines into [such subjects as] ego-soul and what belongs to it, grasped and grasping, the egolessness of persons and things, rising and disappearing, individuality and generality; he skilfully ascertains the

[3] Faculties of systematic cognition, analysis, and discriminative knowledge.

fourfold logical analysis;[4] he enjoys the bliss of self-mastery; he enters successively upon the stages; he knows the differences obtaining in the various elements of enlightenment. The grading of the stages is arranged by me lest the Bodhisattva-Mahasattva, not knowing what is meant by individuality and generality and failing to understand the continuous development of the successive stages, should fall into the philosophers' wrong way of viewing things.

"Mahamati, at the eighth stage the Bodhisattva-Mahasattvas, Sravakas, and Pratyekabuddhas cease cherishing discriminative ideas that arise from the Citta, Manas, and Manovijnana. From the first stage up to the sixth, they perceive that the triple world is no more than the Citta, Manas, and Manovijnana—that, as it is born of a discriminating mind . . . there is no falling into the multitudinousness of external objects except through [the discrimination of] the Mind itself. The ignorant, turning their self-knowledge towards the dualism of grasped and grasping, fail to understand, for there is in them the working of habit-energy which has been accumulating since beginningless time owing to false reasoning and discrimination.

"Mahamati, at the eighth stage there is Nirvana for the Sravakas and Pratyekabuddhas and Bodhisattvas; but the Bodhisattvas are kept away by the power of all the Buddhas from [being intoxicated by] the bliss of the samadhi, and thereby they will not enter into Nirvana. . . .

"The Sravakas and Pratyekabuddhas at the eighth stage of Bodhisattvahood are so intoxicated with the happiness that comes from the attainment of perfect tranquillisation, and, failing to understand fully that there is nothing in the world but what is seen of the Mind itself, they are thus unable to overcome the hindrances and habit-energy growing out of their notions of generality and individuality . . . they have the discriminating idea and knowledge of Nirvana. Their thoughts are possessed by the notion of Nirvana . . . like the ignorant, they are desirous of enjoying Nirvana for themselves. . . . Mahamati, when the Bodhisattvas face and perceive the happiness of the samadhi of perfect tranquillisation, they are moved with the feeling of love and sympathy owing to their original

[4] Analysis in terms of: it is, it is not, it both is and is not, it neither is nor is not.

vows . . . made for all beings, saying, 'So long as they
do not attain Nirvana I will not attain it myself.' Thus they
keep themselves away from Nirvana. But the fact is that
they are already in Nirvana because in them there is no
rising of discrimination. With them the discrimination of
grasped and grasping no more takes place; as they [now]
recognise that there is nothing in the world but what is
seen of the Mind itself, they have done away with the
thought of discrimination concerning all things. They have
abandoned adhering to and discriminating about such notions as the Citta, Manas, and Manovijnana, and external
objects, and separate essences; however, they have not
given up the things promoting the cause of Buddhism; because of their attainment of the inner insight which belongs
to the stage of Tathagatahood; whatever they do all issues
from their transcendental knowledge. . . .

"Mahamati, they will exercise themselves to make those
who have not yet attained the truth attain it. For the
Bodhisattvas, Nirvana does not mean extinction; as they
have abandoned thoughts of discrimination evolving from
the Citta, Manas, and Manovijnana, there is for them the
attainment of the recognition that all things are unborn."

PART V: Some Mahayana Philosophies

Introduction

For the most part, the selections in the present volume are
limited to ones which reveal the genius of Buddhism in terms
readily understandable to all religiously sensitive minds. But
they would give an inadequate and one-sided picture if they
were limited entirely to such materials. And those of my
readers who are spoiling for an intellectual tussle will be glad
to be introduced, at least briefly, to some of the keen thinkers
who have endeavored to defend their Buddhist faith by philosophical argument, and have been confident that it can provide
a sound solution to the major problems which in all times and
places exercise philosophical minds.

Such thinkers have appeared, of course, in each of the
historically influential Buddhist schools. Among the Theravadins the two most important philosophies were those of the

Vaibhesikas and the Sautrantikas, whose differences I shall not take the space to expound. The outstanding individual interpreter of Theravada Buddhism, by general consent, is Buddhaghosa, a converted Brahmin who lived in the first half of the fifth century A.D. His greatest work, the *Visuddhimagga* (or "Path to Purity") is a classic systematization and compendium of Theravada doctrine. It does not readily lend itself to helpful abbreviation, and I have not included any selections from it.

But we must not quite pass by the Mahayana philosophers. Their attempt to give a philosophic clarification and justification for the religious ideal expressed in the preceding section is of absorbing interest; in fact, the selection from the *Lankavatara Sutra,* in its criticism of philosophic interpretations of Nirvana and reasoned defense of its own view, has inevitably taken the form of such a clarification. The most famous of the individual Mahayana philosophers are Asvaghosa, Nagarjuna, Asangha, and Vasubandhu, who were active in North India during the later formative period of the Mahayana perspective. Besides these great men, many of the influential Mahayana sutras employ to a greater or less extent systematic reasoning in defense of the doctrines they teach, and some of these discursive elaborations are more easily followed by a Western reader than the terse dialectical arguments of the renowned philosophers. I shall give samples of Mahayana speculation from each of these two areas.

Asvaghosa lived about the end of the first century A.D. He wrote one of the most influential biographies of Buddha, but the work of greatest philosophic significance attributed to him is the *Awakening of Faith in the Mahayana.* This book, animated by a deep religious zeal, defends a form of philosophic idealism; its authenticity, however, is under dispute and its idealistic position is more profoundly reasoned elsewhere. Nagarjuna's date is less satisfactorily established; he probably lived about a century later than Asvaghosa. One of the most brilliant dialectical minds that any country has ever produced, he maintained a position which in terms of comparison with Western philosophies would be called a form of "nihilism"; only emptiness (or the "Void") is real. Asangha and Vasubandhu were brothers, who lived some time in the fourth century A.D. They expounded a philosophy which in the West would be described as a kind of subjective idealism, holding that mental representations constitute phenomenal reality.

But it is very misleading to refer to these philosophies in

terms of such analogies with Western speculative systems, and if the reader approaches them merely in this fashion he will find himself confronted by a baffling conundrum instead of making progress toward significant understanding. Why? Well, in the first place, just as typical Western philosophies must be understood in the framework of scientific-theoretical presuppositions that are characteristic of the Western mind, so these philosophies must be understood in the framework of the presuppositions characteristic of the Buddhist mind; and it of course explores the nature of goodness, reality, and truth in the context of determined search for spiritual liberation, as the East conceives this process. Hence Buddhist philosophies should be classified in a manner that reflects this framework, and by distinguishing marks appropriate to such an orientation.

In the second place, when this is done the basic lines of division would probably be as follows. Most generally, Mahayana philosophies would either be mainly concerned with practical problems, seeking clarification of the moral values and spiritual techniques involved (in which case they would be distantly analogous to systems of ethics in the West), or they would be largely concerned also with the questions about reality and truth which one who accepts these values and follows these procedures is likely to confront (in which case they would show certain analogies to metaphysical and epistemological philosophies in the West). The analogy, however, always needs to be interpreted in the light of the radical difference of presuppositions that is inescapably present. The most significant division of this second type of speculation would be between philosophies which believe it possible to use the reasoning mind to clarify and establish the nature of the ultimately real and those that reject this conviction, holding that the reasoning mind must discover and accept its own drastic limitations, and the illusoriness of what it has taken for granted, so that a supreme realization that lies beyond discriminative thought and speech may become possible. The former group of philosophies will be led by their inherent logic to some kind of metaphysical idealism, although they will defend it in different ways. The latter group will be led to what in Western terms would be a kind of nihilism—it would, however, be more accurately called a super-rational mysticism. It would be more correct to describe it thus because, according to these philosophies, our understanding acceptance that "all is empty" as measured by the standards of ordinary experience and logic is the necessary and sufficient condition of realizing that which is supremely true but inexpressible in terms of experience and logic.

The following selections include samples of "idealism" and of "nihilism," both in the succinct form given these doctrines by brilliant Mahayana philosophers and also in the form of a more discursive exposition, as contained in two interesting documents that are equally philosophical in their own way.

In reading the two keen dialectical arguments that follow, one should never lose sight of the following considerations:

(a) The ulterior purpose of both Nagarjuna and Vasubandhu is religious rather than metaphysical. They are aiming to clear away obstructions which, especially in the case of vigorous intellects, stand in the way of realizing the spiritual integrity that transcends ordinary experience and ordinary ways of thinking. The concluding sentences of each selection reveal this aim.

(b) Nagarjuna's technique for doing this in the Madhyamika Karikas *is to employ analytic reason (which, he holds, has its relative value) to undermine the categories of reason. And he does not hesitate to use his critique of causality to help destroy even the basic Buddhist concept of Nirvana, as a concept. As stanzas XIX and XX of Chapter XXV show, we have here the dialectical correlate of the doctrine of the* Lankavatara Sutra *that Nirvana is found in sharing the woes of those in Samsara and is not a different realm. The reality of Nirvana he does not mean to deny. An essential condition for entering it is to leave behind the idea that it can be understood as a concept.*

(c) Vasubandhu's technique in the selection here used is to destroy belief in physical reality, by undermining the concepts of atom, of an aggregate of atoms (composing an object), and of perceptual qualities. He leaves, as real, subjective impressions which can only exist in a mind. This prepares the way for an intuitive realization of the true and absolute nature of mind, which is the intellectual aspect of Enlightenment. The latter, culminating feature of his teaching is developed in a longer document not yet translated into English.

1. Nagarjuna's Analysis of Causality and of Nirvana

EXAMINATION OF CAUSALITY

I

There absolutely are no things,
Nowhere and none, that arise [anew];
Neither out of themselves, nor out of non-self,
Nor out of both, nor at random.

II

Four can be the conditions
(Of every thing produced)—
Its cause, its object, its foregoing moment,
Its most decisive factor.

III

In these conditions we can find
No self-existence of the entities.
Where self-existence is deficient,
Relational existence also lacks.

IV

No energies in causes,
Nor energies outside them.
No causes without energies,
Nor causes that possess them.

V

Let those facts be causes
With which co-ordinated other facts arise.
Non-causes will they be,
So far the other facts have not arisen.

VI

Neither non-Being nor Being[1]
Can have a cause.
If non-Being, whose the cause?
If Being, whatfor the cause?

[1] In *The Conception of Buddhist Nirvana*, Dr. Stcherbatsky uses the Latin form "Ens."

VII

Neither a Being nor a non-Being,
Nor any Being-non-Being—
No element is really turned out.
How can we then assume
The possibility of a producing cause?

VIII

A mental Being is reckoned as an element,
Separately from its objective [counterpart].
Now, if it [begins] by having no objective counterpart,
How can it get one afterward?

IX

If [separate] elements do not exist,
Nor is it possible for them to disappear.
The moment which immediately precedes
Is thus impossible. And if 'tis gone,
How can it be a cause?

X

If entities are relative,
They have no real existence.
The [formula] "this being, that appears"
Then loses every meaning.

XI

Neither in any of the single causes
Nor in all of them together
Does the (supposed) result reside.
How can you out of them extract
What in them never did exist?

XII

Supposing from these causes does appear
What never did exist in them,
Out of non-causes then
Why does it not appear?

XIII

The result is cause-possessor,
But causes are not even self-possessors.
How can result be cause-possessor,
If of nonself-possessors it be a result?

XIV

There is, therefore, no cause-possessor,
Nor is there an effect without a cause.
If altogether no effect arises,
[How can we then distinguish]
Between the causes and non-causes?

EXAMINATION OF NIRVANA

I

If every thing is relative,
No [real] origination, no [real] annihilation,
How is Nirvana then conceived?
Through what deliverance, through what annihilation?

II

Should every thing be real in substance,
No [new] creation, no [new] destruction,
How would Nirvana then be reached?
Through what deliverance, through what annihilation?

III

What neither is released, nor is it ever reached,
What neither is annihilation, nor is it eternality,
What never disappears, nor has it been created,
This is Nirvana. It escapes precision.

IV

Nirvana, first of all, is not a kind of Being,
It would then have decay and death.
There altogether is no Being
Which is not subject to decay and death.

V

If Nirvana is Being,
It is produced by causes—
Nowhere and none the entity exists
Which would not be produced by causes.

VI

If Nirvana is Being,
How can it lack substratum;[1]

---

[1] Underlying ground, out of which things arise.

There whatsoever is no Being
Without any substratum.

VII

If Nirvana is not a Being
Will it be then a non-Being?
Wherever there is found no Being,
There neither is a [corresponding] non-Being.

VIII

Now, if Nirvana is a non-Being,
How can it then be independent?
For sure, an independent non-Being
Is nowhere to be found.

IX

Co-ordinated here or caused are [separate things]:
We call this world phenomenal;
But just the same is called Nirvana,
When from causality abstracted.

X

The Buddha has declared
That Being and non-Being should be both rejected.
Neither as Being nor as a non-Being
Nirvana therefore is conceived.

XI

If Nirvana were both Being and non-Being,
Final deliverance would be also both,
Reality and unreality together.
This never could be possible!

XII

If Nirvana were both Being and non-Being,
Nirvana could not be uncaused.
Indeed both Being and non-Being
Are dependent on causation.

XIII

How can Nirvana represent
A Being and a non-Being together?
Nirvana is indeed uncaused,
Both Being and non-Being are productions.

XIV

How can Nirvana represent
[The place] of Being and of non-Being together?
As light and darkness [in one spot]
They cannot simultaneously be present.

XV

If it were clear, indeed,
What a Being means, and what a non-Being,
We could then understand the doctrine
About Nirvana being neither Being nor non-Being.

XVI

If Nirvana is neither Being nor non-Being
No one can really understand
This doctrine which proclaims at once
Negation of them both together.

XVII

What is the Buddha after his Nirvana?
Does he exist or does he not exist,
Or both, or neither?
We never will conceive it!

XVIII

What is the Buddha then at lifetime?
Does he exist, or does he not exist,
Or both, or neither?
We never will conceive it!

XIX

There is no difference at all
Between Nirvana and Samsara.
There is no difference at all
Between Samsara and Nirvana.

XX

What makes the limit of Nirvana
Is also then the limit of Samsara.
Between the two we cannot find
The slightest shade of difference.

XXI

[Insoluble are antinomic[2]] views
Regarding what exists beyond Nirvana,
Regarding what the end of this world is,
Regarding its beginning.

XXII

Since everything is relative, [we do not know]
What is finite and what is infinite,
What means finite and infinite at once,
What means negation of both issues.

XXIII

What is identity, and what is difference?
What is eternity, what noneternity,
What means eternity and noneternity together,
What means negation of both issues?

XXIV

Bliss consists in the cessation of all thought,
In the quiescence of plurality.
No [separate] reality was preached at all,
Nowhere and none by Buddha!

2. Vasubandhu's Argument for Subjective Idealism*

[A questioner has just asked whether there is not a realm
of separate, really existing outer elements which are the objects
of our several kinds of sense consciousness. Vasubandhu re-
plies]:

The Stanza says:

X

That realm is neither one thing,
    Nor is it many atoms;
        Again, it is not an agglomeration,
    Because the atom is not proved.

[2] Contrasting.
* C. H. Hamilton, *Buddhism, A Religion of Infinite Compassion*,
Copyright, 1952, The Liberal Arts Press, Inc., pp. 126-32.

How can this be said? The meaning is that if there really are external bases of cognition which respectively become objects of sense representation, then such an outer realm must either be one, as in the assertion of the Vaisesikas[1] that there is form having parts; or it must be many, as in the affirmation that there are very many real atoms which in agglomeration and combination act together as objects. But the external object cannot logically be one, because we cannot grasp the substance of the whole apart from the parts. Also it logically is not many, because we cannot apprehend the atoms separately. Again logically, they do not in agglomeration or combination make objects, because the theory of single real atoms is not proved.

(Question) How can you say it is not proved?

(Answer) The Stanza says:

XI

One atom joined with six others
>   Must consist of six parts.
>   If it is in the same place with six,
The aggregate must be as one atom.

If one atom on each of its six sides joins with another atom, it must consist of six parts, because the place of one does not permit of being the place of the others. If there are six atoms in one atom's place, then all the aggregates must be as one atom in quantity because, though revolving in mutual confrontation, they do not exceed that quantity; and so aggregates also must be invisible.

(Objection) The Vaibhasikas[2] of Kasmir say: The theory that atoms join together is wrong because they do not have spatial divisions—dismiss such an error as the above—but aggregates have the principle of joining together because they do have spatial divisions.

(Answer) This also is not so, for the Stanza says:

XII

Since it is stated that atoms do not join,
>   Of what then is the joining of the aggregates?
>   If joining is not proved of the latter,
It is not because they have no spatial divisions.

[1] One of the six orthodox schools of Indian philosophy. It championed an atomic pluralism in metaphysics.
[2] One of the Theravada philosophical schools.

Now we must examine the principle and tendency of their statement. Since apart from atoms there are no aggregates, and there is no joining of atoms, then of what is the joining of the aggregates? If you change the statement to save your position and say that aggregates also do not join one another, then you should not say that atoms are without combination because of having no spatial divisions. Aggregates have spatial divisions and yet you do not grant their combination. Therefore the noncombining of atoms is not due to their lack of spatial division. For this reason the single real atom is not proved. Whether atomic combination is or is not admitted, the mistake is still as we have said. Whether spatial division of atoms is or is not admitted, both views are greatly in error.

(Question) For what reason?

(Answer) The Stanza says:

XIII

If the atom has spatial divisions
> It logically should not make a unity;
> If it has none, there should be neither
> > shadow nor occultation;[3]
Aggregates being no different [would likewise be]
> without these two.

If the six spatial divisions of the single atom are different, several parts making up the body, how can unity be proven? If the single atom is without different spatial divisions, then when the light of the rising sun strikes upon it how does a shadow occur on the other side, since there is no other part where the light does not reach? Again, if we assert that atoms are without spatial divisions, how can there be mutual occultation of one by another, since there is no remaining portion of the one to which the other does not go, by which we may speak of mutual obstruction of one by another? Since they do not mutually obstruct, then all the atoms must revolve in the same place; and the quantity of all aggregates is the same as one atom. The error is as we have said above.

(Question) Why not admit that shadow and occultation pertain to aggregates but not to atoms?

[3] One object standing in the way of another.

(Answer) Can it be that, different from the atoms, you admit aggregates which cast shadows and cause occultation?

(Objector) Not so!

(Answer) If that is the case, the aggregates must be without these two phenomena. That is, if aggregates are not different from the atoms, then shadow and occultation must not belong to the aggregates. The intelligence analyzes, arranges and distinguishes, but whether it sets up atoms or aggregates, both are unrealities.

(Question) Of what use is it to consider and choose between atoms and aggregates when you still cannot get rid of external sense quality?

(Answer) Here again, what is this quality?

(Objector) I mean that the object of vision is also the real nature of the color green, and so on with all the other sense qualities.

(Answer) We must judge whether this "object of vision, etc." which is the "real nature of green, etc." is one or many.

(Objector) Suppose we say [one or the other], what is the error?

(Answer) Both views are in error. The fault of multiplicity is as explained before. Unity also is irrational.

The Stanza says:

XIV

Assuming unity, there must be no walking progressively

At one time, no grasping and not grasping,

And no plural, disconnected condition;

Moreover, no scarcely perceptible, tiny things.

If there is no separation and difference, and all colored things which the eye can reach are asserted to be one thing, then there can be no reason in walking progressively on the ground, for if one step is taken it reaches everywhere: again there cannot be simultaneously a grasping here and a not grasping there, for the reason that a unitary thing cannot at one time be both obtained and not obtained. A single place, also, ought not to contain disconnected things, such as elephants, horses, etc. If the place contains one, it also contains the rest. How can we say that one is distinguished from another? Granting two things present, how comes it that in one place there can be both occupancy and non-occupancy—that there can be a seeing of emptiness between? Moreover, there should also be no such scarcely perceptible tiny things as water animalcules, because being in the same single space with the coarse things they should be of equal measure. If you say it is by characteristic aspect that one object differs from another, and that they do not become different things from any other reason, then you certainly must admit that this discriminated thing repeatedly divided becomes many atoms. Now it has already been argued that an atom is not a single real thing. Consequently, apart from consciousness, sense organs such as the eye, and sense objects such as color, are all unprovable. From these considerations we best prove the doctrine that only representations exist.

(Question) The existence or nonexistence of anything is determined by means of proof. Among all means of proof immediate perception is the most excellent. If there are no external objects, how is there this awareness of objects such as are now immediately evident to me?

(Answer) This evidence is inadequate, for the Stanza says:

XV

Immediate awareness is the same as in dreams.
At the time when immediate awareness has arisen,
Seeing and its object are already nonexistent;
How can it be admitted that perception exists?

Just as in time of dreaming, although there are no outer objects, such immediate awareness may be had, so also must the immediate awareness at other times be understood. Therefore to adduce this as evidence is inadequate. Again, if at a certain time there is this immediate awareness, such as the color now evident to me, at that time along with the object the seeing is already nonexistent: (1) because such awareness necessarily belongs to the discriminative action of the intellective consciousness, and (2) because at that time the visual and other sense consciousness have already faded out. According to those who hold the

doctrine of momentariness[4] at the time when this awareness arises the immediate objects—visible, tangible, audible, etc.—are already destroyed. How can you admit that
at this time there is immediate perception?

(Objection) But a past immediate experience is required before intellective consciousness can remember; for
this reason we decide that there is a previously experienced
object. The beholding of this object is what we concede to
be immediate perception. From this the doctrine that external objects truly exist is established.

(Answer) If you wish to prove the existence of external
objects from "first experiencing, later remembering," this
theory also fails.

(Objector) Why so?

(Answer) The Stanza says:

XVI (First part)
As has been said, the apparent object
is a representation.
It is from this that memory arises. . . .

As we have said earlier, although there is no external
object, a sense representation, visual, etc., appears as an
outer object. From this comes the later state with its
memory associate, the discriminated mental representation,
appearing as a seemingly former object. Then we speak
of this as a memory of what has been already experienced.
Therefore, to use a later memory to prove the real existence
of a previously seen external object cannot in principle be
maintained.

(Question) If, in waking time as well as in a dream,
representations may arise although there are no true objects, then, just as the world naturally knows that dream
objects are nonexistent, why is it not naturally known of
the objects in waking time, since they are the same? Since
it is not naturally known that waking objects are nonexistent, how, as in dream consciousness, are the real objects all nothing?

(Answer) This also is no evidence, for the Stanza says:

[4] The radical Theravada doctrine of the impermanence of everything. See above, p. 85 ff.

XVI (Second part)
. . . Before we have awakened we cannot know
That what is seen in the dream does not exist.

Just as in the unawakened state we do not know that
dream objects are not externally real, but do know it on
awaking, even so the world's falsely discriminated recur-
rent impressions are confused and fevered as in the midst of
a dream, all that is seen being wholly unreal; but before the
true awakening is attained this cannot be naturally known.
But if there is a time when we attain that world-trans-
cending knowledge, emancipatory and nondiscriminative,
then we call it the true awakening. After this, the purified
knowledge of the world which is obtained takes precedence;
according to the truth, it is clearly understood that those
[phenomenal] objects are unreal. The principle is the same.

3. Ultimate Reality Is Absolute Mind

*The Surangama Sutra as a whole is a very variegated affair;
much of it is puzzling and amusing to a Western philosopher.
However, its first four chapters contain a sustained argument
in the form of a dialogue, aiming to reveal the true nature of
mind and to establish the reality of absolute mind. The approach is reminiscent of many arguments in idealistic philosophies of the West. I have selected only the passages which
seem essential to the basic line of reasoning followed, and
have divided the argument into sections, giving each a title.
Again, the reader must not miss the religious spirit and purpose
which animates the discussion.*

Thus have I heard; once on a time Buddha was residing in
the city of Sravasti, in the Jetavana vihara,[1] with the congregation of Great Disciples (Bhikshus) 1250 men in all;
all of them perfect Arhats, firmly established in the Divine
Life, distinguished for their superiority to all worldly influences, having perfectly mastered all human knowledge,
and enabled, by the reception of Divine Truth, embodied in
the doctrine of Buddha, to assume countless forms for the
salvation of all sentient creatures, and for the benefit of
ages yet to come. . . . Besides these there were countless
[1] Guest house.

Pratyeká Buddhas, all of them Arhats; and Sravakas, who had come together to the place where Buddha was, and joined themselves with the disciples; it was now just the time of the free discussion held in the midst of the Summer Retreat. . . .

Then Buddha addressed Ananda: "You and I, Ananda, are of one blood, related by the consanguinity of our parents; tell me then, what it was that first stirred your heart in my religious system—what excellences did you see of such persuasive character as to induce you to forsake and quit the fascinations of the world?"

Ananda replied thus to Buddha: "Seeing in Tathagata the thirty-two superior marks, of such superlative beauty, your person bright and ruddy as crystal, and ever reflecting in myself that these marks were not those which the lusts of the flesh produce." . . .

a. Where is mind, as functioning through vision, located?

Buddha replied: "Well said, Ananda! but I now interrogate you!—when first you were conscious of a feeling of preference for the thirty-two superior marks of Tathagata, using what means of sight [did you arrive at this state] and who was it that felt the pleasure of preference for me?"

Ananda replied: "World-honoured One! In this way I arrived at this pleasurable preference, by using my mind and my sight. My eyes gazing on you beheld the superlative excellences of Tathagata, and my mind was sensible of the birth of the delight of love; it was thus that this condition was produced that made me desire to come out of the tangled influences that bound me to life and death."

Buddha replied to Ananda: "According to your words just uttered, the true ground of your pleasurable affection is to be sought in the mind and the eye. But if you know not the precise location of these powers, then you can never get rid of the confusing mists that affect your conduct— just as though a king of a district, on account of the ravages of a band of robbers, were to equip a military force to expel them, the first requisite would be that the soldiers should know whereabouts the robbers were secreted. So, as it is on account of the false judgments of your mind and sight that you are detained in the stream of perpetual transmigrations, I demand of you:—where is the local habitat of this mind and this sight of which you speak?"

Ananda, replying to Buddha, said: "World-honoured One! all the ten different kinds of being which exist in the world agree in considering that the intelligent mind resides within the body; whilst it is evident to every one . . . that the seeing eye is in my head."

Buddha replied to Ananda thus: "Ananda, at this moment you are seated in the preaching-hall of Tathagata; look out now and see the trees of the Jetavana, and tell me where are they situated?"

"World-honoured One! this great-storied religious preaching-hall is situated in the garden of Anathapindaka . . . and so the trees of the Jetavana must be of necessity outside the hall."

"Ananda, as you sit here in the hall, what is it that [your eyes] first behold?"

"World-honoured One, as I sit in the hall I first of all see Tathagata. Next I behold the great Assembly. Then looking outside, I see the varied trees of the garden."

"Ananda, as you behold the trees outside the hall, what is the medium through which you gaze on them?"

"World-honoured One! the windows of this great preaching-hall being opened—therefore, as I sit here, I am able to obtain the extensive view which meets my eye beyond the hall!" . . .

Buddha then addressed Ananda: "According to your statement, whilst your body is located in the preaching-hall, the windows being open, you are enabled to gaze at the garden trees; tell me, then, if it is likewise possible for any person within this hall not to be able to see Tathagata and yet to behold the objects without the precincts?"

Ananda replied, saying: "World-honoured One, it is clearly impossible to suppose that any one within the hall, not being able to see Tathagata, could yet behold the trees and rivulets outside the place."

"Ananda! apply the same reasoning to your assertion with respect to the mind . . . if, according to your former statement, the groundwork of this perceptive faculty is within your body, then its first exercise would be to make itself acquainted with the inner parts of the body itself; so that all men should first be sensible of . . . all that is

within them, and afterwards . . . those things which are
without. But how is it, then, in fact, that we never meet
with a man who is really able to see his own internal
organs? . . . or will it not follow on your own admission,
that not being able to see that which is within, he cannot
know what is without? You must admit, therefore, that this
hypothesis regarding the seat of the knowing faculty, viz.,
that it is within the body, cannot be maintained."

Ananda, bowing his head to the ground, again addressed
Buddha: "From what I gather, as I listen to the words of
Tathagata, it is plain that I must understand the truth to be
that my understanding faculty . . . is really located *without* the body. . . . As men are unable to see that which
is within themselves, but can only take knowledge of what
is without, it seems to follow that the intelligent mind (or
perceptive faculty) must be like a lamp placed *outside* a
house, which cannot illuminate that which is within; this
I take to be the true solution, agreeable to the system of
Buddha and incapable of being refuted." . . .

Buddha replied: "Well, then! take your assertion about
the intelligent mind dwelling outside the body; there must,
therefore, be an external connection between your body
and this mind, and when this personal connection is not
in action, then what the external mind perceives you yourself cannot know; and since (as far as you are concerned)
the knowledge of a thing is the personal knowledge you
possess of it, the intelligent mind (apart from this) knows
nothing. For instance, I now show you my hand, soft as the
material of the Talas tree; at the moment when your eyes
perceive it, does not the intelligent mind also discriminate
as to the properties of the hand?"

Ananda replied: "Yes, certainly, World-honoured One."

Buddha continued: "If, then, your intelligent faculty
immediately discriminates as to the character of that which
is presented to your eyes, how can you say that this faculty
resides without the body (and is so disconnected from it)?
You may be satisfied, therefore, that this hypothesis is also
untenable."

Ananda again replied: "World-honoured One, according
to what you say—viz., that because the intelligent mind
does not apprehend inner truths, therefore it does not reside
within; and, because of the necessary connection of mind

and body, the former cannot be located without the body . . . I now consider further, and conclude that the power of [seeing and] knowing is fixed in one place."

"But what is that place?" asked Buddha.

Ananda said: "It appears to me that this intelligent faculty, which has been proved to be incapable of knowing that which is within, and yet sees that which is without, lies hid as it were within the sense itself. Just as if there were a man who took a glass [lens], and held it up before both his eyes; this, although exterior to the eye, yet being joined to it, prevents not the eye from exercising its faculty of sight, and of distinguishing one object from another. So my intelligent faculty, . . . because it dwells in (or is joined with) the organ of sense, is yet no impediment in the clear perception of that which is without, because, as I suppose, it is secreted in the organ itself." . . .

"Then," Buddha continued, "if your intelligent faculty corresponds to [a power hid behind] this glass lens of which you speak, how is it, when you behold the distant hills and rivers, that you do not preceive the eye itself? . . . But if you do not see the eye, then how can you say that the intelligent faculty lies secreted within the organ? . . . You must be content, therefore, to give up this hypothesis also.". . .

Ananda, replying to Buddha, said: "World-honoured One! I have also heard you, discoursing with Manjusri and other eminent disciples, when you were engaged in the discussion of the question of the true condition [of Being], say, that the intelligent mind was located neither within nor without.

"As far as I can understand the question, it seems that we cannot say that the mind is placed within us, or else there is the difficulty of not seeing that which is within; and we cannot say that it is situated outside us, or else there is the difficulty about the relationship of mind and body; hence we are driven to the conclusion that there is a medium somewhere, so that the mind is neither within the body nor beyond it, *but between the two.*"

"You speak of between the two," said Buddha; "take care that this phrase does not deceive you, so that your 'between the two' means 'nowhere.' Let us investigate it. Where is the place of this middle point? Does it reside in the sense which perceives or in the thing perceived? . . .

"If your intelligent mind resides in the middle of the sense and the object of sense, then the substance of this mind is either united with the two, or separated and distinct from the two.

"If united with the two, then there is a confusion of substance, so that the mind can no longer be regarded as a substantial unit; but there will be a mutual opposition betwixt the two bonds, preventing the possibility of the middle entity of which you speak.

"But if there be no such union, then this intelligent mind must partly partake of the character of the sense which you say has the power of knowing, and partly of the object of sense which you say has no such power. The mind, therefore, has no distinct character; and if so, by what mark may you recognise it, as it exists in the middle of these two opposing powers? You may conclude, therefore, that this hypothesis is not capable of proof."

Ananda addressed Buddha, saying: "World-honoured! formerly I saw Buddha in the society of Mogallana, Subhuti, Pourna, Sariputra, four great disciples, discoursing on the law; on this occasion I heard the following assertion, frequently repeated, that the nature of the intelligent and discriminating mind is such, that it could not be said to be within the body, nor without it, nor in the middle point, but that that was rightly named the mind which in its very nature is without a local habitation, and without preference. I should be glad to know, therefore, whether I may not define the intelligent mind as that which is 'indefinite,' and 'without partiality.' " . . .

b. If it has no location, how determine its reality and nature?

Tathagata, stretching out his golden-coloured arm, bent together his five fingers, and said: "Do you see me doing this, Ananda?" "Yes, indeed," Ananda replied; "I see you." "What do you see?" said Buddha. "I see," Ananda replied, "Tathagata raising his arm, bending his fingers into the form of a shining fist, dazzling alike my mind and eye." Buddha said: "Now, what is the instrument by which you see all this?" Ananda said: "I and all here present see this by the use of our eyes."

Buddha addressed Ananda: "Answer me truthfully! . . . if it is your eyes which see the fist, of what good [or account] is the mind which you say my fist dazzles?" Ananda replied: "Tathagata seems now to inquire as to the particular locality in which this mind of which I speak resides; and yet it is by means of this mind that I, of whom you inquire, am able to investigate the question on which we are speaking. I take it, therefore, that this mind is the power by which I investigate."

Buddha replied: "No, no, Ananda, this is not your mind." Ananda, in an agitated manner, quickly leaving his seat, with raised hands stood upright before Buddha and said: "If this is not my mind, tell me what should it be called?" Buddha answered: "This is but the perception of vain and false qualities, which, under the guise of your true nature, has from the first deceived you." . . .

At this time the World-honoured One began his explanation to Ananda and the rest of the congregation, desiring to excite in them a consciousness of that mind which springs not from any earthly source. Sitting on his lion throne, therefore, he touched the top of Ananda's head and spoke thus: "Tathagata ever says, every phenomenon that presents itself to our knowledge is but a manifestation of the mind . . . which is the true substratum of all. Ananda, if all the varieties of being in the collection of worlds, down to the single shrub, and the leaf, or the fibre of the plant, tracing all these to their ultimate elements—if all these have a distinct and substantial nature of their own (as you say)—how much more ought the pure, excellent, and effulgent mind, which is the basis of all knowledge, to have attributed to it its own essential and substantial existence?

"If, then, you examine this question and still prefer to call the discriminating and inquiring faculty by the name of mind, you must at any rate distinguish it from the power that apprehends the various phenomena connected with the mere senses, and allow the latter a distinct nature. Thus, whilst you now hear me declaring the law, it is because of the sounds you hear that there is a discriminating process within you; yet, after all sounds have disappeared, there still continues a process of thought within, in which the memory acts as a principal element, so that there is a mind acting as it were on the mere shadows of things.

"I do not forbid you to hold your own opinion on the question of this discriminative faculty, but I only ask you to search out the . . . question itself. If, after you have removed the immediate cause of sensation, there is still a discriminative power in the faculty of which we speak, then that is the true mind which you justly designate as yours; but if the discriminative power ceases to exist after the immediate cause which called it into exercise is removed, then this power is only a shadowy idea, dependent entirely on the presence of external phenomena. . . . Searchers after truth . . . seldom attain to the last deliverance found in the condition of an Arhat, and all this because they do not shake off the mistaken notion that this perishable and uncertain process of thought (which depends entirely on accidents) is true and real. . . .

"Ananda, taking the instance of my closed hand, I suppose that if I had no hand there could be no closing it; and if you had no eyes there could be no seeing it; so that by means of your sense of sight, and my right manipulation of my fingers, the whole idea is completed of 'your seeing my fist.' Is this right or wrong?" Ananda replied: "It is right; oh, World-honoured One! for if I had no sight I could not see; whereas, by means of this sense, and your right manipulation, the idea is formed in my mind of your fist, resulting from the agreement of [the necessary] conditions, in each case."

Buddha replied. "This agreement of conditions, as you term it, is not a correct explanation. For, consider: if a man has no hand, there is clearly an end of 'making a fist'; but if a man has no eye, there is not the same complete end of 'seeing'; for, just think a moment. Suppose you were going along a road, and you were to meet a blind man, and ask him, 'Do you see anything?' That blind man would reply to you: 'I see only darkness before my eyes.' Now, although there is no such thing as, in his case, seeing a variety of objects, yet still there is a distinct observation on his part, and the object before his eyes is 'darkness.' What, then, is wanting why this observation should not be called 'seeing'?"

Ananda said: "How can you speak of an 'act of seeing,' when the same darkness is always before the eyes of all blind people?"

able?" The Rajah replied: "World-honoured One! this body of mine, without doubt, in the end, after various changes, will perish."

Buddha said: "Maharajah! you have not yet experienced this destruction of the body; how, then, do you know anything about it?"

"World-honoured One!" replied the King, "with respect to this transient, changeable, and perishable body; although I have not yet experienced the destruction of which I speak, yet I observe the case of things around me and ever reflect that all these things are changing—old things die, and new things succeed; there is nothing that changes not! thus the wood that now burns will be soon converted into ashes; all things gradually exhaust themselves and die away; there is no cessation of this dying out and perishing. I may certainly know, then, that this body of mine will finally perish.". . .

Buddha said: "Maharajah! you confess that from witnessing these ceaseless changes, you arrive at the conviction that your body must perish! Let me ask—when this time for your body to perish arrives, are you cognisant of anything connected with yourself that will not perish?" Prasenadjit Rajah, with his hands clasped before Buddha, replied: "Indeed, I am cognisant of no such [imperishable thing]."

Buddha said: "I will now explain to you the character of that 'nature' which admits of neither birth nor death. Maharajah: When you were a little child, how old were you when you first saw the River Ganges?" The Rajah replied: "When I was three years old, my tender mother led me by the hand to pay my devotions by this stream.". . .

Buddha said: "Maharajah, let us take up your own illustration respecting your gradual alteration of appearance, through every decade of your life. You say that at three years of age you saw this river; tell me then, when you were thirteen years old, what sort of appearance had this river then?" The Rajah replied: "Just the same as it had when I was three years old; and now I am sixty-two there is no alteration in its appearance."

Buddha said: "You now are become decrepit, white-haired, and wrinkled in face, and so your face has grown during successive years. Tell me, then, has the sight which enabled you to see the Ganges in former years become also wrinkled and increasingly so with your years?" The King answered: "No! World-honoured One."

Buddha said: "Maharajah! although, then, your face has become wrinkled, yet your power of sight has in its natured altered not. But that which becomes old and decrepit is in its nature changeable, and that which does not become so is unchangeable. That which changes is capable of destruction, but that which changes not must be from it origin incapable of birth or death." . . .

Ananda addressed Buddha, saying: "World-honoured! if this sight-power is the same as my mysterious nature, then this nature of mine ought to be clear to me; and if this sight-power is the same as my true nature, then what is my mind, so-called, and what my body?". . .

Buddha replied: "Suppose, then, that in the exercise of this mysterious and excellently glorious vision, you are observing things around you, tell me in what does the 'self'[1] of this power consist—is it due to the bright light of the sun? or is it attributable to the presence of darkness? is it the existence of space which constitutes the groundwork of this 'self'? or is it the presence of obstacles that constitutes this self? Ananda! if the bright presence of light is the groundwork, then, as this presence is the substantial basis of vision, what can be the meaning of seeing 'darkness'? If space is the basis of this 'self-caused' power, then, how can there be such a thing as an interruption of sight by any obstacle? or, if any of the various accidents of darkness be considered as the substantial basis of the 'self,' then, in the daylight the power of seeing light ought to disappear. . . .

"You should be satisfied, therefore, that this subtle power of sight, essentially glorious, depends not for its existence, either on cause or connection; it is not what is termed 'self-caused,' nor yet is it the opposite of this. . . . It is independent of all conditions and also of all phenomena. . . .

"Therefore, Ananda! you ought to know that when you see the light, the seeing does not depend on the light; when you see the darkness, the seeing does not depend on the

[1] "Dynamic essence" would perhaps be a good rendering of this word here.

darkness; when you see space, the seeing is not concerned with the idea of space; and so also with the limitations of space."

d. The power of vision, though changeless, is not, as such, absolute. What is absolute and why?

"These four deductions being settled, then I proceed to say that when we exercise the power of sight through the medium of this very sight-power, even then, seeing does not depend on this sight-power; nay, even while 'seeing,' we may be still at a distance from 'true sight,'—nor by the exercise of sight do we necessarily exercise the power of 'true sight.' . . .

"Ananda! consider a man whose eye is afflicted with a cataract: at night, when the light of the lamp shines before him, he thinks he sees a round shadow encircling the flame, composed of the five colours interlacing one another.

"What think you with regard to the perception of this round effulgence encircling the flame of the night lamp—is the beautiful colour in the lamp, or is it in the eye? Ananda! if it is in the lamp, then why does not a man whose sight is healthy see it? If it is in the sight of the person, then, as it is the result of an act of vision, what name shall we give to the power that produces these colours? . . .

"We conclude, therefore, that the object looked at, i.e., the flame, is dependent on the lamp, but that the circle is the result of imperfect vision. Now all such vision is connected with disease; however, to see the cause of the disease (the cataract) is curative of the disease. . . .

"So, then, just what you and other creatures see now, viz., mountains, rivers, countries, and lands; all this, I say, is the result of an original fault of sight . . . of the cataract, as it were, on the true and ever-glorious power of sight which I possess.

"If, then, this ordinary power of sight be, as it were, a cataract on the eye of my true sight, it follows, as a matter of course, that the pure and bright mind of my true knowledge in seeing all these unreal associations is not afflicted with this imperfection: that which understands error is not itself in error; so that, having laid hold of this true idea of sight, there will be no further meaning in such expressions as 'hearing by the ears,' or 'knowing by the sight.'

"This faculty, then, which we, and all the twelve species of creatures, possess, and which we call sight—this is the same as the cataract on the eye—it is the imperfection of true sight; but that true and original power of vision which has become thus perverted, and is in its nature without imperfection—that cannot properly be called by the same name.". . .

At this time, Ananda and all the great congregation, gratefully attentive to the words of Buddha Tathagata, as he opened out these abstruse points of his argument, their bodies and minds both worn out with their exertion, obtained illumination; this great assembly perceived that each one's mind was coextensive with the universe, seeing clearly the empty character of the universe as plainly as a leaf or trifling thing in the hand, and that all things in the universe are all alike merely the excellently bright and primeval mind of Bodhi, and that this mind is universally diffused, and comprehends all things within itself.

And still reflecting, they beheld their generated bodies, as so many grains of dust in the wide expanse of the universal void, now safe, now lost; or as a bubble of the sea, sprung from nothing and born to be destroyed. But their perfect and independent soul [they beheld] as not to be destroyed, but remaining ever the same; it is identical with the substance of Buddha. . . .

[Buddha now speaks] "This unity alone in the world is boundless in its reality, and being boundless is yet one. Though in small things, yet it is great; though in great things, yet it is small. Pervading all things, present in every minutest hair, and yet including the infinite worlds in its embrace; enthroned in the minutest particle of dust, and yet turning the great wheel of the Law; opposed to all sensible phenomena; it is one with Divine Knowledge; it is manifested as the effulgent Nature of the Divine Intelligence of Tathagata.". . .

4. Ultimate Reality Transcends What Can Be Expressed in Words

The document, here employed, in abbreviated form, presents the teaching of Hsi Yun, one of the Ch'an (or Zen) masters who lived about 840 A.D. His teaching is reported by P'ei Hsiu, an official and scholar who became a student under Hsi Yun. It gives a more or less systematic disclosure of Ch'an philosophy.

First, it defends the doctrine with which we are now familiar, that universal mind is alone real. This result is then used to explain why one must abandon seeking for anything; universal mind is realized by the cessation of all seeking and by leaving behind the analytic discriminations it uses and trusts. This step is achieved in a flash of sudden awakening.

But at this point the argument shifts. The reader is supposed to be ready now to see that mind itself, and the categories by which it has been explained, are self-contradictory. The real truth lies beyond any kind of verbal expression. This conclusion is ruthlessly applied even to such central Buddhist ideas as that of the Dharma. Buddha was, of course, aware of the truth on these matters, but in his compassion he communicated partial insights; their purpose was to lead people to the stage where they could achieve this fuller realization.

Again comes a shift, this time to the completely nonrational Ch'an technique of using words, not to answer an objector's question but to discourage him from asking it. It is hoped that he may now be able to attain the awareness that the real difficulty lies not so much in his questions being unanswerable as in his continuing in the state of mind that leads him to ask them. This state—of confidence in the power of analytic reason—is precisely that out of which he needs to awake.

The procedure of this essay constitutes as drastic a challenge to the presuppositions of Western philosophy as can well be imagined.

The Master said to me: "All the Buddhas and all sentient beings are nothing but universal mind, besides which nothing exists. This mind, which has always existed, is unborn and indestructible. It is not green nor yellow, and has neither form nor appearance. It does not belong to the categories of things which exist or do not exist, nor can it be reckoned as being new or old. It is neither long nor short, big nor small, but transcends all limits, measures, names, speech, and every method of treating it concretely. It is the substance that you see before you—begin to reason about it and you at once fall into error. It is like the boundless void which cannot be fathomed or measured.

This universal mind alone is the Buddha and there is no distinction between the Buddha and sentient beings, but sentient beings are attached to particular forms and so seek for Buddhahood outside it. By their very seeking for it they produce the contrary effect of losing it, for that is using the Buddha to seek for the Buddha and using mind to grasp mind. Even though they do their utmost for a full kalpa, they will not be able to attain to it. They do not know how to put a stop to their thoughts and forget their anxiety. The Buddha is directly before them, for this (universal) mind is the Buddha and the Buddha is all living beings. It is not the less for being manifested in ordinary beings, nor is it greater for being manifested in the Buddha.

"As to the merits, countless as the sands of the Ganges, which come from performing the six paramitas[1] and vast numbers of similar practices, since you are fundamentally complete in every respect, you should not try to supplement that perfection by such meaningless practices. When there is occasion for them, perform acts of charity, and, when the occasion has passed, remain quiescent. If you are not absolutely convinced that this [mind] is the Buddha, and are attached to the forms, practices, and performances whereby merit is achieved, your way of thinking has no connection with reality and is quite incompatible with the Way. The mind IS the Buddha, nor is there any other Buddha or any other mind. It is bright and spotless as the void, having no form or appearance whatsoever. To make use of the mind to think [in the ordinary sense of the word] is to leave the substance and attach yourself to forms. The Buddha who has always existed exhibits no such attachment to forms. To practice the six paramitas and a myriad similar practices with the intention of becoming a Buddha thereby is to advance by stages, but the Buddha who has always existed is not a Buddha of stages. Only awake to universal mind, and realise that there is nothing whatsoever to be attained. This is the real Buddha. The Buddha and all sentient beings are universal mind and nothing else. . . .

"This universal mind is no mind [in the ordinary sense of the word] and is completely detached from form. So it is with the Buddhas and sentient beings. If they (the latter)

[1] "Perfect duties." See above, p. 145.

can only rid themselves of analytic thinking[2] they will have accomplished everything. . . .

"Our original Buddha-nature is, in all truth, nothing which can be apprehended. It is void, omnipresent, silent, pure; it is glorious and mysterious peacefulness, and that is all which can be said. You yourself must awake to it, fathoming its depths. That which is before you is it in all its entirety and with nothing whatsoever lacking. Even if you go through all the stages of a Bodhisattva's progress towards Buddhahood, stage by stage, when at last, by a single flash of thought, you attain to full realisation, you will only be realising your original Buddha-nature and by all the foregoing stages you will not have added a single thing to it. You will merely regard those kalpas of work and achievement as nothing but unreal actions performed in a dream. . . .

"This pure mind, the source of everything, shines on all with the brilliance of its own perfection, but the people of the world do not awake to it, regarding only that which sees, hears, feels, and knows as mind. Because their understanding is veiled by their own sight, hearing, feeling, and knowledge, they do not perceive the spiritual brilliance of the original substance. If they could only eliminate all analytic thinking in a flash, that original substance would manifest itself like the sun ascending through the void and illuminating the whole universe without hindrance or bounds. Therefore, if students of the Way only regard seeing, hearing, feeling, and knowing as their [proper] activities, upon being deprived of these perceptions, their way towards [an understanding of] mind is cut off and they find nowhere to enter. You have but to recognize that real mind is expressed in these perceptions, but is not dependent on them on the one hand, nor separate from them on the other. You should not start reasoning from such perceptions, nor allow your thinking to stem from them, yet you should refrain from seeking universal mind apart from them or abandoning them in your pursuit of the Dharma. Neither hold to them, abandon them, dwell in them, nor cleave to them, but exist independently of all that is above, below, or around you, for there is no-

[2] I use this phrase, as a clearer rendering, wherever Chu Ch'an uses the word "mentation."

where in which the Way cannot be followed.

"When the people of the world listen for the Way, all the Buddhas proclaim the doctrine of universal mind. If it is held that there is something to be realised or attained apart from mind and, thereupon, mind is used to seek it, [that implies] a failure to understand that mind and the object of its search are one. Mind cannot be used to seek something from mind, for even after the passage of millions of kalpas, the day of success would never come. Such a method cannot be compared to immediately putting a stop to all analytic thinking, which is the fundamental dharma. Suppose a warrior, who did not realise he was wearing a pearl (which he had thought to be lost) on his forehead, were to seek for it elsewhere; though he were to traverse the whole universe, he would never find it. But if a knowing fellow were to point it out to him, he would immediately realise that it was still in its old place. Therefore, if students of the Way are mistaken about their own real mind, not recognising it as the Buddha, they will accordingly seek elsewhere, indulging in various practices and achievements, and relying upon such graduated progress to attain realisation. But after aeons of diligent searching, they will still be unable to attain to the Way. Such methods cannot be compared to immediately putting a stop to all analytic thinking, in the certain knowledge that there is nothing which has absolute existence, nothing on which to lay hold, nothing on which to rely, nothing in which to abide, nothing subjective or objective. It is by not allowing wrong thinking to take place that you will realise Bodhi[3] and, at the moment of realisation, you will but be realising the Buddha who has always existed in your own mind. Kalpas of striving will prove to have been so much wasted effort, just as, when the warrior found the pearl, he merely discovered what had been on his own forehead all the time, and just as his finding of it was not dependent on his efforts to find it elsewhere. . . .

"If students of the Way desire to become Buddhas, they need not study anything of the Dharma whatsoever. They should only study how to avoid seeking for or clinging to anything. If nothing is sought, the mind will remain in its 'unborn' state and, if nothing is clung to, the mind will not

[3] "Illumination."

go through the process of destruction. That which is neither born nor destroyed is the Buddha. The eighty-four thousand methods for counteracting the eighty-four thousand forms of delusion are merely figures of speech for attracting people towards conversion. In fact none of them exist. Relinquishment [of everything] is the Dharma and he who understands this is a Buddha, but the renunciation of ALL delusions leaves no Dharma on which to lay hold.

"If the student of the Way wishes to understand the real mystery, he need only put out of his mind attachment to anything whatsoever. To say that the real Dharmakaya[4] of the Buddha is like the void means that it actually is void and that the void is in fact the Dharmakaya. . . . The void and the Dharmakaya do not differ from each other, neither do sentient beings and Buddhas, the phenomenal world and Nirvana, or delusion and Bodhi. When all such forms are left behind—that is Buddha. Ordinary people look outwards, while followers of the Way look into their own minds, but the real Dharma is to forget both the external and the internal. The former is easy enough, the latter very difficult. Men are afraid to forget their own minds, fearing to fall through the void with nothing to which they can cling. They do not know that the void is not really void but the real realm of the Dharma. This spiritually enlightened nature is without beginning or end, as old as space, neither subject to birth nor destruction, neither existing nor not-existing, neither defiled nor pure, neither clamorous nor silent, neither old nor young, occupying no space, having neither inside nor outside, size nor form, colour nor sound. It cannot be looked for or sought, comprehended by wisdom or knowledge, explained in words, contacted materially or reached by meritorious achievement. . . .

"If a man, when he is about to die, can only regard the five aggregates of his consciousness as void, the four elements which compose his body as not constituting an ego, his true mind as formless and still, his true nature not as something which commenced at his birth and will perish at his death but as remaining utterly motionless, his mind and the objects of his perceptions as one—if he can only awake to this in a flash and remain free from the entangle-

[4] "Essential substance" would be a good rendering here.

ments of the Triple World,[5] he will indeed be one who leaves the world without the faintest tendency towards rebirth. If he should behold the lovely sight of all the Buddhas coming to welcome him, surrounded by every kind of splendour, and yet feel no desire to go towards them; if he should behold all sorts of evil forms surrounding him and yet have no feeling of fear, but remain oblivious of self and at one with the Absolute, he will indeed achieve the formless state. . . .

"Since the mind of the Bodhisattva is like the void, everything is relinquished by it. When analytic thinking concerning the past does not take place, that is relinquishment of the past. When analytic thinking concerning the present does not take place, that is relinquishment of the present. When analytic thinking concerning the future does not take place, that is relinquishment of the future. This is called complete relinquishment of the Triple World. Since the time when the Tathagata entrusted Kasyapa with the Dharma until now, the mystical transmission has been from mind to mind, yet these minds were identical with each other. A transmission of void cannot be made through words, and any transmission in concrete terms cannot be that of the Dharma. Hence the mystical transmission is made from mind to mind and those minds are identical with each other. It is hard to come in contact either with one who is capable of transmitting or with that which is transmitted, so that few have received this doctrine.

"In fact, however, mind is not really mind and the reception of the transmission not really reception. . . .

"When the Tathagata was alive, he wished to preach the Vehicle of the Truth, but people would not have believed him and, by scoffing at him, would have become immersed in the sea of sorrow. On the other hand, if he had said nothing, that would have been selfishness, and he would not have been able to spread widely the knowledge of the mysterious Way for the benefit of all sentient beings. So he adopted the expedient of preaching the Three Vehicles.[6] As, however, these vehicles include both the greater and the lesser, unavoidably there is both shallowness and depth (in the teaching as a whole). None of them represents the

[5] The worlds of the past, present, and future.
[6] See above, p. 146 ff.

real Dharma. So it is said that there is only a One-Vehicle Way for, wherever there is division into this or that, there is no truth. However, there is no way of expressing universal mind. Therefore the Tathagata called Kasyapa to the Seat of the Law and commanded him to practise this branch of the Dharma separately, saying that, when a silent understanding of it is obtained, the state of Buddhahood is reached."

Question: "What is the Way and what must one do to follow it?"

Answer: "Is then the Way something objective? [For that is what] your wish to follow it [implies]."

Question: "What are the instructions for practising Dhyana[7] and studying the Way which have been transmitted by all the various teachers?"

Answer: "Words which are used to attract the dull-witted should not be relied upon."

Question: "If these teachings are meant to attract the dull-witted, I have not heard the Dharma which is intended for people of the highest capacity."

Answer: "If they are really people of the highest capacity, where can they find others to be followed? If they seek from within themselves they will still find nothing tangible. How much less can they do so from elsewhere? You should not look to what, in instructing others, is called the Dharma, for what Dharma could that be?"

Question: "Then we should not seek for anything at all?"

Answer: "By conceding this you would save yourself a lot of mental effort."

Question: "But in this way everything would be eliminated. There cannot be just nothing."

Answer: "Who teaches that there is nothing? What is this nothing? [But you implied that] you wanted to *seek* for something."

Question: "Since there is no need to seek, why do you also say that we should not eliminate everything?"

Answer: "If you do not seek, that is enough. Who told you to eliminate anything? Observe the Void which lies before your eyes. How can you set about eliminating it?"

[7] "Meditation." This is the Sanskrit word for which Ch'an and Zen are transliterations.

Question: "If I can reach to this Dharma, will it prove to be like the Void?"

Answer: "When have I said to you of the Void that it is like or unlike something? I spoke in that way as a temporary expedient, but you are reasoning [literally] from it."

Question: "Do you mean, then, that one should not reason so?"

Answer: "I have not prevented you, but reasoning is related to attachment. When attachment arises, wisdom is shut out."

Question: "Should we, then, not allow any attachment to arise from it [the search for the Dharma]?"

Answer: "If attachment does not arise, who can say what is right [or wrong]?"

Question: "When I spoke to your Reverence, just now, in what way was I mistaken?"

Answer: "You are one who does not understand what is said to him. What is this about being mistaken?"

Question: "Up to now, everything you have said has been in the nature of refutation, but none of it contains any guidance as to what is the true Dharma."

Answer: "The true Dharma contains no confusion but, by implying such a question you make confusion for yourself. What is this 'true Dharma' which you seek?"

Question: "Since I have given rise to confusion by my question, what is your Reverence's answer [to my problem]?"

Answer: "Observe things as they are and do not worry about other people." He also said: "Take the case of a mad dog which barks at anything that moves. He does the same when it is only the wind stirring the grass and leaves."

"Regarding this Dhyana Sect of ours, since the doctrine was first transmitted, it has never been taught that people should seek [empirical] knowledge or look for explanations of things. We merely talk about 'studying the Way' using the phrase simply as a term to arouse people's interest. In fact, the Way cannot be studied. If concepts based on [factual] study are retained, they only result in the Way being misunderstood." . . .

Question: "Since there is nothing on which to lay hold, how should the Dharma be transmitted?"

Answer: "It is transmitted from mind to mind."

Question: "If mind is used for this puropse, how can it be said that mind does not exist?"

Answer: "Obtaining absolutely nothing is called receiving transmission from mind to mind. The understanding of mind implies [the realisation that] there is no mind and no Dharma."

Question: "If there is no mind and no Dharma, what is meant by 'transmission'?"

Answer: "It is because you people, on hearing of transmission from mind to mind, take it to mean that there is something to be obtained, that Bodhidharma said:

" 'The nature of the mind, when understood,
No human words can compass or disclose.
Enlightenment is naught to be obtained,
And he that gains it does not say he knows.'

"If I were to make this clear to you, I doubt if you could stand up to such knowledge." . . .

"If you will now and at all times, whether walking, standing, sitting, or lying, only concentrate on eliminating analytic thinking, at long last you will inevitably discover the truth. Because your strength is insufficient you may not be able to leap beyond the phenomenal sphere with a single jump but, after three, five, or perhaps ten years, you will certainly have made a good beginning and will be able to go on of your own accord. It is because you are not capable of this [eliminating analytic thinking] that [you feel] the necessity of using your mind to 'study Dhyana' and 'study the Way.' How will the Dharma be able to help you? So it is said: 'All that was spoken by the Tathagata was for the purpose of influencing men.' It was like using yellow leaves for gold to stop the crying of a child, and was decidedly not real. If you take it for something real, you are not one of our sect and, moreover, what relation can it have to your real self? So the sutra says: '[To know that] in reality there is not the smallest thing which can be grasped is called supreme, perfect wisdom.' If you can understand this meaning, you will then see that the Way of the Buddhas and the way of the devils are equally wrong. In reality, everything is pure and glistening, neither square nor round, big nor small, long nor short; it is beyond passion and phenomena, ignorance and Enlightenment." . . .

Stepping into the public hall, [His Reverence] said:

"The knowledge of many things cannot compare for excellence with giving up the search. The sage is one who puts himself outside the range of objectivity. There are not different kinds of mind, and there is no doctrine which can be taught."

As there was no more to be said, everybody went away. . . .

PART VI: Devotional Buddhism in China and Japan

Introduction

We return now to Mahayana literature that is devotional rather than philosophical. And we shall specifically have in mind the spread of Mahayana Buddhism in China and Japan, where expressions of its devotional spirit naturally reflect ideals and emphases that are characteristic of these two peoples. In Tibet and Mongolia, Buddhism took forms quite divergent from those typical of any of the other Buddhist countries; it has seemed best not to include any samples of these.

There are devotional writings, of course, which reveal the point of view of each of the many sub-schools of Mahayana Buddhism. But by far the majority of those which have exercised a wide appeal, especially in China and Japan, express either the viewpoint of the Pure Land School or that of the Meditation School ("Ch'an" in China, "Zen" in Japan). Accordingly, the following selections are chosen from the literature, so far as it is available in English, of these two schools. The sutra from which the brief selection on the layman's ideal is taken, though different in origin, became very popular in the Mahayana countries, particularly in Japan, and its exaltation of the Buddhist layman is in harmony with one of the major developments of the Pure Land perspective (notably that revealed by the Shin sect in Japan), and also with one of the emphases in Zen.

The central theme of the Pure Land School is faith in and devotion to Amitabha (in Japan, Amida). Amitabha, it will be recalled, achieved Buddhahood on the express condition that he could receive at death all who sincerely call upon his name and carry them to his Western Paradise, where they might pursue the quest for ultimate perfection under far happier auspices than when surrounded by the conditions of earthly existence. He made forty-eight vows, which are recited daily by many Chinese and Japanese Buddhists; the eighteenth of these is the vow in which this condition is specifically laid down. One cannot be long in company with Japanese Buddhists of the Jodo or Shin sects without hearing the phrase "nembutsu" ("calling upon the name of Amida Buddha"). The conception of the compassionate Bodhisattvas, who postpone their own entrance into Nirvana through loving concern for the salvation of others, though not at all limited to the Pure Land School, is in feeling and in basic doctrine essentially harmonious with its religious emphasis. These forms of Mahayana faith imply, in their underlying presuppositions, a philosophic idealism; at the heart of ultimate reality is the compassionate wisdom revealed in the Infinite Love and Unquenchable Light of Amitabha.

The ideas of the Meditation School presuppose rather a philosophic nihilism, interpreted in the manner explained in the previous section. Through the various recognized spiritual disciplines, with emphasis on open-hearted searching and on the use of competent instruction, the aspirant awakens into an experience and insight that transcend the possibility of explanation in rational speech and, for those who have achieved it, do not require any such explanation. Reasoned argument may be necessary in the process of guiding seekers toward this awakening—as illustrated in Nagarjuna and Hsi Yun —but at the crucial point it must be turned against itself, revealing its own utter inadequacy and the inescapable need of leaving it behind. Many of the Ch'an and Zen masters developed a successful technique of shocking their disciples past this difficult point, by asking paradoxical questions which could only be answered by taking the leap to a superrational intuition.

What is the aspirant expected to trust when he sees that he can no longer trust reason? The "heart"—i.e., that capacity for comprehensive integrity in his nature which can use logical reason as long as it furthers his quest for reality and can transcend it when he sees it become an obstruction to the attainment of his goal.[1] Within the Meditation School the most important difference that historically appeared was between those who believed that "awakening" is a gradual proc-

[1] Similarities are obvious here with many schools of theologians, both Catholic and Protestant, in the West.

ess and those who held that it is gained in a sudden flash, only the preparatory activities being necessarily gradual.

A few words about the history of the Meditation School will not only be of interest on their own account but will also constitute a further introduction to some of the selections in this section. The origin of the school, according to its own interpretation, is an extreme illustration of the Mahayana teaching that Buddha only revealed at any given time as much truth as his followers were able to receive, and only to each disciple as deep a doctrine as he could comprehend. This school maintains that the Master was able to disclose his most profound insight only late in his life to Mahakasyapa,[2] the sole individual among his disciples who could understand it. Mahakasyapa thus became the first patriarch of the Meditation School; he handed on this esoteric wisdom to his successors, of whom, in India, there were twenty-seven. The twenty-eighth, Bodhidharma, left India and went to China, settling in Canton about 520 A.D. He became the first partriarch in China and transmitted the secret truth to five Chinese successors, the last of whom was Hui Neng who flourished around 675 to 700 A.D. One of the following selections is by Seng Ts'an, the third Chinese patriarch, and another is a sermon by Shen Hui, a prominent disciple of Hui Neng.

The first five selections represent the general orientation of the Pure Land School; they express devotional piety toward Amitabha or (in the case of the fifth selection) toward one of the revered Bodhisattvas.

The first selection contains one of the most popular descriptions of Amitabha's Western Paradise, reminding the Christian reader at many points of the glowing description of the heavenly Jerusalem in the Revelation of St. John.

The second is a similar description in the form of religious poetry. It has been traditionally ascribed to Hui Yuan, a Buddhist philosopher who lived about 400 A.D. This ascription is, however, questioned by some scholars who are experts in the history of Chinese Buddhism.

The third consists of a letter and a poem written by Honen Shonin, founder of the Jodo sect of Japanese Buddhism. He lived from 1133 to 1212 A.D. He had found himself unable to make progress in the path of the Buddha by any of the other recognized disciplines; but he discovered that by repeatedly calling upon the name of Amida, in sincere faith, the burden

[2] Or, simply, Kasyapa.

*on his heart was removed and assurance of ultimate salvation
was gained. The letter expounds the basic principles of his
teaching; the poems need no special comment.*

*In the fourth I have selected songs in praise of Amitabha
written by Shinran Shonin, a younger contemporary of Honen
and at first his disciple. Later he founded the Shin sect of
Japanese Buddhism, affirming in more uncompromising form
than Honen the doctrine of salvation by faith in Amida alone.
These songs were translated by Beatrice Lane Suzuki.*

*The fifth is of special interest to those accustomed to West-
ern ideas of hell. It brings out the fact that in the East hell
is not thought of as everlasting (except for those who make
it so by their continued evil conduct), and that the loving compassion of a Bodhisattva may be so deep that he wishes even to
share the tortures of hell, that he may bring hope to its inmates
and lead them to salvation. Kshitigarbha (Ti Ts'ang in Chinese)
vowed that he would assume whatever forms and use whatever
methods might be necessary in order to deliver all suffering
creatures, including those who languish in hell. The selection
describes the joyful and grateful meeting of the souls who have
found deliverance through his devoted love.*

1. The Pure Land of Amitabha

This world Sukhavati, Ananda, which is the world system
of the Lord Amitabha, is rich and prosperous, comfortable,
fertile, delightful, and crowded with many Gods and men.
And in this world system, Ananda, there are no hells, no
animals, no ghosts, no Asuras,[1] and none of the inauspi-
cious places of rebirth. And in this our world no jewels
make their appearance like those which exist in the world
system Sukhavati.

And that world system Sukhavati, Ananda, emits many
fragrant odours; it is rich in a great variety of flowers and
fruits, adorned with jewel trees, which are frequented by
flocks of various birds with sweet voices, which the Tathagata's miraculous power has conjured up. And these
jewel trees, Ananda, have various colours, many colours,
many hundreds of thousands of colours. They are variously
composed of the seven precious things, in varying com-
binations,[2] i.e. of gold, silver, beryl, crystal, coral, red

[1] See above, p. 158.
[2] This phrase abbreviates several pages of the text.

pearls, or emerald. Such jewel trees, and clusters of banana trees and rows of palm trees, all made of precious things, grow everywhere in this Buddha-field. On all sides it is surrounded with golden nets, and all around they are covered with lotus flowers made of all the precious things. Some of the lotus flowers are half a mile in circumference, others up to ten miles. And from each jewel lotus issue thirty-six hundred thousand kotis of rays. And at the end of each ray there issue thirty-six hundred thousand kotis of Buddhas, with golden-coloured bodies, who bear the thirty-two marks of the superman, and who, in all the ten directions, go into countless world systems, and there demonstrate Dharma.

And further, Ananda, in this Buddha-field there are nowhere any mountains—black mountains, jewel mountains, Sumerus,[3] kings of mountains, circular mountains or great circular mountains. But the Buddha-field is everywhere even, delightful like the palm of the hand, and in all its parts the ground contains a great variety of jewels and gems. . . .

And many kinds of rivers flow along in this world system Sukhavati. There are great rivers there, one mile broad, and up to fifty miles broad and twelve miles deep. And all these rivers flow along calmly; their water is fragrant with manifold agreeable odours; in them there are bunches of flowers to which various jewels adhere, and they resound with various sweet sounds. And the sound which issues from these great rivers is as pleasant as that of a musical instrument, which consists of hundreds of thousands of kotis of parts, and which, skilfully played, emits a heavenly music. It is deep, commanding, distinct, clear, pleasant to the ear, touching the heart, delightful, sweet, pleasant, and one never tires of hearing it; it always agrees with one and one likes to hear it, like the words 'Impermanent, peaceful, calm, and not-self.' Such is the sound that reaches the ears of those beings.

And, Ananda, both the banks of those great rivers are lined with variously scented jewel trees, and from them bunches of flowers, leaves, and branches of all kinds hang down. And if those beings wish to indulge in sports full of heavenly delights on those riverbanks, then, after they have

[3] The standard Indian illustration of a high mountain.

stepped into the water, the water in each case rises as high as they wish it to—up to the ankles, or the knees, or the hips, or their sides, or their ears. And heavenly delights arise. Again, if beings wish the water to be cold, for them it becomes cold; if they wish it to be hot, for them it becomes hot, to suit their pleasure. And those rivers flow along, full of water scented with the finest odours, and covered with beautiful flowers, resounding with the sounds of many birds, easy to ford, free from mud, and with golden sand at the bottom. And all the wishes those beings may think of, they all will be fulfilled, as long as they are rightful.

And as to the pleasant sound which issues from the water (of these rivers), that reaches all the parts of this Buddha-field. And everyone hears the pleasant sound he wishes to hear, i.e., he hears of the Buddha, the Dharma, the Sangha, of the [six] perfections, the [ten] stages, the powers, the grounds of self-confidence, of the special dharmas of a Buddha, of the forms of analytic knowledge, of emptiness, the signless, and the wishless, of the uneffected, the unborn, of non-production, non-existence, non-cessation, of calm, quietude and peace, of the great friendliness, the great compassion, the great sympathetic joy, the great evenmindedness, of the patient acceptance of things which fail to be produced, and of the acquisition of the stage where one is consecrated [as a Tathagata]. And, hearing this, one gains the exalted zest and joyfulness which is associated with detachment, dispassion, calm, cessation, Dharma, and brings about the state of mind which leads to the accomplishment of enlightenment. And nowhere in this world system Sukhavati does one hear of anything unwholesome, nowhere of the hindrances, nowhere of the states of punishment, the states of woe and the bad destinies, nowhere of suffering. Even of feelings which are neither pleasant nor unpleasant one does not hear here, how much less of suffering! And that, Ananda, is the reason why this world system is called the "Happy Land" [Sukhavati]. But all this describes it only in brief, not in detail. One aeon might well reach its end while one proclaims the reasons for happiness in the world system Sukhavati, and still one could not come to the end of [the enumeration of] the reasons for happiness.

Moreover, Ananda, all the beings who have been reborn

in this world system Sukhavati, who are reborn in it, or
who will be reborn in it, they will be exactly like the Para-
nirmitavasavartin Gods:[4] of the same colour, strength,
vigour, height and breadth, dominion, store of merit, and
keenness of super-knowledge; they enjoy the same dresses,
ornaments, parks, palaces and pointed towers, the same
kind of forms, sounds, smells, tastes and touchables, just
the same kinds of enjoyment. And the beings in the world
system Sukhavati do not eat gross food, like soup or raw
sugar; but whatever food they may wish for, that they perceive as eaten, and they become gratified in body and mind,
without there being any further need to throw the food
into the body. And if, after their bodies are gratified, they
wish for certain perfumes, then the whole of that Buddha-
field becomes scented with just that kind of heavenly perfume. But if someone does not wish to smell that perfume,
then the perception of it does not reach him. In the same
way, whatever they may wish for comes to them, be it
musical instruments, banners, flags, etc.; or cloaks of different colours, or ornaments of various kinds. If they wish
for a palace of a certain colour, distinguishing marks, con-
struction, height and width, made of various precious
things, adorned with hundreds of thousands of pinnacles,
while inside it various heavenly woven materials are spread
out, and it is full of couches strewn with beautiful cushions
—then just such a palace appears before them. In those
delightful palaces, surrounded and honoured by seven
times seven thousand Apsaras,[5] they dwell, play, enjoy and
disport themselves.

. . . And the beings who are touched by the winds,
which are pervaded with various perfumes, are filled with
a happiness as great as that of a monk who has achieved
the cessation of suffering.

And in this Buddha-field one has no conception at all
of fire, sun, moon, planets, constellations, stars, or blinding
darkness, and no conception even of day and night, except
[where they are mentioned] in the sayings of the Tathagata.
There is nowhere a notion of monks possessing private
parks for retreats.

And all the beings who have been born, who are born,

[4] See above, p. 31.
[5] Celestial nymphs.

who will be born in this Buddha-field, they all are fixed on the right method of salvation, until they have won Nirvana. And why? Because there is here no place for and no conception of the two other groups, i.e., of these who are not fixed at all, and those who are fixed on wrong ways. For this reason also that world system is called the "Happy Land." . . .

And further again, Ananda, in the ten directions, in each single direction, in Buddha-fields countless like the sands of the river Ganges, Buddhas and Lords countless like the sands of the river Ganges glorify the name of the Lord Amitabha, the Tathagata—praise him, proclaim his fame, extol his virtue. And why? Because all beings are incapable of falling away from the supreme enlightenment if they hear the name of the Lord Amitabha, and, on hearing it, with one single thought only raise their hearts to him with a resolve connected with serene faith.

And if any beings, Ananda, again and again reverently attend to this Tathagata, if they will plant a large and immeasurable root of good, having raised their hearts to enlightenment, and if they vow to be reborn in that world system, then, when the hour of their death approaches, that Tathagata Amitabha, the Arhat, the fully Enlightened One, will stand before them, surrounded by hosts of monks. Then, having seen that Lord, and having died with hearts serene, they will be reborn in just that world system Sukhavati. And if there are sons or daughters of good family, who may desire to see that Tathagata Amitabha in this very life, they should raise their hearts to the supreme enlightenment, they should direct their thought with extreme resoluteness and perseverance unto this Buddha-field, and they should dedicate their store of merit to being reborn therein.

2. The White Lotus Ode

What words can picture the beauty and breadth
Of that pure and glistening land?
That land where the blossoms ne'er wither from age,
Where the golden gates gleam like purest water—
The land that rises in terrace on terrace

Of diamond-clad steps and shining jade—
That land where there are none but fragrant bowers,
Where the Utpala lotus unfolds itself freely.
O hear the sweet tones from hillside and grove,
The All-Father's praise from the throats of the birds!

And the ages fly by in an endless chain,
Never broken by summer's or winter's change.
The burning sun can never more frighten.
The icy storms' power long ago is subdued.
The clouds full of light and the green-mantled forests
Now cradle all things in their endless peace.
Now the soul is set free from the haunts of darkness
And rests secure in the dwelling of truth.
See, all that was dim and beclouded on earth
Here is revealed, appropriated, secured.

There ne'er was a country so brightened with gladness
As the Land of the Pure far off to the West.
There stands Amitabha with shining adornments,
He makes all things ready for the Eternal Feast.
He draws every burdened soul up from the depths
And lifts them into his peaceful abode.
The great transformation is accomplished for the
    worm
Who is freed from the body's oppressive sorrows.
It receives as a gift a spiritual body,
A body which shines in the sea of spirits.

And who indeed is it with grace in his tones,
Who sends his smile out to the dwellings of the
    suffering;
And who indeed is it whose glance is like the sun
Who shows his compassion on life and is victor?
Yes, it is God himself, who sits on the throne
And, by his Law, redeems from all need.
With gold-adorned arm, with crown of bright jewels,
With power over sin, over grief, over death.
None other is like to our God in his greatness,
And none can requite his compassion's great power!

3. Honen's Letter and Poems*

I have carefully examined into the qualifications necessary in these latter evil days for all sentient beings to attain birth into the Pure Land of Perfect Bliss, and I find that no matter how meagre one's religious practices may be, he should not give way to doubt, for ten repetitions of the sacred name are quite enough, indeed even one. And it matters not how great a sinner a man may be, he should not give way to doubts; for, as it says, Amida does not hate a man, however deeply stained with sin he may be. And though the times be ever so degenerate, let him not doubt. For even sentient beings who will live in the period after the Law has perished, can be born into the Pure Land. How much more men of our own times! Even though we be indeed unclean, we need not doubt the possibility of attaining *Ojo*,[1] for it is specifically stated that we are but ordinary mortals, tainted with evil passions.

There are indeed many Pure Lands in the ten quarters of the universe, but we seek for the Pure Land in the West, because it is in this one that all sentient beings, who have committed the ten evil deeds and the five deadly sins, can find *Ojo*. The reason why we give ourselves up to Amida alone among all the Buddhas, is that He welcomes those who have repeated His sacred name, even three or five times. And the reason we choose the *nembutsu*[2] out of all the other forms of religious discipline is because it is the one prescribed in the Original Vow of that Buddha. If we are but born into the Pure Land by embarking upon Amida's Original Vow, then none of our cherished desires remain unfulfilled. And this embarking upon the ship of the Original Vow depends upon our faith.

It is a joy beyond all other joys to have attained all these things that are so difficult of attainment: first of all being born a human being, then coming in contact with the Original Vow, then having one's religious aspirations aroused, then getting free from the long round of transmi-

* Coates and Ishizuka, *Honen the Buddhist Saint,* Copyright, 1925, by The Chion-in, Kyoto, pp. 402-06, 542-45.
[1] Birth in the Pure Land.
[2] Calling on the name of Amida Buddha.

213

grations, and finally being born into the Pure Land. While believing that even the man who is so sinful that he has committed the ten evil deeds and the five deadly sins may be born into the Pure Land, as far as you are concerned, be not guilty even of the smallest sins. And if a sinful man may thus be born into that land, how much more a good man! And as to this act of repeating the *nembutsu,* believe that ten repetitions, yea even one, will never be in vain, and so continually practise it without ceasing. If by repeating the *nembutsu* once a man may thus reach *Ojo,* how much more so if he repeats it many times!

As Amida Buddha has already verified the words of His Vow, "unless it happens as I vow, I shall not accept enlightenment," and is now in reality in that blissful land, as He said, He surely will come and meet us when we are about to die. The revered Shaka[3] himself will indeed rejoice when he looks with delight upon our escape from the transmigratory round by following his teachings, and in like manner will also all the Buddhas of the six quarters rejoice, when they see that we have, by believing what they have endorsed, been born into that Pure Land, from whose pure blessedness we shall never fall.

Let your joy, therefore, be as high as the heavens above and as deep as the earth beneath. Let us then, whether walking, standing, sitting, or lying, or wherever we are, always be returning thanks for the great blessedness of having in this life come in contact with the Original Vow of the Amida Buddha. It is in these words of the Vow where He graciously says, "Or even ten times calling" that we should above all put our trust, and it is to the clause where Zendo[4] says that of a certainty we shall be born into the Pure Land, that we should above all else direct our faith. . . .

You should not say, as some do, that because you put your trust in Amida and believe in the *nembutsu,* it is all right to have nothing to do with the merciful vows of the many Buddhas and Bodhisattvas. On the other hand you should not think lightly of despising in the least those excellent *Hokke* and *Hannya* Sutras. Even though you may believe in the Amida Buddha, your faith is quite one-sided

[3] Sakyamuni, i.e., Gautama Buddha.
[4] The Chinese founder of the Pure Land doctrine (A.D. 613-681).

if you despise the many Buddhas, or doubt Shaka's holy teachings. If your faith is not right, it is not in harmony with the mind of the Buddha Amida, and it is certain His merciful Vow has nothing to do with you.

There are those who say that the effort to avoid sin and improve oneself is making light of Amida's Vow, and the frequent repetition of the *nembutsu,* and the effort to pile up a large number of them, is equivalent to doubting his saving power, and many such like things one sometimes hears. But do not for a moment be misled by such misconceptions. Is there any place in any of the sutras where Amida encourages men to sin? Certainly not. Such things come from those who make no effort to get away from their own evil deeds, and who go on in their former sinful life. By such utterly unreasonable and false sayings they would mislead ignorant men and women, urging them forward in the committing of sin and stirring up their evil passions within them. Now such persons are nothing less than a company of devils, and their work heathenish, and you ought to think of them as enemies to your reaching birth into that Pure Land of Perfect Bliss. Again, to say that frequent repetitions of the sacred name mean the encouragement of the principle of self-effort[5] shows utter ignorance of facts and is a deplorable blunder. Even one repetition or two of the sacred name must be said to be the *nembutsu* of salvation by one's own power, if one does it with that thought in his heart; while a hundred or a thousand repetitions day and night for a hundred or a thousand days, so long as one does it with an entire trust in the merits of the great Vow, looking up in confidence to Amida with every repetition, constitute the *nembutsu* of salvation by Amida's power alone. And so the *nembutsu* of those who possess the so-called mental states,[6] no matter how many times they may call upon the sacred name, moment by moment, day and night, can by no means be called the *nembutsu* of salvation by one's own power, so long as they are really looking up to Amida, and trusting to his saving power alone.

Again in reference to the three mental states, there are

---

[5] I.e., trust in one's own effort rather than in Amida's grace.
[6] See the next paragraph. The three are: sincerity, absence of doubt, and earnest longing for the Pure Land.

some who say that if a man understands them when he repeats the *nembutsu*, of course he will possess them, but in the case of ignorant people who do not know even the names of those states, how is it possible for them to have them? Now this too, I must repeat, is a great misconception. Even though one is so ignorant as not to know the names of these three mental states, if he only puts implicit trust in Amida's Vow, with no doubt in his heart at all, and thus calls upon the sacred name, he is already in possession of these mental states. And so, if one practises the *nembutsu* with this simple faith, these three mental states arise of their own accord within him. There are, then, even among the most unlettered, those who practise the *nembutsu*, and when they come to face death, they accomplish their birth into the Pure Land with complete composure of mind. . . .

[Poems handed down as Honen's by his disciples]:

The Seasons

O mist of spring, thou hidest all things beautiful and
    bright,
  As if there did not shine the true, imperishable light!

    I gaze and gaze each passing day
      On the geranium sweet,
    And for the happy day I yearn
      My Amida to meet.

    If from Buddha Amida
      My heart its col'ring gains,
    It will be like the beauteous boughs
      In autumn's crimson stains.

    If in the winter of our sin,
      Amida's name we call,
    Warm rays from Him will chase away
      The cold and snowdrifts all.

Sacrifice

Dear life itself is not too dear
    For woman's love to give.
For joys eternal, then, why fear
    To sacrifice and live?

My Mountain Home

Above the thatch of my mountain home
The white clouds morning and evening hover.
Ah! When shall the hour of that day come
That the *Ojo* purple[1] me shall cover?

Invocation Alone

Ill seems each occupation
That would free the heart from blame,
Compared with invocation
Of the Buddha's sacred name.

Seek the Land of Bliss in Youth

To seek the Land of Bliss
   In early years
Will leave for life's fair end
   No doubts or fears.

The Cicada

Like the cicada that has cast
Its shell but sings its rapturous lay,
The voice of him who calls His name
From the frail body of this clay,
His heart to scenes of Paradise
Already having flown away.

Amida's Light

There is no place where the moonlight
   Casts not its cheering ray;
With him who has the seeing eye
   Alone that light will stay.

Sincerity

In quest of *Ojo,* need it be that any fall?
Sincerity of heart is lacking, that is all.

Nembutsu

Ten times Amida's name shall pass my lips
      Ere I repose,
My last long slumber shall begin some time,
      And when—who knows?

[1] The rich color glowing over that which one is about to attain.

[Poems written by Honen's own hand]:

The Pine of a Thousand Years

Pine of a thousand earthly years,
    I dwell beneath thy shade,
Till by the Lord of Boundless Life
    My welcome home is made.

The Little Pine

'Tis called the little pine—I marvel why;
Its towering branches seem to touch the sky.

The Heart of Man

The heart of man is like the water of a mere:
You know not whether it will be turbid or clear.

Precious Memory

First in the Blessed Pure Land
    When I attain my birth,
Shall be the precious memory
    Of friends I left on earth.

The Glorious Vision

The Pure Land's glorious vision
    Is bliss that man may claim,
If he but worthily repeats
    Amida's Sacred Name.

4. Shinran's Songs to Amida

Since the attainment of Buddhahood by Amitabha,
Ten kalpas have now passed away;
The Light radiating from the Dharmakaya has no limits:
It illumines the world's blindness and darkness.

The Light of His wisdom is measureless,
All conditional forms without exception
Are enveloped in the dawning Light;
Therefore take refuge in the True Light.

Amida's Light is like a wheel radiating without bounds.
Buddha declared that all things embraced by His Light
Are freed from all forms of being and non-being.
Take refuge in the One who is universally enlightened.

The clouds of Light have, like space, no hindrances;
All that have obstructions are not impeded by them;
There is no one who is not embraced in His Soft Light;
Take refuge in Him who is beyond thought.

Nothing can be compared to His Pure Light;
The result of encountering this Light
Destroys all karma bondage:
So take refuge in Him who is the Ultimate Haven.

Amida Buddha's illumining Light is above all,
So he is called the Sovereign Buddha of Flaming Light,
The darkness of the three evil paths[1] is opened:
Take refuge in the Great Arhat.

The radiance of His Light of Truth surpasses all,
So He is called the Buddha of Pure Light;
Those who are embraced in the Light
Are cleansed from the dirt of karma and attain
　　　　emancipation.

However far His light illumines, love penetrates,
The joy of faith is attained,
So we are told.
Take refuge in the Great One who gives comfort.

He is known as the Buddha of the Light of Prajna[2]
Because He dispels the darkness of ignorance;
The Buddhas and the beings of the Three Vehicles
All join in praising Him.

As there is a constant flow of Light,
He is known as the Buddha of Constancy;
Because of perceiving the power of light with uninterrupted
　　　　faith,
We are born into the Pure Land.

[1] Those of hungry ghosts, the animal world, and hell.
[2] "Transcendental wisdom," the ultimate source of all knowledge.

As the Buddha of Light knows naught of measurement,
He is known as the Buddha of Unthinkable Light;
All other Buddhas praise the *Ojo*
And the virtues of Buddha Amida are extolled.

As His Wondrous Light transcends form and description,
He is known as the Buddha of Inexpressible Light;
His Light has the power to enlighten all beings:
So he is praised by all the Buddhas.

As His Light surpasses that of the Sun and the Moon,
He is known as the Sun-and-Moon-Surpassing Light;
Shakamuni could not praise Him enough:
Take refuge in the One who is peerless.

At the first discourse given by Amida,
The holy multitudes were beyond calculation;
Those who wish to go to the Pure Land
Should take refuge in the Buddha who commands great
        numbers.

The numberless great Bodhisattvas in the Land of Bliss
After one birth more will become Buddhas;
When they have taken refuge in the virtues of Fugen[3]
They will come back to this world in order to teach beings.

For the sake of all beings in the ten quarters
They gather up all the Dharma-treasures of Tathagatahood,
And to save them lead them to the Original Vow.
Take refuge in the Ocean of the Great Heart.

Together with Kwannon[4] and Seishi,[5]
He illumines the world with the Light of Mercy;
Leading all those in ripe condition for the Dharma,
He knows no time for rest.

Those who reach the Land of Purity and Happiness,
When they return to this world of five defilements
Like Buddha Shakamuni work without cessation
For the welfare of all beings.

[3] One of the great Mahayana Bodhisattvas. In Sanskrit, Samant-abhadra.
[4] Japanese for Avalokitesvara. (In Chinese, Kwan Yin.)
[5] Another famous Bodhisattva.

The miraculous power and self-mastery
Enjoyed by them is beyond calculation;
They have accumulated virtues beyond thought:
Take refuge in the Honoured One who is peerless.

Sravakas and Bodhisattvas in the Land of Happiness,
Men and gods all radiant in Prajna,
In form and appearance are equally majestic;
But different names are given according to this world.

They are incomparably perfect in features,
Exquisite in bodily form, their equals cannot be found;
Appearing from the Void, yet they have infinite form:
Take refuge in the Power to whom all beings are equal.

Those who aspire to the Land of Happiness
Must abide "in the group of perfect faith."[6]
None are to be found there who long for wrong or unsettled
      faith,
And they are praised by all the Buddhas.

When all beings in every condition within the ten quarters,
Endowed with all excellent virtues,
Hearing the name of Amida with sincerity of heart,
Attain faith; how they will rejoice at what they hear!

"Because of my Vow that if they should not be born [in
      the Pure Land]
I will not attain enlightenment."
When the right moment for faith arises, joy is instantly felt,
And rebirth is definitely confirmed, once for all.

The Buddha Land of Happiness, with everything belonging
      to it,
Is the product of the power of Dharmakara.[7]
There is nothing compared to it above or below the heav-
      ens:
Take refuge in the Great Mind-Power.

[6] The group of those who have no doubt of their birth in the Pure
Land.
[7] Amida's name while he was still in the stage of Bodhisattvahood.

The splendid views of the Land of Happiness,
Shakamuni with all his unobstructed wisdom declared
To be really beyond all expression:
Take refuge in the Buddha whose glory is beyond descrip-
tion.

Rebirth [in the Pure Land] for all the periods of time
Not only is assured for beings of this world,
But for all in the Buddha-lands of the ten quarters;
Their number is indeed measureless, numberless, and in-
calculable.

Those beings who, hearing the Holy Name of Amitabha
Buddha,
Feel joyous and adore him,
Will be given treasures of merit
And benefits great and incomparable.

Although the great chiliocosm may be filled with flames,
Yet he who hears the Holy Name of the Buddha,
Always in accord with steadfastness,
Will freely pass [to the Pure Land].

Amida's mysterious limitless Power
Is praised by innumerable Buddhas;
From the Buddha-lands in the East,
As many as the sands of the Ganges, numberless Buddhas
come.

From the Buddha-lands in the remaining nine quarters,
Come the Bodhisattvas to see him;
Shakamuni the Tathagata composing songs,
Praises his virtues infinite.

All the countless Bodhisattvas of the ten quarters,
In order to plant the root of merit,
Pay homage to the Bhagavat[8] and praise him in song:
Let all beings take refuge in Him.

[8] "Lord."

5. The Bodhisattva Who Saves Even From the Depths of Hell

At that time those beings who had been saved from perdition, thanks to the compassionate heart of Tathagata, met together with Ti-ts'ang in the Tao-li[1] heaven for a great assembly. In every section there were countless millions. They all came with incense and flowers, which they offered before the face of Buddha. These multitudes who now flocked around Ti-ts'ang before the throne never again need return to evil; for they have attained the highest and most all-embracing wisdom. These multitudes who have passed through endless kalpas of birth and death, birth and death, and have wandered through the two regions of pain, now stand in the Tao-li heaven with the proof of experience, for Ti-ts'ang's solemn pledges and his great all-embracing mercy have proved themselves effective. After having attained this place, their hearts are filled with the most unspeakable joy.

Now, without turning away their eyes for a moment, they look to Tathagata with holy veneration. And the "World-Honoured One" stretches out his golden arms and blesses the various forms in which the Bodhisattva Ti-ts'ang has incarnated himself through the endless kalpas. He lays his hands on their heads and says: "As I stand in the five unclean worlds and try to instruct and influence the refractory creatures there, I find that out of ten there are usually one or two who cling to evil. It is for this reason that I constantly take various forms and make use of countless different methods to save the unfortunate. I change myself into a heavenly god like Brahma, into a god of transmutations, into a king, a minister, or a relative of a minister. I manifest myself as a 'pi-ch'iu,'[2] or a nun, as a man who devotes himself to Buddhism in the quiet of his own home, as a woman who gives herself to meditation in the stillness of home. I do not hold obstinately to my Buddha body. I take upon myself all the above-mentioned bodily forms in order to be able to save all. You see how

[1] The central heaven, embracing all the others.
[2] Those at the second stage of spiritual advancement.

through these continuous kalpas I have tried, with pain and unceasing effort, to save all these rebellious creatures, and bring them to obedience, so that they may give up the false and devote themselves to the true. Nevertheless, there still remain some who are under the burden of sin's retribution. If they should fall completely into the power of evil, it would be a frightful time for them.

"As I stand here in the Tao-li heaven I call upon all, both those who now live in this world of sorrow, and those who shall live in that new world which shall issue forth at (Maitreya's) appearance. I desire to save all, so that they may escape from grief and want, and receive Buddha's mark on their bodies."

At this time all the various bodily incarnations of Ti-ts'ang were gathered together from the different worlds into one body. Tears ran from Ti-ts'ang's eyes and nose, as with heart-felt longing and deep sadness he looked up to Buddha and said:

"For endless kalpas I have been under Buddha's special guidance, so that I have received unspeakable divine strength and wisdom. This has prepared me to enter into the most varied physical forms. I have revealed myself in the most widely different worlds, in number as many as the sands of the river Ganges. In every one of these worlds I revealed myself in millions of forms. Every single incarnation has saved millions of people and led them to a reverent understanding of the 'three great jewels' [Buddha, the doctrine, and the order] as well as to eternal redemption from birth and death, and into the state of joy of Nirvana.

"Moreover, if there should still be anything lacking in the way of good works, be it but a hairbreadth, a grain of sand, or a speck of dust, I will carry it all on to completion.

"Therefore, thou World-honoured One, be not anxious for the generations that are to come! Be not anxious for the generations that are to come! Be not anxious for the generations that are to come!"

Then Buddha lifted up his voice and praised Ti-ts'ang, saying: "Good, good—I share your joy! When you shall have fulfilled this great promise and after endless kalpas shall have finished this work of salvation, then will you truly have shown yourself to be the possessor of the tenderest heart and the highest wisdom!"

Selections 6–9 express the orientation of the Ch'an School, with special emphasis on the doctrine of sudden awakening.

The sixth consists of two paragraphs from Tao Sheng, a philosopher who was contemporary with Hui Yüan (A.D. 400). He lived before the Ch'an School had, as such, become established in China, but he taught the doctrine of sudden awakening and gave it a reasoned defense. These paragraphs, translated by Dr. Walter Liebenthal, reveal the general philosophical position underlying this doctrine. What is necessary is to give up error and become an unruffled pond; then the sun of the Buddha will be reflected in us as he is.

The seventh is a popular poem by Seng Ts'an, third Ch'an patriarch in China (about A.D. 600). Note how, according to it, through trust in the heart we can leave behind, in a flash, the obstructing alternatives of logical reason, and can attain the transcendent realization that is our true goal. This does not separate us from the world of the senses, however; it is simply accepting that world in its true reality and meaning.

The eighth is a group of passages from a very interesting sermon by Shen Hui (died A.D. 760), a disciple of the sixth Ch'an patriarch. It teaches, in the form of an earnest exhortation, all the basic principles of the doctrine of sudden awakening. It is not necessary, Shen Hui holds, to engage in prolonged meditation as the arahats and pratyekabuddhas do; one should just throw away the errors due to the dust of evil passions; instantaneous realization is possible if the essential conditions for it are met. And when that realization comes one will see that all the concepts (Buddha, dharma, etc.) by which he had been helpfully guided up to that point are really, as rational concepts, meaningless. This sermon is also translated by Dr. Liebenthal.

The ninth selection illustrates the famous koan *device* of the Ch'an or Zen school. The master asks a question that is intrinsically incapable of being answered in any rational way. His purpose is to shock those of his disciples who are ready for it into a leap to the superrational insight of which the koan *can serve as the medium.*

In this particular illustration the lesson is that by the discriminations of analytic thought we have built a glass house in which we are now imprisoned. We outgrow our bottle and must get out. How? It is broken by clearly recognizing that it is of our own ignorant making.

6. Tao Sheng on Nirvana and the Buddha's Way

The Inner Order of Things is that of Nature. To get in mystical union with Nature is Illumination. Now, that Order is free from distinctive features; Illumination, however, implies change. (A problem is raised which I shall answer.) The basis of Existence is unchanging, unruffled, like the surface of a pond, as long as it is not stirred by unceasing reflections of outside objects. Error has ruffled its surface and thus we have lost mastery over our fate. We grope along for a way; when we have found it we desist from erroneous moves. Returning to the original perfect state, we wonder why we ever started on the journey. For we started from the goal. (This point has never been clear to me.) But when I studied the tendencies of life, I understood that Reality is not reflected in the images of what surrounds us here, but real is what existed before this began to exist.

The Cosmic Body of the Buddha is real; his Human Bodies are phenomenal, and shaped as they are needed in each case. How to understand this? To one who sees things as they really are, all illusions which he had formerly acquired vanish forever; in that moment his earthly career ends. Beyond the Three Worlds he lives in solitary bliss; in union with Cosmic Order he haunts the shapeless. This very shapelessness enables him to assume any shape; his very separation from the World places him in the midst of it. Though he is able to assume any shape, the actual shape is determined by our expectations. The Buddha cannot shape his Human Bodies; as a shadow answers a form, so he appears. His stature may be minute or enormous; his life may last long or short—these are reflections of the Buddha, produced by the expectations of various Beings; his Real Body is not among them.

If he is not called he does not appear. Not that he is not ready to appear, nay—Beings, by their indolence, cut themselves off from his presence and make it impossible for him to establish contact. The Buddha is like the sun; when he is high in the sky, all kinds of articles are reflected in a pond. The reflections and forms are shaped by the articles themselves, not by the sun. And there must be a clear pond, or else the Buddha cannot appear. Not that he does not want to appear, nay—the Beings themselves, if they do not fulfil the required condition, make it impossible for him to appear. It follows that the Buddhas, whether six chang or eight ch'ih tall, are nothing but images reflected in the pond of our heart. The Buddha is not an individual, how can there be two of them?

7. Seng Ts'an's Poem on Trust in the Heart

The Perfect Way is only difficult for those who pick and
    choose;
Do not like, do not dislike; all will then be clear.
Make a hairbreadth difference, and Heaven and Earth are
    set apart;
If you want the truth to stand clear before you, never be
    for or against.
The struggle between "for" and "against" is the mind's
    worst disease;
While the deep meaning is misunderstood, it is useless to
    meditate on Rest.
It[1] is blank and featureless as space; it has no "too little" or
    "too much";
Only because we take and reject does it seem to us not to
    be so.
Do not chase after Entanglements as though they were real
    things;
Do not try to drive pain away by pretending that it is not
    real;
Pain, if you seek serenity in Oneness, will vanish of its own
    accord.
Stop all movement in order to get rest, and rest will itself
    be restless;
Linger over either extreme, and Oneness is forever lost.
Those who cannot attain to Oneness in either case will fail.
To banish Reality is to sink deeper into the Real;
Allegiance to the Void implies denial of its voidness.
The more you talk about It, the more you think about It,
    the further from It you go;

[1] I.e., the Buddha-nature.

Stop talking, stop thinking, and there is nothing you will
    not understand.

Return to the Root and you will find the Meaning;

Pursue the Light, and you will lose its source;

Look inward, and in a flash you will conquer the Apparent
    and the Void.

For the whirligigs of Apparent and Void all come from
    mistaken views;

There is no need to seek Truth; only stop having views.

Do not accept either position,[2] examine it or pursue it;

At the least thought of "Is" and "Isn't," there is chaos and
    the Mind is lost.

Though the two exist because of the One, do not cling to
    the One;

Only when no thought arises are the Dharmas without
    blame.

No blame, no Dharmas; no arising, no thought.

The "doer" vanishes along with the deed,

The deed disappears when the doer is annihilated.

The deed has no function apart from the doer;

The doer has no function apart from the deed.

The ultimate Truth about both Extremes is that they are
    One Void.

In that One Void the two are not distinguished;

Each contains complete within itself the Ten Thousand
    Forms.

Only if we boggle over fine and coarse are we tempted to
    take sides.

In its essence the Great Way is all-embracing;

It is as wrong to call it easy as to call it hard.

Partial views are irresolute and insecure,

Now at a gallop, now lagging in the rear.

Clinging to this or to that beyond measure,

The heart trusts to bypaths that lead it astray.

Let things take their own course; know that the Essence

Will neither go nor stay;

Let your nature blend with the Way and wander in it free
    from care.

Thoughts that are fettered turn from Truth,

Sink into the unwise habit of "not liking."

[2] Adoption or rejection.

"Not liking" brings weariness of spirit; estrangements serve
    no purpose.

If you want to follow the doctrine of the One, do not rage
    against the World of the Senses.

Only by accepting the World of the Senses can you share
    in the True Perception.

Those who know most, do least; folly ties its own bonds.

In the Dharma there are no separate dharmas, only the
    foolish cleave

To their own preferences and attachments.

To use Thought to devise thoughts—what more misguided
    than this?

Ignorance creates Rest and Unrest; Wisdom neither loves
    nor hates.

All that belongs to the Two Extremes is inference falsely
    drawn—

A dream-phantom, a flower in the air.[3] Why strive to grasp
    it in the hand?

"Is" and "Isn't," gain and loss, banish once for all!

If the eyes do not close in sleep there can be no evil dreams;

If the mind makes no distinctions, all Dharmas become
    one.

Let the One with its mystery blot out all memory of com-
    plications.

Let the thought of the Dharmas as All-One bring you to the
    So-in-itself.[4]

Thus their origin is forgotten and nothing is left to make us
    pit one against the other.

Regard motion as though it were stationary, and what be-
    comes of motion?

Treat the stationary as though it moved, and that disposes
    of the stationary.

Both these having thus been disposed of, what becomes of
    the One?

At the ultimate point, beyond which you can go no further,

You get to where there are no rules, no standards,

To where thought can accept Impartiality,

To where effect of action ceases;

Doubt is washed away, belief has no obstacle.

Nothing is left over, nothing remembered;

[3] A pure fantasy.
[4] "Essence of reality." Cf. "Truly so," fourteen lines below.

Space is bright, but self-illumined; no power of mind is
    exerted.
Nor indeed could mere thought bring us to such a place.
Nor could sense or feeling comprehend it.
It is the Truly-so, the Transcendent Sphere, where there is
    neither He nor I.
For swift converse with this sphere use the concept "Not
    Two";
In the "Not Two" are no separate things, yet all things are
    included.
The wise throughout the Ten Quarters have had access to
    this Primal Truth;
For it is not a thing with extension in Time or Space;
A moment and an aeon for it are one.
Whether we see it or fail to see it, it is manifest always and
    everywhere.
The very small is as the very large when boundaries are
    forgotten;
The very large is as the very small when its outlines are not
    seen.
Being is an aspect of Non-being; Non-being is an aspect
    of Being.
In climes of thought where it is not so, the mind does ill
    to dwell.
The One is none other than the All, the All none other
    than the One.
Take your stand on this, and the rest will follow of its own
    accord;
To trust in the Heart is the "Not Two," the "Not Two" is
    to trust in the Heart.
I have spoken, but in vain; for what can words tell
Of things that have no yesterday, tomorrow, or today?

8. Shen Hui's Sermon on Sudden Awakening

Sermon of the monk from Nan-yang, in which is taught the
Ch'an doctrine of salvation through Sudden Awakening
and direct understanding of [one's own true] nature.

"Dharma of incomparable bodhi—all the Buddhas
highly praise its profundity. Friends! Come each of you,
open your heart to incomparable bodhi. Buddhas and

Bodhisattvas who all are good, truly reliable friends, are met with very rarely indeed. What you have never heard before you will hear to-day; whom you have never met before you will meet to-day. The *Nirvana Sutra* says: 'The Buddha asked Kasyapa: Is it difficult to hit a needle point placed on the earth with a sesame seed thrown out of the highest heaven? It is indeed, said Kasyapa. Yet, said the Buddha, less difficult it is than that a true cause and a true condition together meet.' What is a true cause and a true condition? Friends, that you open your heart to the truth is the true cause; that Buddhas and Bodhisattvas, your good, truly reliable friends, arrive at the dharma of incomparable bodhi, so that you may attain final salvation, that is the true condition; that both together meet is good. The mouth of the indifferent is full of bad language, their mind full of bad thoughts; long will they revolve in the wheel-of-life without being saved. May each of you open his heart to the truth! I shall lead your confession. May each of you pay homage to the Buddha! [The assembly joins in.]

"We pay homage to all the Buddhas of the past, to all of them.

We pay homage to all the Buddhas of the future, to all of them.

We pay homage to all the Buddhas of the present, to all of them.

We pay homage to the holy Dharma, the sutra-pitaka of the Prajnaparamitas.

We pay homage to all the great Bodhisattvas and the monks who have attained more or less complete illumination."

[The leader resumes.]

"Let us all from the depth of our hearts confess! Let the three stirrings of my friends be pure."

[The assembly joins in.]

"All the past, future, and present stirrings of my body, my mouth and my mind, the four unforgivable sins, I now sincerely confess from the depth of my heart. From these sins may I be delivered. Never shall I commit them again." . . .

[The leader.]

"Friends, all who are present, you have this occasion to join our congregation; you may now, each one of you, open

your heart to incomparable bodhi, strive for the dharma
of incomparable bodhi. If you want to attain this bodhi, you
must believe the words of the Buddha, rely upon the doctrine of the Buddha. What are the words the Buddha has
said? The Sutra says:[1]

" 'All bad things you shall not do; all good, things you
shall obediently do.

" 'You shall purify your mind. That all the Buddhas have
taught.'

"That is what all the Buddhas of the past have preached.
'All bad things you shall not do,' defines discipline (sila).
'All good things you shall obediently do,' defines insight
(prajna). 'You shall purify your mind,' defines meditation (samadhi). Friends, these three points are integral
parts [of the same doctrine]; not until [this is understood]
may one speak of Buddhism. Which are the points that are
one? Sila, samadhi, prajna. Not to let illusion rise is sila;
to be free of it is samadhi; to know about this is prajna.
These are the points that are one.

"Everybody must observe sila, the Rules of Conduct. If
you do not observe the Rules of Conduct, the good dharma
cannot grow. If you aim at incomparable bodhi you must
first observe the Rules of Conduct, then you can enter
[Nirvana]. If you do not observe the Rules of Conduct, you
will not even be incarnated in a scabby jackal, how much
less in the dharmakaya of a Tathagata, the reward of his
meritorious deeds. Friends, if you study incomparable
bodhi without purifying the three stirrings, without observing the Rules of Conduct, and declare that you may become
a Tathagata, [you try something] impossible.

"If you practise sila and prajna by action while bent on
sila, prajna, and samadhi without action, you are miscalcu-
lating.[2] If you practise samadhi by action this will lead to
incarnations among men and gods [a fruit which is] not
equal to incomparable bodhi. Friends, for a long time you
drift in the Ocean of Samsara, during many mahakalpas
as innumerable as the sands of the Ganges River, unable to
attain salvation, because you did not even once open your
heart to the truth. Maybe you did not meet the Buddhas

[1] This quotation is from the Anguttara-Nikaya.
[2] I.e., true self-transformation cannot be achieved by actively trying
for it.

and Bodhisattvas, your truly reliable friends. But even if you had met them you would not have opened your heart to the truth; in fact it is this reason that makes you drift in the Ocean of Samsara during many mahakalpas as innumerable as the sands of the Ganges River without being able to attain salvation.

"Or did you open your heart but only to the truth of the two Vehicles [Theravada] which lead to incarnations among men and gods? When the Karma [warranting your happy sojourn on these planes] is exhausted, resourceless you will drop back [into lower ones]. The Buddhas who arise in this world are as numerous as the Ganges sands; the great Bodhisattvas arising are as numerous as the Ganges sands. Those human beings whom each of these Buddhas and Bodhisattvas, their good friends, arises to save are as numerous as the Ganges sands. Why did you not meet them? That you are now wandering in Samsara without attaining salvation is surely due to the fact that the condition of your bodhi is absent, for on all the Buddhas and Bodhisattvas of the past, your truly reliable friends, you have never spent a single thought.

"Or [your failure may be due to the fact that] there are good friends [spiritual guides] who do not quite understand what incomparable bodhi really is. Teaching Sravaka doctrines of the two Vehicles which lead to incarnations among men and gods, they resemble one who puts dirty food in a precious vessel. In this simile a precious vessel stands for a friend who opens his heart to the truth, dirty food for the doctrines of the two Vehicles which lead to incarnations among men and gods. [Such a friend], though he reaps the sweet fruit of an incarnation among gods, which is not too bad, will again share the lot of the common people of our days when his Karma is exhausted.

"Friends, now open your minds to the teaching which is in accordance with the Prajnaparamita, [yielding results] excelling those [gained by] the Sravakas and Pratyekabuddhas, in no point distinct from those which Sakyamuni has prophesied for Maitreya. The numbers of kalpas which the two-Vehicle [Theravada] saints spend in meditation are [great]. . . . When the [prescribed] number of kalpas during which they practise meditation is full, the Bodhisattva Mahasattvas, if there is an occasion, preach them the Law. Then, opening their heart to the truth for the first time, they are in no way distinct from my friends who now open their heart to the truth. For, as long as they were absorbed in meditation, the two Vehicles were unfit to grasp the dharma of incomparable bodhi preached to them. A sutra says: 'The Heavenly Maiden said to Sariputra, common people may lose their bearing, and regain it again, but not the Sravakas.' . . .

"Friends, all of you, each single one, possesses the nature of a Buddha. The good friends [the Bodhisattvas] do not take the bodhi of the Buddha and hand it out to you, nor do they settle things for you. Why? The *Nirvana Sutra* says that [the Buddha] has already foretold your destination, namely, that all the Beings are from the beginning in Nirvana; from the beginning are they endowed with the gift of immaculate wisdom. Why do they not recognize this fact? [Why do they] wander in Samsara and cannot attain salvation? Because their view is obstructed by the dust of evil passions. They need the direction of a good friend; then they will recognize [that they are Buddhas], cease to wander, and attain salvation.

"When thus my friends [are told to] discard as useless all they have learned before, then those who have spent fifty or more, or [only] twenty years in practising meditation, hearing this, might be very much puzzled. [I therefore explain.] By 'discard' is meant 'give up' deceiving yourself about the Doctrine, not the Doctrine itself. For all the Buddhas of the ten directions could not discard the true Doctrine, much less so your good friend. As the air in which we walk, stand, and lie, unable to separate ourselves from it, such is the dharma of incomparable bodhi; one cannot separate from it. All actions and operations are inseparable from the sphere of the dharma. In a sutra [Vimalakirti] says: 'I can remove my disease but not the dharma of the disease.'[3]

"Friends, listen attentively, I speak to you of self-deception. What does self-deception mean? You, who have assembled at this place today, are craving for riches and the pleasures of intercourse with males and females; you are thinking of gardens and houses. This is the coarse form of

---

[3] I.e., I cannot remove the law that existence involves the possibility of disease.

self-deception. To believe that it must be discarded is the fine form of self-deception. That you do not know.

"What is the fine form of self-deception? When you hear one speaking of bodhi you think you must have that bodhi; and so when you hear one speaking of Nirvana, of emptiness, of purity, of samadhi, you think you must have that Nirvana, that emptiness, that purity, that samadhi. These are all self-deception; these are fetters, heresies. With that deception in mind you cannot attain salvation. If [unaware of the fact that] you are saved, that you are guiltless from the very beginning without anything additional required—you think of [leaving the world and] abiding in Nirvana, this Nirvana becomes a fetter [binding you to life]; in the same way purity, emptiness, samadhi, become fetters. Such thoughts impede your progress to bodhi. . . .

"Get conscious of the fact that in the natural state [your mind] is tranquil and pure, completely blank; [then it] is also unsupported and unattached, unbiased like empty space, reaching everywhere, that is, identical with the tathata-kaya[4] of the Buddhas. Tathata is [the quality] inherent in the absence of self-deception. Because we understand this fact we preach freedom from self-deception [or attachment]. One who looks at [things] free from self-deception, though fully seeing, hearing, feeling, and knowing, is always blank [unconcerned about this or that] and tranquil; in one act he practises sila, samadhi, and prajna simultaneously and fulfils the ten thousand conditions of virtue. Then he possesses the 'wisdom of the Tathagata which is wide and large, profound and far-reaching.' What means 'profound and far-reaching'? When [one's own] nature is clearly seen, then samadhi is profound and far-reaching; when one's nature is not seen, it is not profound and far-reaching.

"Use all your strength, my friends, so that you may attain salvation by Sudden Awakening. When your eyes see a form, clearly distinguish every form, and yet no [desire] is evoked by these varying forms, when in their midst you remain unaffected, among them attain salvation, then you have accomplished the samadhi of forms. When your ears hear a sound. . . . When your nose smells a fragrance.

---

[4] "True substantial essence."

. . . When your tongue tastes something savory. . . . When your body feels a touch. . . . When your manas[5] distinguishes a dharma, and yet no [desire] is evoked by these varying dharmas, when in their midst you remain unaffected, among them attain salvation, then you have accomplished the samadhi of dharmas. When in this manner all the organs distinguish well, that is original prajna; when no [desire] arises, that is original samadhi. . . .

"I shall explain in short to my friends what is meant by identity of the sinner and the saint, using the simile of empty space. In itself empty space neither changes nor ceases to change. In daylight those are right who think it to be bright; at night those are right who think it to be dark. Yet, whether bright or dark, it is the same space. Brightness and darkness alternate while the space itself neither changes nor ceases to change. The same applies to sin and saintliness. Don't distinguish between truth and error; in reality saintliness is not different [from sin]. A sutra says: 'It is the same if one contemplates one's own true nature or the Buddha.' It follows that freedom from attachment [to external things, which replaces meditation in Ch'an Buddhism], enables you to look into the heart of all the Buddhas of the past, and yet it is nothing else than what you yourselves experience to-day. A sutra says: 'Contemplating the Tathagata, [I am aware that he] neither arrives out of the future, nor departs to the past, nor lasts in the present.' Who seeks the dharma [truth] should not seek it in the Buddha, the Dharma, the Sangha. Why? Because the Buddha-nature [of each Being] is found in his own heart. . . .

"Set yourselves your own rules, penetrate to your own heart! Then you have penetrated to the understanding of all the sutras. [No scholarship is needed.] When the Buddha was still living there were Beings of every description who left their families and followed him. All the Buddhas of the past preached to the eight kinds of listeners, not selectively or privately. As the sun at midday illuminates every spot, as the dragon king[6] sends rain impartially and equally, so that the grasses and trees are watered, each kind in accordance with its need, so are the Buddhas when

[5] The analytic faculty of mind.
[6] A nature-power occasionally referred to in earlier literature.

they preach the Law. Then their mind is open to every need, showing no preference to one or the other, and Beings of every description understand their message. A sutra says: 'The Buddha uses one and the same language in order to preach the Law; the Beings understand each in his own way.'

"Friends, when you study prajnaparamita, you must read extensively the *Mahayana Sutras*. There are Ch'an teachers who do not like Sudden Awakening but want you to awaken [gradually] by using the expedients that [the Buddhas] offer, but that is a method good only for a very inferior type of Being. As in a clear mirror one sees one's face [undistorted], so in the *Mahayana Sutras* one sees the true picture of one's own heart. First, you must not doubt; trusting the word of the Buddha you must purify the three stirrings, then you can enter Mahayana. The School of Sudden Awakening relies exclusively upon the word of the Tathagata for its practice. I am telling you the pure truth. Bestir yourselves: Come and ask if you have any doubt. Fare you well!" . . .

9. A Zen "Koan"

Riko [Li-k'u], a high government officer of the T'ang dynasty, asked Nansen [Nan-chuan][1]: "A long time ago a man kept a goose in a bottle. It grew larger and larger until it could not get out of the bottle any more; he did not want to break the bottle, nor did he wish to hurt the goose; how would you get it out?"

The master called out, "O Officer!"

To this Riko at once responded, "Yes!"

"There, it is out!"

This was the way Nansen produced the goose out of its imprisonment.

10. The Mahayana Layman's Ideal

This selection portrays the ideal layman from the Mahayana viewpoint. He lives in the world and fulfills his social responsibilities; while doing so he exemplifies all the virtues that a devout follower of the Master and an aspirant for enlighten-

[1] A famous Ch'an master (A.D. 748-834).

*ment should. Though not yet having achieved Bodhisattvahood,
with its self-sacrificing zeal to save others, he is portrayed as
exemplifying something of this virtue and as superior to the
monks who have withdrawn from the world.*

At that time, there dwelt in the great city of Vaisali a
wealthy householder named Vimalakirti. Having done
homage to the countless Buddhas of the past, doing many
good works, attaining to acquiescence in the Eternal Law,
he was a man of wonderful eloquence;

Exercising supernatural powers, obtaining all the Dhara-
nis,[1] arriving at the state of fearlessness;

Repressing all evil enmities, reaching the gate of profound truth, walking in the way of wisdom;

Acquainted with the necessary means, fulfilling the
Great Vows, comprehending the past and the future of the
intentions of all beings, understanding also both their
strength and weakness of mind;

Ever pure and excellent in the way of the Buddha, remaining loyal to the Mahayana;

Deliberating before action, following the conduct of
Buddha, great in mind as the ocean;

Praised by all the Buddhas, revered by all the disciples
and all the gods such as a Sakra[2] and Brahman king, the
lord of this world;

Residing in Vaisali only for the sake of the necessary
means for saving creatures, abundantly rich, ever careful
of the poor, pure in self-discipline, obedient to all precepts;

Removing all anger by the practice of patience, removing all sloth by the practice of diligence, removing all distraction of mind by intent meditation, removing all ignorance by fullness of wisdom;

Though he is but a simple layman, yet observing the
pure monastic discipline;

Though living at home, yet never desirous of anything;

Though possessing a wife and children, always exercising pure virtues;

Though surrounded by his family, holding aloof from
worldly pleasures;

Though using the jeweled ornaments of the world, yet
adorned with spiritual splendor;

[1] Magic spells.
[2] Indra, the chief of the gods.

Though eating and drinking, yet enjoying the flavor of the rapture of meditation;

Though frequenting the gambling house, yet leading the gamblers into the right path;

Though coming in contact with heresy, yet never letting his true faith be impaired;

Though having a profound knowledge of worldly learning, yet ever finding pleasure in things of the spirit as taught by Buddha;

Revered by all as the first among those who were worthy of reverence;

Though profiting by all the professions, yet far above being absorbed by them;

Benefiting all beings, going wheresoever he pleases, protecting all beings as a judge with righteousness;

Leading all with the Doctrine of the Mahayana when in the seat of discussion;

Ever teaching the young and ignorant when entering the hall of learning;

Manifesting to all the error of passion when in the house of debauchery; persuading all to seek the higher things when at the shop of the wine dealer;

Preaching the Law when among wealthy people as the most honorable of their kind;

Dissuading the rich householders from covetousness when among them as the most honorable of their kind;

Teaching kshatriyas [i.e. warriors] patience when among them . . .

Removing arrogance when among brahmans . . .

Teaching justice to the great ministers . . .

Teaching honesty to the ladies of the court when among them . . .

Teaching loyalty and filial piety to the princes . . .

Persuading the masses to cherish the virtue of merits . . .

Protecting all beings when among the guardians as the most honorable of their kind;

——Thus by such countless means Vimalakirti, the wealthy householder, rendered benefit to all beings.

EPILOGUE: Buddha's Pity

My children,

The Enlightened One, because He saw Mankind drowning in the Great Sea of Birth, Death and Sorrow, and longed to save them,

For this He was moved to pity.

Because He saw the men of the world straying in false paths, and none to guide them,

For this He was moved to pity.

Because He saw that they lay wallowing in the mire of the Five Lusts, in dissolute abandonment,

For this He was moved to pity.

Because He saw them still fettered to their wealth, their wives and their children, knowing not how to cast them aside,

For this He was moved to pity.

Because He saw them doing evil with hand, heart, and tongue, and many times receiving the bitter fruits of sin, yet ever yielding to their desires,

For this He was moved to pity.

Because He saw that they slaked the thirst of the Five Lusts as it were with brackish water,

For this He was moved to pity.

Because He saw that though they longed for happiness, they made for themselves no karma of happiness; and though they hated pain, yet willingly made for themselves a karma of pain; and though they coveted the joys of Heaven, would not follow His commandments on earth,

For this He was moved to pity.

Because He saw them afraid of birth, old age and death, yet still pursuing the works that lead to birth, old age and death,

For this He was moved to pity.

Because He saw them consumed by the fires of pain and sorrow, yet knowing not where to seek the still waters of samadhi,

For this He was moved to pity.

Because He saw them living in an evil time, subjected to
    tyrannous kings and suffering many ills, yet heedlessly
    following after pleasure,
For this He was moved to pity.

Because He saw them living in a time of wars, killing and
    wounding one another; and knew that for the riotous
    hatred that had flourished in their hearts they were
    doomed to pay an endless retribution,
For this He was moved to pity.

Because many born at the time of His incarnation had
    heard Him preach the Holy Law, yet could not re-
    ceive it,
For this He was moved to pity.

Because some had great riches that they could not bear to
    give away,
For this He was moved to pity.

Because He saw the men of the world ploughing their fields,
    sowing the seed, trafficking, huckstering, buying and
    selling; and at the end winning nothing but bitterness,
For this He was moved to pity.

Bibliography

This bibliography only aims to include a few general books on Buddhism in English which one who has begun to read these selections would find especially helpful.

Anesaki, M. *History of Japanese Religion*. London: Kegan Paul, Trench, Trubner and Co., 1930.

Arnold, Sir Edwin. *The Light of Asia*. London: Kegan Paul, Trench, Trubner and Co., 1891.

Brewster, E. H. *The Life of Gotama the Buddha*. New York: E. P. Dutton and Co., 1926.

Burlingame, E. W. *Buddhist Parables*. New Haven: Yale University Press, 1922.

Conze, E. *Buddhism, Its Essence and Development*. New York: Philosophical Library, 1952.

————— *Buddhist Texts Through the Ages*. New York: Philosophical Library, 1954.

Davids, Mrs. C. A. F Rhys. *Buddhism*. New York: H. Holt and Co., 1912.

————— *Gotama the Man*. London: Luzac and Co., 1928.

Davids, T. W. Rhys. *Buddhist India*. New York: Putnam's, 1903.

————— *Early Buddhism*. London: Constable and Co., 1910.

Eliot, Sir Charles. *Hinduism and Buddhism*. 3 vols. London: E. Arnold and Co., 1921.

————— *Japanese Buddhism*. London: E. Arnold and Co., 1935.

Fung, Yu-Lan. *History of Chinese Philosophy* (trans. by D. Bodde). Vol. II. Princeton: Princeton University Press, 1953.

Hackmann, H. *Buddhism As A Religion*. London: Probsthain, 1910.

Hamilton, C. H. *Buddhism*. New York: The Liberal Arts Press, 1952.

Hodous, L. *Buddhism and Buddhists in China*. New York: Macmillan, 1924.

Horner, I. *Women Under Primitive Buddhism*. London: G. Routledge and Sons, 1930.

Johnston, R. F. *Buddhist China*. London: J. Murray, 1913.

Keith, A. B. *Buddhist Philosophy in India and Ceylon*. Oxford: The Clarendon Press, 1923.

Lee, S. C. *Popular Buddhism in China*. Shanghai: Commercial Press, 1939.

McGovern, W. M. *Introduction to Mahayana Buddhism*. London: Kegan Paul, Trench, Trubner and Co., 1922.

Oldenberg, H. *Buddha, His Life, His Doctrine, His Order*. London and Edinburgh: Williams and Norgate, 1882.

Pratt, J. B. *The Pilgrimage of Buddhism*. New York: The Macmillan Co., 1928.

Rodhakrishnan, S. *Gotama the Buddha*. Bombay: Hind Kitabs, 1945. (Reprinted in his translation of the *Dhammapada*, Oxford University Press, 1950.)

————*Indian Philosophy*. Vol. I. London: Allen and Unwin, 1927. (Rev. Ed. 1931.)

Reichelt, K. L. *Truth and Tradition in Chinese Buddhism*. Shanghai: The Commercial Press, 1927, 1934.

Reischauer, A. K. *Studies in Japanese Buddhism*. New York: Revell, 1917.

Saunders, K. J. *Epochs in Buddhist History*. Chicago: University of Chicago Press, 1922.

Smith, F. H. *The Buddhist Way of Life*. London: Hutchinson's University Library, 1951.

Steinilber-Oberlin, E. *The Buddhist Sects of Japan*. London: Allen and Unwin, 1938.

Subhadra Bhikkhu. *The Message of Buddhism*. London: Kegan Paul, Trench, Trubner and Co., 1922.

Suzuki, B. L. *Mahayana Buddhism*. London: D. Marlowe, 1948.

Suzuki, D. T. *Introduction to Zen Buddhism*. New York: Philosophical Library, 1949.

Thomas, E. J. *History of Buddhist Thought*. New York: A. A. Knopf, 1933.

————*The Life of Buddha as Legend and History*. New York: A. A. Knopf, 1927.

Waddell, L. A. *The Buddhism of Tibet*. Cambridge (England): W. Heffer and Sons, 1939.

Ward, C. H. S. *Buddhism*. Vol. I (Hinayana) 1947, Vol. II (Mahayana) 1952. London: The Epworth Press.

Glossary

The purpose of this glossary is to explain words in the text that may be unfamiliar to Western readers, especially Sanskrit terms. If the Pali equivalent is also sometimes used in the West, it is added in parentheses. Where the Pali form is the one ordinarily used, it alone is given.

Amitabha (in Japanese, *Amida*). The Buddha who is the main object of devotion in the Pure Land School of Chinese Buddhism, and the Jodo and Shin Schools in Japan.

Ananda. Buddha's cousin and closest personal companion among his disciples.

Anathapindika. A lay patron of early Buddhism, giver of the famous Jeta grove and monastery.

anatta. "No soul" (doctrine) of Buddhism.

apsara. Celestial nymph.

arhat (*arahat*). The perfected disciple; one who has completed the discipline required to attain liberation.

arya (*ariya*). Noble; the noble ones; the elect.

asavas. The "cankers" which obstruct spiritual achievement (e.g., sensual longing, desire for continued separate existence, ignorance).

asura. Demonic power, devil.

atman. The soul, conceived as one in reality with Brahman.

Avalokitesvara (in Chinese, Kwan Yin). A Bodhisattva conceived as merciful to those in special need.

bhikkhuni. Nun.

bhikshu (*bhikkhu*). Mendicant monk.

bodhi. Enlightenment.

Bodhidharma. The twenty-eighth Ch'an patriarch in India and the first in China.

bodhisattva. One moved by compassionate zeal to aid his fellow men toward salvation, hence willing to postpone his own entrance into Nirvana to this end.

Brahman. The ultimate divine reality, for Hinduism.

brahmana (usually spelled Brahmin). A member of the highest, namely the priestly, caste.

Buddha. The Illumined One. The main title of the founder of Buddhism after his enlightenment.

Ch'an. See *Zen.*

citta. Memory recognition; the faculty of systematic cognition.

deva. Heavenly being, god.

dharani. Words or sentences possessing magic power.

dharma (dhamma). Rule of duty or of social obligation (Hinduism). The truth; the saving doctrine or way (early Buddhism). Reality; essential quality; any reality (Mahayana Buddhism).

dharmakaya. Literally, "body of the law." In Mahayana thought, one aspect of ultimate reality.

dhyana. "Meditation." It is the Sanskrit word of which Ch'an and Zen are Chinese and Japanese transliterations.

dukkha. Suffering, pain, misery, sorrow, unhappiness.

fetters. The main forms of attachment that bind a living being to the wheel of worldly existence.

gatha. Verses; poem composed of them.

Hinayana. "The lesser vehicle"; one of the two major divisions of Buddhism. See *Theravada.*

Indra. One of the great Hindu gods.

Isipatana. The deer-park near Benares (now called Sarnath), where Buddha preached his first sermon.

jataka. A story or legend about Buddha's birth or previous forms of existence.

jina. Conqueror.

jivatman. The soul, as a separate individual.

kalpa. An age, epoch of time.

Kapilavastu. The capital city of the Sakya tribe, where Buddha grew to adulthood.

karma (kamma). The principle of causality in moral experience.

Kondanna. A disciple of Buddha, the earliest convert to his preaching.

koti. A large number.

kshatriya. Member of the warrior caste, the second highest in the Indian social scheme.

Kshitigarbha (in Chinese, Ti Ts'ang). A Bodhisattva who seeks to save even those in hell.

Kusinara. The place where Buddha died.

Maghavan. Bountiful Lord (an epithet given to Indra).

Mahakasyapu (or *Kasyapa*). One of Buddha's disciples; according to Zen tradition, its first patriarch.

Mahayana. "The greater vehicle"; one of the two major divisions of Buddhism.

manas. The discriminative and deliberative faculty of mind.

manovijnana. Discriminative knowledge.

Mara. The Evil One; the great tempter.

Mogallana. One of Buddha's chief disciples.

moksha. Ultimate release or liberation (of the soul from the cycle of birth and death).

mudra. Gesture (of the hand).

muni. A sage.

nayuta. A large number.

Nirvana (Nibbana). The state achieved by the conquest of craving; the spiritual goal of Buddhism.

paramita. Perfection, ideal virtue.

Paranirvana. "Beyond Nirvana," the state into which one who has attained Nirvana passes at death.

prajna. Transcendental wisdom or insight.

prapti. A force maintaining the living equilibrium of the factors composing a personality.

pratyeka-buddha. One seeking salvation independently of others.

Pure Land. One of the schools of Chinese and Japanese Buddhism, emphasizing devotion to *Amitabha.*

purusha. The soul, conceived as individual or (sometimes) as universal (the soul of the universe).

Rajagaha. The capital city of the Magadha people.

raja. King; chief; ruler.

rishi. A sage (usually a hermit).

Sakra. A name for Indra.

Sakya. The tribe into which Buddha was born.

Sakyamuni. The sage of the Sakyas, i.e., Buddha.

samadhi. Complete concentration, absorbed contemplation.

samana. An ascetic.

Samantabhadra. One of the great Bodhisattvas. In Japanese, *Fugen.*

samsara. The ocean of birth and death, i.e., of successive individual existences in transmigration.

Sangha. The order of Buddhist monks.

Sariputra (sariputta). One of Buddha's chief disciples.

skandhas. The five factors constituting an individual person.

Sautrantika. One of the Theravada philosophical schools.

sravaka. "Hearer"; a disciple not yet capable of independent progress.

sunya. The Void; emptiness; the realm of transitory and relative existence.

tanha. Craving; selfish or blind demandingness.

Theravada. "The way of the elders." The form of Buddhism prevalent in Ceylon, Burma, and Siam.

Tathagata (*"Ju Lai"* in Chinese). "He who has fully arrived," i.e., the Perfect One. A title of the Buddha.

Ti'en Tai. One of the schools of Chinese Buddhism.

tripitaka. The "Three Baskets," canonical Buddhist scriptures.

Upanishads. Philosophical dialogues or treatises of ancient India.

Uruvela. The town near which Gautama attained enlightenment.

Vaibhasika. One of the Theravada philosophical schools.

Vaisesika. One of the six orthodox schools of Indian philosophy.

Vedas. Ancient Indian scriptures.

Yama. God of the dead; sometimes, death personified.

Zen (in Chinese, *Ch'an*). One of the schools of Chinese and Japanese Buddhism, emphasizing abandonment of striving as the way to enlightenment.